LYNCHINGS

LYNCHINGS

Extralegal Violence in Florida during the 1930s

Walter T. Howard

Authors Choice Press
New York Lincoln Shanghai

Lynchings
Extralegal Violence in Florida during the 1930s

Authors Choice Press
an imprint of iUniverse, Inc.

iUniverse books may be ordered through booksellers or by contacting:

iUniverse
2021 Pine Lake Road, Suite 100
Lincoln, NE 68512
www.iuniverse.com
1-800-Authors (1-800-288-4677)

Originally published by Susquehanna University Press

ISBN-13: 978-0-595-37650-6
ISBN-10: 0-595-37650-9

Printed in the United States of America

Dedicated
to Virginia, Ian,
Christopher, and Stephanie

Contents

Acknowledgments

This book is a history of lynching in the state of Florida during the 1930s. As such, it is the product of a continuing scholarly interest in race relations and antiblack violence that began when I first encountered the ghastly tale of Claude Neal's death in the pages of George Brown Tindall's *Emergence of the New South, 1917–1945.* That shocking encounter initiated my education concerning the scope and meaning of white racial hatred for African Americans, extralegal violence, and the black freedom struggle. While a beginning graduate student at the University of West Florida in Pensacola, I became especially interested in racial violence in Florida during the decade of the Great Depression and Scottsboro. As I wrote my master's thesis on the Neal affair, I was receptive to the suggestion of James R. McGovern that further examination of Florida's extralegal executions in the thirties could contribute to our overall understanding of the peculiar form of American violence known as lynching. I traveled to Tallahassee and Florida State University for further graduate study with the thought that a wide variety of scholars might welcome a detailed statewide study of lynching. This served as the basis for my dissertation, which was nurtured by a committee that included Neil Betten, William Warren Rogers, and Joe Richardson. That undertaking led to this book.

Special thanks go to Neil Betten, colleague and friend, who has been an unwavering source of support and encouragement since I began my research. I am also grateful to the Florida State University history department for the dissertation fellowship that provided research funds for travel. My department chairperson here at Bloomsburg University, James Sperry, was kind enough to arrange the teaching schedule to maximize available time for revising the manuscript, and for that I am appreciative. A word of acknowledgment also goes to Dr. Rob Ralph (church historian at First United Church of Christ in Tampa), John Metcalf (son of the Reverend Walter Metcalf, Tampa), and Dr. Adliel Moncrief (contemporary of Reverend Metcalf) for new information on the important Shoemaker case. Mention should also be made of the helpful interviews granted by *Tampa Tribune* writer Leland Hawes. Researchers and library aides at many locations helped in producing this book: the Andruss Library at Bloomsburg University, the Firestone Library at Princeton University, the Southern Collection at the University of North Carolina at Chapel Hill, the Woodruff Library at Atlanta University, the Tuskegee Institute in Alabama, the Library of Congress, the Franklin D. Roosevelt Library at Hyde Park, New York, the Florida State Archives in Tallahassee, and the Alabama State Archives in Montgomery.

Members of my family sustained me during the time it took to complete this project, constantly telling me I was doing something worthwhile. My only sorrow as I complete this labor is that neither of my parents, Margaret and Lowell Howard, Sr., both of whom would have rejoiced at the publication of this book, are alive to celebrate with me. Still, I know that I owe much of this endeavor to these working-class parents who instinctively taught me the deep meaning of social justice. In the time that I have been transforming this project from a dissertation to a book, my life has been immeasurably enriched by my wife Ginny and our new son, Ian. She read, criticized, and encouraged every phase of my writing; I value her judgment and I appreciate her long-suffering patience as I worked through revising the manuscript. It is to her and Ian, along with Christopher and Stephanie, that this book is dedicated.

LYNCHINGS

Introduction

ON 26 April 1930, vigilantes in Hillsborough County, Florida kidnapped an Hungarian immigrant, John Hodaz, from police custody and drove him to a secluded area about ten miles north of Plant City. There they dragged the terrified man from a car while someone backed another automobile under an overhanging bough of an oak tree. A rope was thrown over the limb, then a perfectly fashioned hangman's noose was placed around Hodaz's neck. One of the lynchers forced the defenseless man on top of the motorized scaffold; several gunmen trained their weapons on the hapless prisoner and fired just as the auto supporting him was withdrawn. One shotgun blast, discharged at close range, tore through the body beneath the heart, ripping a jagged hole in the middle of the victim's torso. Another similar charge took effect on the right side of the chest. Before departing, vigilantes fired five pistol bullets into the lifeless form as it swung from the oak tree. John Hodaz stood accused of violating the "honor" of family and community: he had allegedly bombed the home of a prominent Plant City family against whom he held a personal grudge. He was the first lynch victim of the decade in Florida; fourteen more would fall victim to extralegal violence by 1940.

Lynchings, whether committed in the backwoods of Florida or elsewhere in the United States, call out for scholarly treatment. Several decades ago Richard Hofstadter issued something of a challenge to American historians to reconsider the notion, prevalent at the time, that violence is of only negligible importance in American society.[1] And indeed, the events of the last thirty years—assassinations, riots, wars, and the like—clearly show the American heritage is in large part a violent one. A part of that vexing legacy—lynching—stands as one of the nation's most shocking, troublesome, and confounding species of violent wrongdoing. Contemporary white Americans often associate it with colorful visions of the Old West and romantic notions of frontier vigilantism, a standard item of our national mythology. Black journalists and scholars, however, never indulged in such

13

vapid conceptions. Close observers and chroniclers of extralegal crimes, they knew that in the late 1800s and the early twentieth century lynchings were a routine, everyday sort of villainy that were primarily southern and almost always inflicted upon black, rather than white, people. The Florida-born and Marianna-raised editor of the *New York Age*, T. Thomas Fortune, called lynching an "exhibition of barbarity on the part of the South."[2] And W. E. B. Du Bois certainly embraced no idyllic views of lynch-law tragedies; the vicious practice shook him to the core, as it did many black intellectuals, and prompted him to observe in 1899 that "one could not be a calm, cool, and detached scientist while Negroes were lynched, murdered, and starved."[3]

In his well-known prophetic pronouncement that "race" was to be the great global problem of the twentieth century, Du Bois surveyed the "color line" issue, and injustices like lynching, in an international context.[4] And in fact, lynch-law dramas were played out in the southern United States against the larger background of American imperialism in Latin America and the Philippines as well as European colonial aggression in Africa and Asia. No doubt, Africans from Mozambique punished under the forced labor system of the Portuguese, the tribes "hammered" by British troops in Kenya, or the Filipino guerrilla tortured by U.S. soldiers would have easily understood the feelings experienced by African American communities in places like Georgia, Mississippi, and Florida, where extralegal executions were commonplace at the turn of the century. The embattled Marcus Garvey said as much when he declared that "lynching and burning, and disrespect of Negroes is not confined to any one country. It is spread all over the world; and it means that if we in this present age do not go out and do something to stop lynching, every inch of ground in the world will become unsafe for the Negro in the next twenty years."[5] Himself a victim of a "legal lynching" of sorts, the iconoclastic black nationalist was deported and left behind an America that stood out as unique in the world as an obsessive practitioner of lynch-law atrocities.

Researchers now look on this state of affairs in the early part of the 1900s and read, with a sense of historical perspective, current headlines about lawlessness and violence directed against outsiders and dispossessed social groups. Indeed, a number of historians in recent years have focused their scholarly attention on the dark and violent side of the American past. They understandably look for the roots of disturbing present-day social problems, such as the proliferation of extremist hate groups, occurrences of antiethnic violence, and undeniable incidents of police brutality in our social history. In the process they have made an interesting discovery: the state of Florida—with its sunshine, beaches, and palm trees—has long been plagued by mob violence.

Lynch law in the Sunshine State reached its peak in the 1890s and then gradually declined over the next five decades. Furthermore, in the 1930s, the last phase of the lynching and vigilante era, Florida was the most lynch-prone state in the South. One antilynching organization of the day, the Association of Southern Women for the Prevention of Lynching (ASWPL), reported in a special survey that during those years this southern state had the highest frequency of the practice of lynch law in the country. From 1930 to 1939, Florida went only one year (1933) without a lynching. The next worst state, Mississippi, had two lynch-free years; Georgia and Louisiana had three, and the rest of the lynching states at least four. Virginia had only one extralegal execution in this period. These data clearly reveal that during the thirties Florida ranked first in the South when it came to the frequency of its lynching activities.[6]

The roll call of terror for whites was short. As events proved, Hodaz and the other two white lynch victims of this period stood accused of violating accepted standards of conduct in their communities. For example, as a transplanted New England socialist, Joseph Shoemaker (lynched on 30 November 1935) had challenged the power and values of Tampa's political establishment. Further, Miles Brown (lynched on 1 April 1939), a native white southerner, had murdered a well-known, revered Panama City businessman. In these ways, then, all had violated a code of law and honor or had threatened the established order in the community. Consequently, self-appointed law enforcement groups took the law into their own hands by doing away with these so-called undesirables.[7]

The list of black casualties reads like a litany of horrors. White lynchers dispatched black victims throughout the ten-year period under study in different areas of the state for a variety of unproven allegations. On 28 August 1931 a small Calhoun County mob lynched Richard Smoak and his brother Charlie, two turpentine workers, for a charge of physically assaulting a white "woodsrider." The next year, on 6 June, a man named Henry Woods, accused of killing a white police chief, fell into the hands of a frenzied posse that burned him alive at the stake in Hamilton County. Tampa lynchers, on 31 January 1934, killed Robert Johnson for supposedly attacking and raping a white woman. The most grisly extralegal murder of the thirties occurred on 27 October 1934, when Jackson County mobs tortured, mutilated, castrated, and hanged Claude Neal, a young farmworker charged with rape and murder. Motorized urban lynchers in Ft. Lauderdale slew Reuben Stacey on 19 July 1935, believing he had physically assaulted a white woman. Accused of a similar crime, Buckie Young was shot to death by a mob of unknown size on 11 September 1936 in Madison County. A small vigilante band in Tallahassee on 20 July 1937 shot and

KEY

1. Santa Rosa County
2. Panama City
3. Calhoun County
4. Jackson County
5. Tallahassee
6. Hamilton County
7. Madison County
8. Taylor County
9. Daytona Beach
10. Tampa
11. Plant City
12. Ft. Lauderdale

Florida lynching sites.

killed two teenagers, Richard Ponder and Ernest Hawkins, for an alleged attack on a white policeman. A number of men in Santa Rosa County, responding to charges that J. C. Evans had committed an unspecified "unnatural" sex act on a white child, kidnapped him from police and riddled his body with bullets. Otis Price, accused of raping a white woman, was executed by a Taylor County group on 9 August 1938 when they gunned him down in cold blood. And finally, two lynchers murdered Lee Snell, a taxi driver, in Daytona Beach on 29 April 1939—he had unintentionally struck and killed a white child with his cab.[8]

The lynching of these Florida blacks led to strong condemnation of the injustice of white racial violence. Loud protests of this inequity came from the national media, the national black community, and concerned anti-lynching groups; there was also an increasing threat of involvement by the federal government. The message was clear: fatal violence toward African Americans was inconsistent with the new values embraced by the national community. In the 1930s a changing American society was gradually moving toward the goal of fair treatment for its black citizens, paving the way for the civil rights movement of later decades.

As a form of violence peculiar to the United States, lynching was unjustified disobedience to the rule of law in ordered society, resulting in illegal, deadly violations of the integrity of persons. Strictly speaking, it was the practice of a group of two or more individuals inflicting punishment upon victims without regard to law in the "service of justice, tradition, or race."[9] Practitioners cared little or nothing about legal formalities, automatically presumed the guilt of their victims, and summarily executed them. The victims, of course, had no way to defend themselves or prove their innocence; moreover, in their suffering and death they sometimes became the center of public spectacles. Finally, local communities, county and state officials, and the criminal justice system, directly or indirectly, approved of these crimes and failed to bring perpetrators to justice.[10]

Lynching has a long history in the United States.[11] It was first employed as a brutal (but usually nonlethal) form of vengeance in the Revolutionary War period by vigilant patriots against loyalists, criminals, and other social misfits.[12] Attempting to maintain social organization and minimize lawlessness during the 1800s in open areas of the West, frontiersmen often targeted cattle rustlers, horse thieves, claim jumpers, murderers, Hispanics, and Native Americans for swift extralegal killings. Often seen as valuable property by white folk, slaves in the Old South were rarely lynched; but southerners in the antebellum period did illegally put to death a good number of insurrectionary blacks, abolitionists, criminals, crooked gamblers, or others who dared violate the region's keenly felt sense of honor.[13] Lastly, in an urbanized America around the turn of the century, fatal forms of extralegal violence moved to the city as a mechanism to control and suppress ethnics, immigrants, dissidents, labor activists, political radicals, peace activists, and sometimes kidnappers.[14] Fundamentally, however, lynching became infamous in the post-Reconstruction New South as a powerful and violent instrument of social control aimed at black citizens.[15] In fact, between 1882 and 1968 approximately 4,743 victims were lynched in the United States, and some 3,446 of them were southern blacks. In Florida during this period 257 blacks and 25 whites were killed by vigilantes.[16]

A few statistics reveal the scope of this abuse in Florida and the South generally. From 1889 to 1918, peak lynching years in the United States, nearly two hundred blacks were illegally executed in the Sunshine State. There were, of course, lynchings of blacks throughout the South in this same period. In Georgia (360), Mississippi (350), Texas (263), Louisiana (264), and Alabama (244), the number of extralegal incidents surpassed those in Florida, while in Arkansas, Tennessee, Kentucky, South Carolina, North Carolina, and Virginia fewer blacks were lynched.[17] Moreover, the data further reveal a trend of decline over the years. During the 1890s, 74 blacks fell victim to lynch law in Florida, and in the first ten years of the twentieth century, 51 met death in the same fashion. Between 1910 and 1917, 49 blacks were lynched, and 34 between 1922 and 1929. Finally, 12 blacks were executed by lynchers in the period 1930 to 1940, before this violence at last waned.[18] Lynchings declined in Florida over the years for a number of reasons. Public opposition inside and outside the South, along with white consolidation of power over blacks in the region after 1900, combined with alternatives to illegal executions (legal lynchings in hasty, sham trials and police brutality during arrests) to bring about a reduction of this practice.[19] Still, the rope and faggot would be used now and again by whites to terrorize blacks in an attempt to make them a more pliant people.[20]

For some time now the subject of lynching has fully engaged the interest of historians in a serious way; in fact, the number of books and dissertations dealing with this matter has increased sharply during the last two decades. Yet, according to one recent authoritative account, "the scholarship on lynching has only recently moved beyond its infancy."[21] If that is so, it has occurred in spite of the difficulty of applying traditional research methods to this curiosity that has been so important in the history of race relations in the South. In dealing with such a volatile topic, scholarly investigators must use extra caution in examining and evaluating court records, newspaper accounts, police reports, oral traditions, and the findings of outside observers. Worse still, precisely determining the source and development of extralegal violence in its varied contexts is exceedingly difficult. A few have even suggested that it is rarely possible for scholars to gather enough credible sources to write a reliable, accurate history of lynching.[22] But while this may be the case in some instances, the history of extralegal violence in Florida during the 1930s indicates that the data are obtainable.

Because methodological problems have until recently discouraged historical studies, social scientists—largely sociologists and psychologists—stepped into the breech beginning in the 1920s and 1930s. Using their disciplines' techniques to probe the mysteries of lynching, they set forth a number of interesting theories. Southern sociologists, for example, focused on a deep and abiding strain of virulent white racism as the force that led to lynch law violence, and concluded that the region's institutions were too weak to inhibit it. If white southerners did not sufficiently respect the rule of law and the value of black life, it was primarily because their churches, schools, courts, and police were too underdeveloped and backward to enlighten them on such matters. The implication was that only after the forces of modernization had transformed the area, with the growth of cities and industries, would it set aside its violent, illegal tendencies toward blacks. According to this line of reasoning, once southerners reduced poverty, properly educated their children, provided adequate law enforcement, and put a modern communication and transportation system in place, they would naturally lose interest in barbaric practices like lynching.[23] Few at the time considered the possibility, so well articulated in recent years by Michael Cassity, that modernization (which he refers to as intrusive industrial capitalism) would bring urban crowding, as well as job and housing competition, which in turn was sure to increase antagonism between the races.[24]

In the 1930s and 1940s socioeconomic theories by a wide assortment of analysts—including Arthur F. Raper, John Dollard, Oliver C. Cox, Wilbur Cash, Gunnar Myrdal, and Walter White— argued that lynching had many related causes: the dynamics of white racism, poverty, provincialism, economic frustration, seasonal rhythms, inadequate legal procedures, frontierlike conditions of the rural South, and the proportion of blacks in a locality's population.[25] Moreover, the classic statement of the caste theory comes out of this period. Social scientists who embraced this thesis looked for answers in the social stratification of southern society that existed during the lynch-law era, realizing that caste lines themselves engendered ongoing contention and strife between the races. To maintain caste distinctions and all the advantages that went with them, whites assumed a posture of permanent, unceasing wariness and alertness, standing ready to punish any black infractions. White caste solidarity allowed for no deviations or departures; no dissent or challenge on either side of the color line was permitted. This system of power arrangements within the southern social order paid off for whites in numerous ways, including, according to sociologist Oliver C. Cox, providing a large pool of black workers who were easily exploited and manipulated.[26] Above all, it kept white males in a social position superior to black men, black women, and even white women (whom, argued white patriarchs, lynching was supposed to protect). White men were willing to engage in the ultimate form of extralegal violence to maintain superiority and dominance, knowing that caste solidarity protected them from trial, conviction, and punishment. Recently, the historian George Fredrickson has referred to lynching as "the ultimate sociological method of racial control and repression, a way to use fear and terror to check 'dangerous' tendencies in a black community considered to be ineffectively regimented or supervised."[27]

In the years since the 1940s, lynching theory has grown more complex and sophisticated. The disciplines of the contemporary social sciences (excluding historians, who largely neglected the topic until the late 1970s) offer a useful variety of methods to explain southern lynch law episodes. By and large, sociologists theorized that this lethal custom was best viewed as a violent, coercive instrument of white political and social control over blacks in a biracial society.[28] In fact, over the last few decades in the pages of scholarly journals in sociology, especially the *American Sociological Review* and *Social Forces*, lynching theory has been hotly debated.[29] Recently, two researchers, Stewart E. Tolnay and E. M. Beck, have applied intricate and elaborate quantitative techniques in an effort to increase our understanding of trends and patterns of southern lynchings.[30] Their work, moreover, points out a new direction for historical research that can be seen in one recent study that utilizes computer analysis in a quantitative approach to the history of lynching.[31]

Further, social psychologists such as Neil Smelser, Roger Brown, and T. W. Adorno focused on group dynamics and authoritarian personalities that underlie acts like lynching.[32] In addition to this, psychohistorians have examined what might be called the "psychopathology" of lynch-related behavior—manhunts, torture, mutilations, castrations, homicide, and voyeurism—as well as the southern sexual mythology that whites resorted to in justifying extralegal violence against blacks.[33] Although psychological interpretations may fail to address the issue of temporal or regional variations in lynchings, they are certainly useful at the microlevel to aid in explaining the particulars of case studies. Undoubtedly, more New South family, psychosocial-development, and gender studies are needed before a definitive psychohistory of lynching can be written. But researchers also need to move beyond a Freudian-like psychosexual approach in analyzing mob violence. In this regard the work of antiapartheid white South African scholars is suggestive. Using Jungian categories, they assume that the shared mythological thinking by white racists about blacks is as much historical material as anything preserved in archives. If ritual is the enactment of a myth, the gruesome components of lynching rituals seem like nightmare choreography, and southern lynchers often seemed compelled by the forces of an underground logic of a mythology that demanded a dark and tragic fulfillment.[34]

In the 1980s historians at last took on the task of interpreting lynching. Drawing on the new ideas about social and cultural history prompted by the new directions the profession took in the preceding twenty years, historians of the South have advanced remarkably sophisticated lines of analyses. The first to do so, Jacquelyn Dowd Hall, sees extralegal violence as essentially the by-product of the long, deep traditions of the patriarchal and white supremacist Old and New South.[35] Bertram Wyatt-Brown's *Southern Honor* views lynching, as well as most other forms of southern violence, as ultimately rooted in the long-standing southern code of honor that more often than not fostered and countenanced lynch-law horrors and mob violence.[36] One historian who uses Freudian categories, Joel Williamson, lays out a psychosexual explanation that economic fears and racial hatred were combined with sexual anxiety about black males in such a way that sometimes white southerners were led to savagely attack blacks as acts of psychological release.[37] Finally, Edward L. Ayers, in his *Vengeance and Justice*, proposed a multicausal interpretation that incorporated aspects of the psychosexual and southern honor theses along with the ideas of economic frustration caused by depression and of southern republicanism, which generally depicts lynchers as exercising popular justice as an expression of the will of the white majority.[38]

This study will not challenge these theories; indeed, it will provide ample documentation for almost all of them. Moreover, the story of lynching in Florida during the thirties shows that no single reason can explain the prevalence of this kind of vigilante activity. More explicitly, this book seeks to illustrate and analyze the varied and complicated nature of extralegal violence. The full range of mob terror can be seen in Florida in the 1930s, from simple homicides to the vicious killing of a political radical to the gala, ceremonial kind of lynching that is rich in symbolism. Therefore, assorted theories must be evaluated and tested in light of specific but differing historical circumstances.

In short, this inquiry recognizes that white racism and race relations are not static or uniform in Florida, nor in any other southern state; rather, they vary over time and from place to place.

Extralegal violence has plagued the United States since the late-eighteenth century, reaching its peak in the years between 1880 and 1930, then gradually dying out. In fact, after 1877 it had become a largely southern phenomenon in which blacks were the prime target. Furthermore, this was still the case in Florida during the 1930s. This decade, moreover, comprises a distinct period in the history of the South, especially in regard to race. Although there was continuity from an earlier time in the persistence of segregation, disfranchisement, peonage, and lynching, the decade of the Great Depression and the New Deal brought crucial and stark changes below the Mason-Dixon line. In addition to profound and unsettling agricultural transformations, federal programs, policies, and agencies challenged and eventually modified traditional behavior regarding race. These changes were in no small way responsible for the decline of lynching in the thirties and afterward. As the number of lynch incidents fell during the decade, however, white southerners sometimes resorted to the alternative tactic of "legal lynchings."

The noted Scottsboro case in Alabama serves as a reference point in examining Florida lynchings. In 1931 white southerners in Alabama convicted nine black youths of raping two white women, and sentenced eight of them to death. Although, as events proved, the evidence and facts clearly indicated innocence, white authorities carried out a series of "legal lynchings" by repeatedly convicting and sentencing these victimized young men (even though higher courts of appeal kept overturning these convictions). National, and even international, groups continually involved themselves in the affair until they succeeded in making Scottsboro the major—but certainly not the only—symbol of white racism and parochial justice in the South of the 1930s.

Unquestionably, Florida lynchings in this same period are also important symbols of southern injustice, In fact, two of them stand out from the rest because of their shocking brutality and national impact: the Claude Neal (1934) and Joseph Shoemaker (1935) affairs. Acting on the pretense of defending white womanhood, white lynchers in Jackson County tortured Claude Neal for hours before he finally died. Walter White of the National Association for the Advancement of Colored People (NAACP) brought all the macabre details of this sordid episode out into the open in a masterful exercise of national exposure. He called the attention of the Franklin D.

Roosevelt administration, the Congress, and the Department of Justice to this racial slaying; in the process he influenced congressional deliberations about proposed federal antilynching legislation. In another vicious act, urban vigilantes in Tampa acted to preserve the political establishment in the community by flogging socialist Joseph Shoemaker. His terrible death became for a short while a widely embraced cause célèbre owing in large part to the national agitation by Norman Thomas and the Socialist Party of America. Understandably, then, these two executions and their aftermath merit special consideration. Nonetheless, these two major incidents are woven into the overall tapestry of Florida and southern lynch law in the 1930s.

Florida, a large and diversified state, serves as the focus of this work. In spite of its reputation as a tourist region, it had been an Old South slave state as well as a stalwart member of the Confederate States of America (Confederacy) during the Civil War era. Moreover, it suffered chronic interracial conflict in the Reconstruction and Jim Crow periods (1865–1955). Additionally, north Florida during the thirties was a predominantly rural, agricultural zone whose inhabitants embraced antebellum traditions, values, and attitudes characteristic of the Deep South. The southern part of the state in the twentieth century, on the other hand, consisted primarily of urban enclaves with commercially and industrially based economies much like those found in the Upper South. Since extralegal incidents occurred in both localities, this offers the opportunity to assess the validity of various theories of mob violence in these two very different settings in an attempt to answer two fundamental questions: What motivated southern lynchers in Florida during the 1930s, when extralegal violence was a fading tradition? And what were the reasons for the decline of lynching in Florida and the South?

The first five chapters of this book move forward in chronological fashion. Chapter 1 covers the first three lynchings of the thirties as well as the historical roots of lynch law in this southern state. The second chapter deals with the local, regional, and national impact of the two lynch incidents of 1934, both of which were apparently motivated by the long-standing compulsion of the "rape complex." The course of events on the local and national level surrounding the three Florida lynchings of 1935–36, including the Shoemaker case as an illustration of establishment violence, are detailed in chapter 3. Examining the story of the three lynchings in the panhandle in 1937–38, chapter 4 also tells of the "legal lynching" of a young black accused of a sex-oriented, lynchable offense. The next chapter follows the continued use of extralegal violence by Floridians in 1939, and the way antilynching forces inside and outside the state reacted to it. Looking back over the entire decade, chapter 6 enumerates the trends and patterns of Florida lynch law, and then seeks to explain the reasons for this phenomenon's decline. The final chapter surveys the extralegal incidents and some of the racial turmoil that occurred in Florida after 1940, and gives a broad interpretive analysis of the meaning of extralegal violence in Florida.

1

Lynch Law, Florida Style

FLORIDA'S resort to lynch law in the twentieth century reflected the state's roots in the antebellum South. During the nineteenth century Americans in the North and other areas of the country (as well as Europeans) imagined the state as little more than a southern frontier area. To them, the mention of "Florida" conjured up images of alligators and swamps and palms, palmettos, cypress, and canebrakes, or perhaps of General Andrew Jackson dispensing summary justice to the unfortunate Alexander Arbuthnot and Robert Ambrister. In any case, visitors to north Florida in the 1840s and 1850s would have certainly noticed not only the region's unique flora but also many yeoman farmers who owned few or no slaves, a few large planters with numerous bondsmen, and virtually no urban industry. At the time, port cities were fundamentally trading, not manufacturing, centers. Ambitious men-on-the-make and colorful railroad developers arrived in force in south Florida only at the end of the 1800s; there they found cattle ranchers in places like Hillsborough County and small numbers of Seminole Indians near the Everglades and Big Cypress Swamp. More importantly, this largely rural and underdeveloped state displayed some of the distinct characteristics commonly associated with the western frontier, including the occasional use of vigilante violence to maintain social order. For instance, in the small town of Tampa during the 1850s local vigilantes lynched unwanted, troublesome white criminals who unexpectedly turned up in the years of the Third Seminole War. Likewise, extralegal violence in north Florida was sometimes employed against whites, although blacks more often felt its sting.[1]

Florida had inflicted violence and physical abuse on black people well before the 1930s, and even prior to the 1880s. After a long run as Spanish colonial possession (and a British colony from 1763 to 1783), Florida was admitted to the Union as a slave state on 3 March 1845. Following a fifteen-year influx of white southerners and their chattel into this relatively poor and sparsely settled region, blacks comprised about 45 percent of the total population of some 140,000 on the eve of the Civil War. As elsewhere, white slaveholders were a law unto themselves when it came to disciplining their charges, and the record is replete with vivid examples of how they continually utilized fear, force, and physical punishment to maintain the "peculiar institution."[2] The widely accepted prewar social habit of brutalizing and intimidating blacks carried over after the Civil War into the Reconstruction period, when anxious, disoriented whites used it to reestablish their domination over former slaves. Unending racial violence plagued Florida's postwar years, especially in places like Jackson County, in the panhandle, where ongoing black-white conflict bordered on small-scale race war.[3] One historian of American violence, Richard Maxwell Brown, discovered nine or so vigilante movements, besides the Ku Klux Klan, that operated in both north and south Florida during the late 1860s and most of the 1870s.[4]

Politics, combined with bitter racial hatred and devotion to white racial hegemony, motivated much of the antiblack violence in Florida during the 1880s. The validity of this proposition is dramatically illustrated by the lynching of Charles Savage and Howard James in Madison, Florida, in August of 1882 for the twin sins of being both black and active in the Republican Party. In the aftermath of this and other similar incidents, white Democrats went on to secure their firm hold on power with the new constitution of 1885. It disenfranchised blacks, limited their right to own property, empowered authorities to imprison them for breach of employment contracts, and excluded them from most public accommodations. Customary practices of exclusion now hardened and took on a legal, institutional character. Florida proceeded to put the southern racial caste system into place, knowing that it encouraged whites to commit violent acts against the lives, personal security, and property of black people.[5]

In the 1890s southern whites in Florida fashioned a hard world for blacks to live in. In this state and elsewhere a new generation of blacks, born in freedom and less willing than their parents to humble themselves, must have made many whites feel uneasy. Whites responded by making segregation, disfranchisement, and peonage the common lot of most blacks; moreover, whites expected them to be dutiful and obedient in assuming their subordinate role. Also, this was the decade when "radical" racism reached its zenith in Florida and the South generally. Whites embraced a set of beliefs and values that held blacks to be inferior in every respect, and claimed scientific proof substantiated their racist conclusions. Blacks were thought to be of a lower order, biologically more primitive, intellectually inferior, and emotionally underdeveloped. The ideology of white supremacy hardened toward the end of the nineteenth century, with the primary image of blacks in the white mind changing from docile child to aggressive, dangerous being. Whites also saw black males as sex-mad fiends unable to control their lust for white women.[6]

In this kind of hostile environment, then, Florida and southern lynch law reached its peak. With antiblack passions at full roar, the violence-inspiring frustrations caused by economic depression (in the early 1890s) and the ready availability of scapegoats in the form of a large, vulnerable black population set the stage for a carnival show of lynchings. Although the bloody era got off to a slow start in 1890, when lynchers killed only three blacks, that number tripled the following year. According to official records, twelve blacks were executed by mobs in 1895, and just as many in 1897, the two worst lynch years in the Sunshine State in the nineties. In all, over seventy blacks were lynched in this ten-year period.[7]

Lynchers at this time also indulged their blood lust in the form of multiple executions. These kinds of episodes, involving the simultaneous killing of two or more victims, usually in response to murder or rape allegations, transpired sporadically throughout the decade. In 1893, three blacks suspected of homicide were done away with in November near Lake City, in lynch-prone Columbia County. This event, however, served only as a prelude to the carnage of 1895 and 1897. Madison County, no stranger to extralegal violence, hosted a triple lynching on 19 May 1895, when Samuel Echols, Simeon Crowley, and John Brooks were dispatched in or near Ellaville for the accusation of raping a white woman. In 1895, Bartow, in Polk County, was the scene of an extralegal incident that claimed the lives of three victims, all black and all suspected of rape. On 9 June 1895 lynchers from the town of Mayo in Lafayette County murdered a black man named William Collins for attempted rape, and a few days later killed two or more blacks for supposedly hiding Collins from the mob. One of the largest of the state's multiple lynchings in this or any other decade occurred on 5 March 1897, when lynchers simultaneously executed five black men (suspected of murder) in the community of Juliette, Marion County, and then ten days later killed three more (also accused of murder) in the same locality. Judge Lynch returned once again to Madison County in 1899, this time in the form of a triple lynching in Dunnellon, claiming three of the year's six black victims.[8]

The tragedy of lynching continued in Florida during the opening decades of the new century in the Progressive Era. Although the early 1900s was a period of significant reform in most areas of American life, historians have long recognized that race, the "blind spot" of Progressivism, was the major exception to this generalization. This was certainly the case in Florida, where the state legislature between 1905 and 1909 passed a series of measures that outlawed cohabitation, miscegenation, and racial integration in higher education, in jail accommodations, on common carriers, on electric cars, in public waiting rooms, and at ticket windows. The poll tax came in 1910. Furthermore, according to available records, Florida lynchers in 1900 launched the new century with nine illegal executions (eight blacks and one white) in Hamilton, Hernando, Jackson, Polk, Suwannee, Sumter, and Columbia Counties; and the next year they dispatched seven black victims, five for the allegation of murder, one for rape, and one for train wrecking. In 1910, the bloodiest year of Florida's lynching history, vigilantes killed fifteen blacks and two Hispanics. Also, in that year numerous multiple lynchings took place all over the state: mob violence claimed the lives of two blacks suspected of murder in March in the Tampa Bay area; in Holmes County vigilantes murdered two blacks on 20 July, and a few days later (2 August) they lynched four more—all six were accused of homicide; and then in September, Jackson County and the Tampa Bay area hosted a double lynching. The most multiple lynchings in the annals of lynch law in the Sunshine State occurred in 1911 in Columbia County, where vigilantes executed six blacks charged with murder, and in 1916 in Alachua County, where lynchers killed four black men and two black women suspected of murdering a white.[9]

Antiblack sentiment in Florida continued during the World War I period into the 1920s, when white racists persisted in inflicting extralegal violence on black people, although with slightly less frequency.[10] If lynching statistics are a barometer of race relations, then the fact that Floridians lynched about fifty blacks in both the decades 1900–1909, and 1910–19 but fewer than forty during the 1920s suggests that in the Jazz Age mob fever abated somewhat along with the intensity of white racial hatred and the overall tension level between the races throughout the state.[11]

The prevalence of lynching in Florida between 1880 and 1930, though progressively declining, reveals that whites in this former slave state resorted to such extralegal tactics primarily to intimidate and control a large minority population so as to perpetuate white supremacy, maintain Jim Crow customs and laws, and discipline local black communities. Moreover, the racial caste system, developed and maintained at varying levels of effectiveness in different parts of the state over these years, was still the rule in race relations in the lynching counties and cities of Florida during the 1930s. This suggests that even as late as the thirties, white racism was still the basic cause of most lynchings. Nonetheless, on some occasions angry vigilantes snatched the life of a white man. One such victim was John Hodaz, an immigrant horribly murdered in Hillsborough County in the decade's first recorded lynching.

THE JOHN HODAZ LYNCHING

The mysterious dynamiting of the J. W. Waller home in Plant City stunned the county. The *Tampa Tribune*, which carried all the details of the incident, reported that on 24 April 1930, at about 6:00 A.M., Mrs. Waller opened her kitchen door only to have a bomb go off in her face. The perpetrator had placed dynamite in a tin bucket on the Waller's back porch and then connected it with a string to the doorknob. Opening the door brought an instant explosion that demolished the porch and wrecked the kitchen. The force of the blast hurled Mrs. Waller about ten feet through the air, leaving her unconscious and covered with debris. Reacting quickly to the crisis, the seriously injured woman's husband and neighbors rushed her to the hospital, where doctors amputated her left leg.[12]

The shock to the community of Plant City caused by this catastrophe was compounded by the discovery of four undetonated bombs planted at the H. B. Willaford home. Observers described the Willafords and Wallers as "prominent farmer folk," well liked by their neighbors. These two families lived about one mile from each other. Willaford had awakened that morning to discover a box of explosives with 350 sticks of dynamite under his bedroom window. Fortunately for him, a long fuse to it had burned about three inches and then sputtered out harmlessly. Later in the day he tripped a string on the path leading to his barn, which sprung a rat-trap device designed to set off another charge, but it too failed to detonate. Further, he found another bomb connected to the barn door, ready to go off. Finally, after a thorough search of his property, Willaford came across a fourth dynamite device along a well-trod path near his house. Not surprisingly, friends congratulated this lucky man on his remarkable escape from disaster.[13]

Press accounts of tragedy and near-tragedy in Plant City inflamed local opinion. Tampa papers described in graphic detail the "fiendish plot to destroy the Waller family and the H. B. Willaford family," and they declared that the "bomber had apparently worked for several hours during the night, setting the quiet country scene for wholesale murder." They confidently claimed that the perpetrator of this outrage would soon be apprehended.[14]

Reporters had good reasons for making this claim. Indeed, from the beginning of the investigation, authorities viewed a man named John Hodaz as the chief suspect. He was a forty-one-year-old naturalized citizen, born in Hungary; the *Tampa Tribune* described him as an unmarried person who often appeared quiet, depressed, and sullen. His naturalization papers revealed that he had come to the United States from eastern Europe in 1915. It would later be learned that Hodaz had worked for the U.S. Navy in World War I and had been trained in the use of explosives. Another Tampa paper published a brief story stating that the small Hungarian community in Hillsborough County declared this immigrant to be a Czech, although local Czechs correctly denied this. In response to this claim and denial, the *Tribune* reported that "nobody wants to claim him."[15]

It soon came to light that Hodaz had harbored a grievance against Waller and Willaford. About one year prior to the bombing, both Hillsborough County men had been instrumental in having the Hungarian arrested and prosecuted for a series of domestic burglaries in the Plant City area. In addition to this, Willaford had physically assaulted Hodaz, who then sought refuge in the Waller home. Waller, however, drove him back out onto the street. The humiliated immigrant apparently waited a year and then took his revenge.[16]

Needless to say, law enforcement officials went right to work on this case. Plant City officers, Tampa policemen and Hillsborough County deputies combined their manpower and resources in an intense manhunt for Hodaz. All day on 24 April, and throughout the night, they searched with bloodhounds for the alleged culprit over the countryside and highways surrounding Plant City. According to one account, Hillsborough County Sheriff R. T. Joughlin, "fresh from a moonshine raid," went about spreading a "dragnet" over the greater Plant City area. Efforts to find Hodaz at his usual haunts were unavailing, and law officers monitored major roads throughout the county. Finally, the police in neighboring communities were furnished a description of the suspect.[17]

Local newspapers wasted no time in publishing an astonishing announcement that encouraged unauthorized efforts to track down and punish the dynamiter. They printed an offer, made by Willaford and Sheriff Joughlin, promising a thousand-dollar reward to anyone coming forth with information leading to the bomber's capture, "dead or alive." Everyone in the community seemed to accept without objection this officially sanctioned invitation to a lynching.[18]

With this kind of encouragement, a large unofficial search party organized itself soon after the dynamiting. This unruly crew, consisting of scores of outraged Plant City citizens, looked day and night for Hodaz. Reacting wildly to any rumor, these angry men roamed over Hillsborough County searching frantically for the Hungarian who they believed had set the explosives at the Waller and Willaford homes. At one point, this restless group took a strawberry grower named Otto Keen, who was suspected of hiding the dynamiter, from his house and flogged him for some ten minutes before satisfying themselves that he was not concealing Hodaz. Expressing concern about these extralegal activities, law enforcement officials stated that when the suspect was apprehended, he would promptly be spirited away to an out-of-town jail for safekeeping.[19]

Authorities sought to reassure the public that they were in control of the tense situation. Directing the investigation, Sheriff Joughlin told reporters that he would soon make an arrest. On the day after the bombing, State Attorney J. Parkhill joined the case and called the dynamiting "one of the most dastardly crimes ever perpetrated in Hillsborough County." The state attorney and sheriff followed every lead until the case broke wide open.[20]

On 26 April, two days after the bombing, deputy sheriff Tobey Robinson responded to an anonymous tip and arrested Hodaz in Tampa. The suspect surrendered without a struggle; he was taken into custody at a boarding house at 115 Magnolia Avenue, where he had rented a room under the assumed name of "Alga Diaz" on the night before the bombing. "I told Hodaz what I wanted," stated Robinson, "and he came along without any resistance." The deputy added, "He only asked that he be given the chance to get a lawyer. I handcuffed him and we started out." Robinson searched Hodaz's room and found twelve thousand dollars in Polish government bonds and a file of newspaper clippings about the dynamiting episode. The deputy claimed that his prisoner confessed to planting the undetonated explosives at the Willaford home, but he denied the Waller bombing. Finally, Robinson related that Hodaz swore he was aided by an accomplice, whom he refused to name.[21]

The deputy put Hodaz in his car and headed toward Bartow, in neighboring Polk County. In some unexplained way, however, a band of gunmen knew precisely where to wait for the officer and his prisoner on this route. "I guess I was about five miles southeast of Plant City," explained Robinson, "when I saw a car coming to meet me with his headlights out." He also declared that another auto came up behind him at about the same time. "Four men jumped out wearing masks, each armed, and one holding a flashlight. Three of the guns were shoved into my side, and one against the head of Hodaz, and the flashlight brought out his features in the darkness. I guess they knew him. Not much was said and there were eight men in two cars. They still held guns on me and they put Hodaz in one car. They turned around and told me to drive like hell. As I started four shots were fired."[22]

The kidnappers took Hodaz and brutally lynched him in a secluded wooded area of the county. The next morning a woodcutter found the dead man swinging from a tree that has come to be known in local oral tradition as the "Hodaz Oak." Word of the macabre scene swept through the county, and within an hour of this discovery, a large crowd of curious onlookers— one report estimated the gathering to number in the hundreds—gathered in the pouring rain to view the gaping holes in the deceased's chest. The narrow, winding road through the woods was choked with cars and horse-drawn wagons. The crowd expressed no sympathy for the victim; in fact, one angry man in the throng had to be restrained to keep him from kicking the body of Hodaz. A few men even asked for pieces of the hangman's rope to take home as souvenirs. Sheriff Joughlin and State Attorney Parkhill were among the last to arrive at the site that morning.[23]

At the scene, in a sudden spring rainstorm, justice of the peace A. W. Hawkins hastily impaneled a coroner's jury. Indeed, he selected a jury from the spectators who stood about. This group gathered in the cleared spot beneath the tree and stared up at the mutilated form that hung above. The sheriff took down the body, and jurors watched as the coroner went through a perfunctory examination and declared, "I pronounce this man dead."[24]

After the pronouncement Sheriff Joughlin virtually absolved his deputy of any liability in this affair. He declared that Robinson was merely follow-ing orders in taking Hodaz to Bartow. Even so, neither lawman ever satis-factorily explained how the waiting gunmen knew what route would be used to take Hodaz out of Tampa that day. The deputy speculated that one of the cars driven by vigilantes must have followed him to and from Tampa. While this might have explained the presence of the car that came up from behind, it clearly failed to account for the automobile that came toward him with its lights out. As events attest, investigating authorities never chal-lenged the officer's story. Indeed, the sheriff announced at the lynch scene that he would pay the posted reward money to Deputy Robinson.[25]

The Hillsborough County sheriff took it for granted that few in Plant City would object to his awarding the reward money to his subordinate. This town, where the lynch victim lived and worked before his demise, was a small community of six thousand inhabitants in 1930.[26] Situated just twenty miles from the metropolis of Tampa, the pleasant-looking city was identi-fied as the center of strawberry farming in Florida.[27] Furthermore, unlike many farming towns in the state, Plant City was neither culturally isolated nor economically backward. Attractions and diversions in nearby Tampa offered residents many opportunities for varied ways to pass their leisure time. Moreover, the *Tampa Tribune* and *Tampa Times* kept them well informed about national and international affairs. Plant City citizens lived in a bustling community and drove on paved streets lined with many modern-looking office and commercial buildings; most owned cars and enjoyed the use of electricity in their homes.[28]

In spite of the relatively modern appearance of Plant City in 1930, many who lived in and around this rural community still adhered to the old-fashioned frontier ethics of their fathers. This code of conduct called for the immediate administration of informal justice to criminals or undesirables, bypassing costly, time-consuming legal processes. Although blacks were the most common victims of lynch law in the South, those whom the community viewed as outsiders, especially foreigners, also suffered at the hands of vigilantes.[29]

A number of foreign-born whites lived in Hillsborough County in 1930. Moreover, many of them were clearly visible to the native majority as farm-workers and transients. In a county of some 153,519 people, blacks made up 19 percent of the total population in 1930, and foreign-born whites comprised about 11 percent.[30] The latt͏ ͏luded a small contingent of eastern Europeans.[31] These large min͏ ͏, groups undoubtedly raised the anxiety level of native white sout͏ ͏.ers who were much concerned about maintaining their dominar͏ ͏. the community.[32] By 1930 the native white majority in Hillsboro͏ ͏.ounty had not yet learned to live peacefully with the varied ethn͏i ͏.ups who resided in their midst. They still looked askance at the d͏:´ ͏.nt social customs and cultural practices of the blacks, Cubans, Sr͏ ͏.ds, Italians, and eastern Europeans who lived among them in the ͏.npa Bay area.[33] Varying dress, mannerisms, languages, social habits, and institutions of immigrants sometimes stirred fear and distrust among the dominant social groups in the county. Members of this social stratum, in turn, often used extralegal violence as an instrument of social control against ethnics accused of seriously violating expected standards of behavior.[34]

In addition, economic conditions created by the onset of the Great Depression undoubtedly exacerbated ethnic tensions in Hillsborough County. Hard times in the vicinity of Plant City took the form of bank failures, mortgage foreclosures, falling crop prices, and rural unemployment. In this increasingly constricted local economy, native whites and ethnics competed for the low-income, marginal jobs provided by agricultural and commercial enterprises. In all probability, indigenous agricultural laborers were angered when they could find little or no work, while migrants, many of whom were foreign-born whites willing to accept subsistence-level wages or alternative payments, continued to plant and harvest strawberries and other crops.[35] Lynching a Hungarian immigrant might well have been one way this distressed group vented its frustrations over economic difficulties that it could not control.

It fell to the representatives of the native majority to apprehend and deal with the vigilantes who lynched Hodaz. Not surprisingly, they were pessimistic about the upcoming investigation. Sheriff Joughlin, for example, declared that identifying and capturing the murderers would "be extremely difficult in view of the scanty evidence." He continued, "My regret is that we did not get a chance to question Hodaz concerning an accomplice." State Attorney Parkhill stated that the Hillsborough County grand jury would investigate the lynching in May, but he speculated that apprehending the masked killers would be difficult without eyewitnesses to identify them.[36]

After the coroner's inquest, officials turned the lynch victim's remains over to a Plant City undertaker. Graphic press accounts and wild rumors stirred a morbid curiosity among a great many people. In fact, more than four thousand persons from all over the Tampa Bay area visited the local funeral home to view the Hungarian's body. This throng included men, women, and even children, who "were abnormally curious to see the victim of the hideous lynching."[37]

Soon after the burial of Hodaz, community leaders in the county assessed the situation created by this incident. The *Tampa Tribune* led the outcry over the lynching; along with details of this grisly extralegal execution, it featured a front-page story about how Florida led the nation in lynchings in 1929.[38] It also ran a long and strongly worded editorial titled "An Avoidable Lynching," which stated, "It is unfortunate that Hillsborough County's record for the year has already been marred." Further, the editorial emphatically noted that "this was a lynching which could have been avoided easily. . . . To take the accused man directly back into the territory where indignation centered was a stupid piece of business. He should have been taken in the other direction."[39]

The Tampa paper wrote at length about the causes of this tragedy. Moreover, its analysis went further than noting the obvious motivation of vigilantes seeking vengeance for the Plant City bombing. It explained to the public that a year earlier authorities had unsuccessfully prosecuted the Hungarian for several burglaries and then reluctantly dismissed the charges. The dismissal of charges was allegedly based on the "technicality" of a defective search warrant used to gather evidence for the state's case against Hodaz. This evasion of punishment, editors claimed, was the key factor in motivating a small group of Hillsborough County vigilantes to take the law into their own hands. The lynchers, according to the *Tribune*, were fearful that this man might once again manipulate the legal process to avoid being brought to justice. The editorial concluded, "We'll have to score another black mark against Old Man Technicality, who so often defeats justice and turns loose upon the public criminals who ought to be doing time."[40]

Editors in nearby Orange County followed the Tampa newspaper's lead. The *Orlando Sentinel* took a special interest in this case, and it ran an editorial which argued that the Plant City lynching was actually an understandable protest against legal technicalities. It also characterized Hodaz as "an undesirable citizen, a lawbreaker, and positive menace to society." *Sentinel* editors asserted that "whenever court procedures move with increased swiftness and with greater surety, the incentive to such an affair . . . will be lessened and the number of lynchings will be decreased."[41] The *Tribune* promptly responded in kind to this editorial and declared that "probably uppermost in the inflamed minds of those who did Hodaz to death was the thought that, if left to procedures of the courts, he might escape the penalty for this much more serious offense." It then concluded by asserting that "the lynching was a crime, but it was at the same time a bloody assertion of the lack of confidence in the established process of justice."[42]

The Tampa newspaper continued its analysis of this lynching in a third editorial, which appeared on 2 May 1930. In this piece, however, the *Tribune* made a full disclosure of all the facts and admitted that there was more to the Hodaz affair than a band of vigilantes venting frustration over legal technicalities. Tampa editors at last spelled out the details of the Hungarian's earlier encounter with the law, and in the process cleared up some of the misunderstandings about this case. After his previous arrest, Hodaz had pled guilty to burglary charges, and the court prepared to sentence him to a term in Florida state prison. At this point he retained a private attorney, who withdrew the guilty plea and asked the court to discharge the prisoner on the grounds that the arrest warrant had been technically defective. The court refused to do this, so Hodaz was then tried before a jury on burglary charges. And however strong the prosecution's case, after hearing all the evidence, the jury acquitted this defendant.[43]

The *Tribune* laid out these facts and tried to defend its earlier version of the affair. Editors claimed, "It is our information that the validity of the warrant figured in the trial and probably had something to do with the verdict rendered." Nonetheless, they failed to explain just how the so-called faulty warrant influenced the jury's decision or otherwise affected the trial. Nor did they state why they had failed to mention the jury trial in their previous coverage of the story; instead, they diverted attention from this question by singling out Hodaz's lawyer as the villain, arguing that it was he who had thwarted justice in order to save his client from just punishment.[44]

Other editors in south Florida wrote much less about this lynching and its causes than did the *Tribune* and the *Sentinel.* Nevertheless, they too were critical of this lawless act. The *St. Petersburg Times* for example, lamented the fact that lynch law plagued the United States, while there were no similar customs in other "civilized" nations like England, Canada, and Australia.[45] A *Miami Herald* editorial exclaimed: "Another brutal lynching disgraced the name of Florida. . . . Brave officer! It is the duty of officers of the law to protect their prisoners. The crime calls for investigation and vigorous prosecution."[46]

The lynching did indeed call for thorough investigation and vigorous prosecution of the guilty parties. In this particular instance, however, there would be neither. On 6 May 1930 the Hillsborough County criminal justice system failed to consider the Hodaz lynching when the spring term of the circuit court convened without the customary impaneling of a new grand jury. The *Tribune* announced that this step broke sharply with tradition; in fact, it was the first time in the county's history that no grand jury was convened. Disenchanted editors ran a story titled, "What, No Grand Jury?" Noting the claim "that there is no particular demand for the services of a grand jury at this time," the *Tribune* countered, "There is always some matter which could be investigated by that important body, a recent tragic occurrence near Plant City for example."[47] This article made it clear to the public that, in the final analysis, Hillsborough County officials did not really want to know who executed Hodaz.

This lynching was not an isolated incident of southern vigilante justice. Indeed, the Plant City episode was one of twenty-one such crimes that took place in the South in 1930.[48] This number of extralegal killings, double the figure of 1929, alarmed many concerned groups and organizations, especially the southern-based Commission on Interracial Cooperation (CIC) and the National Association for the Advancement for Colored People. They feared that lynching was making a comeback after declining in the 1920s.[49] In response to this situation the CIC created the Southern Commission on the Study of Lynching (SCSL) to investigate and analyze all the lynchings of 1930. To accomplish this, the SCSL named one white and one black investigator to gather evidence about vigilante-style executions of that year. The white investigator was Arthur F. Raper, a social scientist from the University of North Carolina, and the black investigator was Walter Chivers, a sociologist from Morehouse College.[50]

Arthur Raper inquired into the Hodaz affair. Details clearly raising the possibility of police complicity or misconduct in the slaying immediately attracted the attention of this sociologist. In his final report, Raper bluntly stated, "Police officers were either in connivance with the mob or else extremely stupid." He concluded that "the mob took possession of the accused in the presence of the officer, who did not fire a shot or make any other real effort to protect the accused."[51] Raper's investigation of the Hodaz killing was part of a larger story of educated, native white southerners taking a strong stand against lynching in the 1930s. This change in attitude marked a dramatic development in the history of the modern South.[52] Raper conducted rigorous inquiries into all twenty-one lynchings of 1930 in an effort to compile scientific evidence to enlighten southerners about the evils of lynchings. His findings were compiled, edited, and published by the SCSL in pamphlet form in 1932, with several other CIC members writing additional magazine articles to publicize the information.[53] Finally, these case studies and findings, including a brief analysis of the Hodaz episode, were published in 1933 as *The Tragedy of Lynching*.

Beyond producing this classic study, Raper spoke widely on its conclusions. Throughout the South he addressed civic clubs, churches, and similar groups. Many southerners, he believed, thought lynching terrible and were in fact pleased to have detailed information to buttress their opposition. The SCSL sent Raper's book to educational institutions and libraries all over the South; as a result, thoughtful readers throughout the region had the opportunity to examine the details of the Hodaz slaying in the larger context of the overall story of southern lynchings.[54]

One southerner opposed to this gruesome custom was Florida governor Doyle Carlton, although in this instance he failed to take any action in response to the illegal Hodaz execution.[55] The press reported that when the Plant City tragedy occurred, the state's chief executive was traveling by train to North Carolina on official business and could not be reached for a statement. Even so, upon returning to Florida, Carlton did not make any effort to condemn the crime publicly, nor did he call for any special investigation of this lawless act. He could have acknowledged possible police misconduct in the matter and then demanded that certain Hillsborough County law officers, perhaps Sheriff Joughlin and Deputy Robinson, be brought before him to explain their actions in this matter. The governor, however, took none of these steps.[56] He might have avoided involvement in this case in part because he was already preoccupied with combating the effects of the Great Depression in his state. In addition to this, none of the organizations and groups that usually called on government leaders to respond to such tragedies wrote Carlton after this lynching. The governor, then, was under little pressure to act.

In the Hodaz case none of the lynchers was officially identified, let alone brought to trial. Authorities in this instance clearly refused to take action. County officers, the state attorney, and even the governor failed to investigate aggressively this tragic crime; not one of them was committed to the task of apprehending and prosecuting the guilty parties. Each undoubtedly viewed the lynch victim as an undesirable immigrant and a menacing criminal who deserved his fate, even at the hands of vigilantes.

In the aftermath of the Hodaz affair, and of all the other lynchings of 1930, concerned southerners intensified their attack on lynching. In the fall of 1930 the SCSL began a fact-finding project designed to gather enough information for it to draft a model antilynching law that could be introduced into state legislatures throughout the South. As a part of this exercise, the SCSL asked Governor Carlton in a letter, "What are the powers prescribed expressly by the laws of Florida in reference to the chief executive of the state in case of lynching?" It further sought to "enlist" the governor's counsel in its cause.[57] Carlton immediately responded that Florida had no antilynching law and that "there are no powers conferred by law upon the governor relative to lynching."[58] This communication from the SCSL to Carlton was soon followed by one from the ASWPL that assured him every southern governor had the power to "erase this crime from the records of his state."[59] The Florida governor confidently reasserted his long-standing opposition to the odious custom of extralegal murder.[60]

THE SMOAKS LYNCHING

Governor Carlton dealt with only one lynching in 1931. It occurred in northwest Florida in Calhoun County, a rural district of about 1,080 square miles, bordered on the east by the Apalachicola River and to the north by the Chipola River. This excellent water transportation network, along with abundant forests, stimulated a vibrant lumber and naval stores industry that was more important to the local economy than agriculture.[61] In fact, in 1932 the value of agricultural products in this sparsely settled county was about the same as it had been in 1900,[62] and in 1930 only 12.8 percent of the total land area was utilized for farming.[63]

Not surprisingly, then, one of the prime sources of employment in Calhoun County was the lumber industry and the turpentine camps. Furthermore, this was especially true for blacks, who comprised about 19 percent of the total population of 7,238 in 1930.[64] Black laborers in the county turpentine camps suffered from low pay, inadequate housing, and perpetual debt to the company store.[65] Such harsh circumstances virtually reduced these blacks to a state of peonage. Moreover, white bosses and coworkers sometimes victimized black workers in and out of the workplace through brutal, disciplinary violence. In the 1920s, in fact, federal authorities indicted several Calhoun County naval stores operators for abusing black workers.[66] Such violence served to maintain the caste system while also coercing fearful compliance from black labor; this social dynamic was the basic cause of the 1931 Calhoun County lynching.[67]

On 18 August 1931 Charlie and Richard Smoak, two blacks, ages fifteen and twenty-three, respectively, were working in the woods near Youngstown in Calhoun County for the Youngstown Naval Stores Company. A white man named Frazier Williams was also working that day as a "woodsrider." For some unknown reason, Williams argued bitterly with these two black youths, and one of them struck him over the head, knocking him unconscious. When he regained consciousness, his assailants were gone, so he mounted his horse and rode in his injured condition to the small hamlet of Youngstown. Reportedly, he was briefly hospitalized in nearby Panama City for about one week before he fully recovered and returned to work.[68]

As soon as authorities learned of the assault on the white man they arrested the Smoaks brothers. A Bay County deputy sheriff incarcerated them in the Panama City jail because he mistakenly believed that the assault had occurred in Bay County. To no one's surprise, there was talk around Youngstown of a "lynching party," but because Williams was recovering so quickly, nothing materialized (1–2). In any event, Calhoun County sheriff R. J. Flanders proceeded to Panama City, where he secured the two youths and brought them to jail in Blountstown, the county seat. This trip was carried off without incident or threat to the black suspects. On 21 August, Richard was charged with assault with intent to commit first-degree murder, and Charlie was charged "as a principal in the second degree" (2).

The family of the two youngsters naturally worried about this turn of events. The parents, Jim and Susanna Smoak, also worked for the Youngstown Naval Stores Company and lived near Youngstown; both were reportedly "intelligent" blacks, and Susanna was literate. On 23 August, Jim traveled to Panama City seeking help for his two sons. He sought out C. C. Smith, a white man, whom he consulted about procedures to obtain the release of his two children. When Smith referred him to a Calhoun County attorney, Jim journeyed back to Blountstown and talked with this lawyer, convincing him to take the case (2–3).

Jim Smoak also turned for help to his white employers. On 25 August, C. B. Waller, manager of the Youngstown Naval Stores Company, suggested to him that the boys might be released from jail on bond. He told the concerned father that he wanted them to work at a turpentine camp run by his brother, George Waller, at California Bayou, near Panama City. He even assured Jim that he would pay their bond. On 28 August, C. B. Waller and C. C. Land, another turpentine camp operator, took care of the five hundred dollar bond on each brother so that near 5 P.M. that day the police released Richard and Charlie Smoak from custody (3–5).

The carefully fashioned plan now called for George Waller to transport the three Smoaks to California Bayou in order to meet Susanna, who had already moved the other children and just a few belongings to the new job site. A sullen Waller, however, delayed this trip until just about dark, when he and his three passengers climbed into his two-door Ford sedan. Waller drove, Jim sat next to him in the front seat, and the two youths sat in the rear seat (5–6).

At dusk the car left Blountstown, proceeding south on State Road Number 6, the most direct route to California Bayou. Soon afterward, however, Waller stopped at a store and filling station at Scotts Ferry, about fifteen miles south of Blountstown. There he bought a cold drink and candy for the two youths. At this point Jim grew uneasy, because it was now sometime after dark and they were a long way from their destination. He did not feel comfortable with the long delay. When they finally left Scotts Ferry, Waller informed the Smoaks that he was going by a school in nearby Kinard to pick up a niece who was teaching there; she would go to California Bayou with them. This meant that they would have to turn off State Road Number 6; for the first time during the trip, Waller deviated from the direct route to their destination, and this understandably alarmed Jim Smoak (6–7).

That they turned off the paved road onto a quiet, dark, and deserted dirt road only heightened Jim's apprehension. After traveling a few miles in this new direction Waller began to complain that something was wrong with the lights, as they began to blink. It turned out that these blinking lights were a signal to other men waiting ahead. Waller's car slowed to a halt, and suddenly a group of armed men stepped out of the bushes along the road and promptly surrounded the car (7–8).

There are two differing accounts of what happened next. According to Waller's recollections, the eight to twelve men in the hostile crowd ordered the two black youths out of the car, then told him and Jim to drive quickly down the road. He also maintained that since all the men wore masks, he did not recognize any of them, by either their appearance or voices. Furthermore, the men, armed with "pistols and guns," supposedly intimidated Waller into driving away from the kidnapping scene as fast as he could. Finally, he later swore that he heard no shots as he departed with Jim in the front seat (8).

Jim Smoak related an altogether different story of the crime. He stated that when the car stopped, a small mob of about five or six men approached the automobile. They all wore masks of a sort, the lower portion of their faces was covered with handkerchiefs, and there were shotguns and rifles, as well as pistols. Jim also related that he immediately recognized one of the men in the mob as C. B. Waller, who angrily shouted at Jim to shut his mouth, that they were not after him but rather the two boys. Someone in the crowd jerked the youths out of the backseat on Waller's side of the car and ordered them to comply quietly. In a moment of panic Charlie began to run; he was gunned down on the spot in front of his father's eyes. George Waller instantly started the car and drove off with Jim in the front seat next to him (9–10). Jim later revealed that as the auto sped from the lynch scene, he heard a volley of shotgun fire and knew immediately that both of his sons had been killed. Charlie died from pistol and rifle shots, and nearly all wounds were in the back. Richard was shot in the front in two or three places by shotgun blasts at close range. The killers then threw the two bodies in a ditch along the side of the road, and simply left (10–13).

At about 8:45 P.M. George Waller called Sheriff Flanders, informing him of the evening's tragic events. He then lodged Jim Smoak in the black quarters at nearby Kinard. The grief-stricken father was ordered to remain there until Waller retrieved him for the coroner's inquest, which was held that very night. En route back to the lynching scene, Waller reportedly threatened Jim's life in order to ensure favorable testimony at the inquest. Waller swore to the coroner's jury that a crowd of men took the boys away from him and that he did not recognize any of the masked kidnappers. Fearing for his safety and that of his remaining family, Jim was coerced by circumstances into swearing that Waller's testimony was true. In effect, the coroner's jury whitewashed the case at the lynching scene itself, just hours after the murders (11).

What the jurors did not know was that the Wallers had met at Susanna Smoak's home the day before the slaying, and there they evidently planned the extralegal execution of the woman's children. On this day, they also cynically informed Smoak that her two sons would be released from jail and brought to California Bayou. But when they did not appear after their release, she understandably grew worried. The day after the lynching, George Waller carried her to Youngstown to pick up a few of her belongings, keeping cruelly silent about the tragic events of the previous day. The first that she heard about her children being lynched was from friends in Youngstown; one can only imagine her shock and dismay (14–15).

The lynching destroyed the Smoak family. By the time Susanna Smoak arrived in Youngstown, Jim had already fled to parts unknown. The stunned mother hurriedly buried her sons and moved to the nearby hamlet of Cottondale (about twenty miles north of Youngstown) in such haste that she left all her possessions behind. She later asked state attorney John

H. Carter to help her reclaim her belongings; he asked C .B. Waller (undoubtedly one of the lynchers) to haul her things to Cottondale on his truck. Waller, however, flatly refused to honor this request. Smoak obviously feared for her safety if she were to return to Youngstown, and she had no money to hire someone to retrieve her family's personal belongings (15).

While Jim and Susanna Smoak attempted to recover from the terror of the murder of their sons, this lynching case was brought before the Calhoun County grand jury by State Attorney Carter. Late in 1931, much to the consternation of the state attorney, that body was determined to follow the example of the coroner's jury and whitewash the entire affair. Carter kept in close contact with Governor Carlton about this matter, and wrote him declaring, "I summoned a great number of persons before the grand jury, including Frazier Williams, as well as George and C. B. Waller." He hastened to add that "of course, no indictments were returned, as the evidence was wholly incomplete." He concluded his letter to the governor, "The general opinion seems to be that the matter had died down, and nothing further will ever come of it. This is exactly the situation I wanted."[69] Carter took advantage of this and conducted his own investigation into the affair.

Governor Carlton's interest in this case prompted the state attorney's extraordinary investigative efforts. The governor had read about the lynching in several Florida newspapers that confused the details of the case. The *St. Petersburg Times*, the *Tampa Tribune*, the *Miami Herald*, and the *Tallahassee Democrat* mistakenly reported that the Smoaks who were lynched were father and son, not brothers, and they all incorrectly stated that the lynch victims had been dragged from their homes by the mob and then murdered.[70] The governor responded to these stories about the lynching by ordering an official investigation into the crime. He also declared his regret, adding that the killers "lynched not only the Negroes, but the state of Florida."[71] These statements earned him a flattering telegram from the CIC's Will Alexander, which read in part, "Let us commend heartily your vigorous statement relative to the Blountstown lynching and your expressed determination to do everything possible to apprehend and punish the culprits." He continued, "This case of mob murder was peculiarly flagrant and indefensible. Florida owes it to herself and the South to bring the perpetrators to justice as the only possible means of vindicating in some degree our laws and our civilization."[72]

During September and October 1931, the governor's office received sporadic protests over the lynching. For example, the Panama City physician who treated Frazier Williams wrote that this double lynching was "one of the worst crimes ever committed in the state."[73] A man from Brooklyn, New York, defined the slaying of the Smoaks as a "barbaric act" that left a "stench in the nostrils of the whole civilized world."[74] The most potent protest, without a doubt, came in the form of a heartfelt letter from Susanna Smoak herself: she implored the governor to find and punish her sons' lynchers.[75] Carlton was moved to forward the letter to State Attorney Carter, along with an urgent request to aid this "family in the course of [his] investigation."[76] On 5 November Carter wrote Carlton, informing him he would help Smoak if he could, and promising a genuine attempt to find the vigilantes.[77] The governor wrote Smoak, assuring her that he would conduct an investigation into the matter that would go beyond the grand jury's inquiry.[78]

After the grand jury dismissed the affair, the state attorney secretly conducted his own inquiry into the lynching, as he had promised the governor. He hired a private investigator who located Jim Smoak in south Alabama; Carter traveled out of the state to talk with Smoak in person, and the black man rewarded this effort by relating all the details of the lynching to the state attorney, but when Carter suggested the possibility that the father of the slain boys might return to Calhoun County to testify against the lynchers, Jim quickly refused even to consider it. Smoak rightly believed his life would be in danger, because C. B. Waller knew he had recognized him as one of the lynchers. In any event, Carter remained in constant contact with Jim Smoak through Susanna, and could see him upon two or three days' notice.[79]

Upon completion of his special investigation, Carter sent a detailed report of the whole affair to Governor Carlton on 5 March 1932. In an accompanying letter, he declared that he would ask the grand jury, scheduled to meet in April 1932, to return indictments for first-degree murder against C.B. and George Waller. He also revealed his beliefs about the case to the governor, and they were none too optimistic: "I realize that the case depends upon the testimony of two Negroes, and in Calhoun County, a Negro's word is not worth much where it conflicts with a white man's." He continued, "However, the circumstances are so strong, and the lynching was such a cold-blooded affair that I feel it my duty to leave no stone unturned to bring the guilty parties, or some of them, to justice."[80] The governor, in appreciation of this effort, wrote the state attorney with a sense of resignation in the face of overpowering forces of racial prejudice and discrimination. "I hope you can secure an indictment even though a conviction may not be possible," he said, and wistfully added, "Certainly these men should not escape punishment for such a dastardly crime."[81]

Carter followed through on his pledge to the governor. In the spring of 1932, before "one of the best grand juries convened in Calhoun County," he presented evidence that positively identified three participants in the lynching. Nevertheless, no indictments were returned because "the case rested upon Negro testimony." He expressed his disappointment to Carlton, writing, "I have done my very best to apprehend the guilty parties, and have them billed. But unless I secure additional evidence, it will be useless to present the case to future grand juries. I will keep you advised of further developments."[82] The governor wrote Carlton, "I am sure that you are doing everything that could be done in this matter."[83]

The reaction by officers in the criminal justice system to this double lynching in Calhoun County was all too typical in rural southern regions. A black in that county had no voice in court because of the influence of local white public opinion. Carter knew that the white lynchers in this case had to be tried in a local court, and that an all-white jury would give greater weight to the white man's testimony than to a black's. The assumption here was based on the deep, pervasive white conviction that it was dangerous to allow blacks to vindicate their rights against whites.[84] Not surprisingly, then, Jim and Susanna Smoak were never brought in to testify in a court of law regarding the execution of their two sons.

The Henry Woods Lynching

After the Smoaks slayings, the eighth of eleven that occurred in the South in 1931, Governor Carlton faced one final lynching on his watch.[85] In 1932 Henry Woods was murdered by a mob in Hamilton County, a thinly settled region of some 9,454 residents.[86] An area entirely cut off from the rest of Florida by the Suwannee River and its tributary, the Withlachooche, it contained some of the best farmland in the state; over 40 percent of its total land area was devoted to farming in 1930. Sea island cotton was the chief agricultural crop, although there was a healthy lumber and turpentine industry as well.[87] A secluded and backward county classified as 100 percent rural, Hamilton County was plagued by one of the highest illiteracy rates in the state; in fact, in 1930 about 30 percent of its children between the ages of seven and nine did not even attend school.[88] Above all, this was a Jim Crow county, where blacks, who comprised slightly over one-third of the total population (1930), were coerced by whites into accepting second-class citizenship. Racial exclusion by law and custom set them apart as a separate group targeted for special, unfair treatment; they were forbidden to vote, to hold office, to sit on juries, to attend white schools, to attend white churches, and to hold anything but the most menial, low-paying jobs. In agriculture most blacks were tenants and sharecroppers who endured the economic burden of peonage and perpetual debt all of their lives. In addition, whites socially segregated blacks, believing them to be an inferior people; blacks, then, clearly understood that whites in Hamilton County would not tolerate black assaults on a white person, especially if that white person was a police officer.[89]

Henry Woods, a Jasper black, was lynched in Hamilton County on 6 June 1932, for this very kind of attack. Chief of police Ira J. Fowler arrested Woods for allegedly stealing an automobile, and the suspect violently resisted. In the ensuing scuffle, Woods killed the white police chief. Almost immediately an intense manhunt was organized by Hamilton County sheriff J. H. Hunter, law officers from nearby Columbia County, and a posse of fifteen hastily deputized men. A few days after the murder of Fowler, the enraged posse cornered Woods in a field about three miles from Jasper. Reportedly, some farmers had captured, tied up, and held the black suspect for lawmen, expecting to collect a $250 reward; the angry law officers, however, had no intention of bringing Woods in for trial. Instead, seeking vengeance outside the law, these authorities were bent on lynching the black man as soon as they found him.[90]

When Woods fell into the hands of the posse, which by then was little more than a vigilante mob, they quickly executed him. There were conflicting versions of the details of this lynching. The skimpy story carried by the Associated Press merely related that a posse led by police officers shot and killed Woods.[91] A Lake City resident familiar with the facts of the case wrote a letter to the CIC's Will Alexander that outlined another, more ghastly account. According to this report, the posse first riddled Wood's body with bullets; then, while he was still alive, it took him to "some secluded spot putting him on a brush heap after slicing the body with knives." Finally, the letter claimed that the vengeful lawmen and their posse burned his body as their last act of violence.[92]

The CIC director forwarded this letter to Governor Carlton along with a plea for an investigation.[93] The correspondence reached the governor's office in mid-August, but the state's chief executive ordered no inquiries, nor did he issue a public statement deploring the lynching. Carlton may have been unresponsive because he had only a few months left in office, or he may simply have been weary of dealing with these affairs of illegal executions. Oddly enough, the press in Florida also had little to say about the incident; when it had occurred in early June, newspapers, preoccupied with the round of recently held summer primary elections, either ignored the extralegal murder altogether or mentioned it only in passing. Analysis of election returns apparently monopolized all available editorial space in major dailies throughout the state. And perhaps because papers in Florida and the rest of the country paid so little attention to this crime, precious few protest letters or telegrams were sent to the governor's office. In short, a lame-duck governor ignored this extralegal killing, and distracted editors conveniently disregarded it as hardly newsworthy during the primary season.

More difficult to understand is why the black press and the NAACP were silent as well about this lynching. In the early 1930s the association was temporarily diverted from its ongoing antilynching work by extraordinary financial woes and, worse still, by internal dissension.[94] Bitter disputes between leaders such as W. E. B. Du Bois and Walter White, compounded by the membership's apprehension over events surrounding the Scottsboro case in Alabama, were central concerns of the association in the dark days of the Great Depression.[95] Indeed, it was not until 1933 that the NAACP was able to commit itself to a reinvigorated, sustained antilynching drive throughout the rest of the decade. In any event, the fate of Henry Woods, for whatever reasons, fell between the cracks in the dark days of 1932.[96]

2

Protecting White Women

ALTHOUGH there were no lynchings in Florida in 1933, vigilantes committed twenty-eight such crimes elsewhere in the South.[1] To combat this continuing abuse, southern antilynching groups carried on their campaign to educate the region's citizens about the evils of lynching. Part of this educational effort was provided by University of North Carolina law professor James H. Chadbourn, a legal scholar who worked for the Commission on Interracial Cooperation's Southern Commission on the Study of Lynching. His well-researched volume, *Lynching and the Law*,[2] was published in 1933, and in early January 1934 a fresh copy was forwarded to Florida's new governor, David Sholtz. Whether Sholtz read (or even bothered to skim through) the book is not known; in any case, it was intended to enlighten all southerners about an important issue. It consisted of a survey of all existing legislation relating to lynching, an examination of court decisions concerning these laws, and a model antilynching statute. Sholtz thanked the SCSL for the study and confidently assured them that, as governor, he already had the necessary powers to stop lynching activity in his state. Finally, he declined a request that he push for an antilynching bill in Florida.[3]

THE ROBERT JOHNSON LYNCHING

In mid-January 1934, just a few weeks after the SCSL sent *Lynching and the Law* to Sholtz, the Florida branch of the ASWPL met with the governor. At this meeting Sholtz gave Jane Cornell, head of the Florida Council of the association, his assurance that there would be no lynchings in Florida if he "had two hours to get to the scene of the disturbance." He also asserted that he had "sufficient power to apprehend and punish lynchers," which he would "use to the utmost should a lynching occur in Florida."[4] Actually, Sholtz could do little to apprehend or punish lynchers if local authorities failed to act aggressively in such cases. In fact, by law he could not even call

47

out the National Guard to the site of a threatened execution if county officials did not request it.[5]

Only a few days after Governor Sholtz had conferred with representatives of the Florida ASWPL, a lynching occurred in Tampa, the second of
1934. On 28 January 1934 Robert Johnson, a forty-year-old black, was
arrested by Tampa police. He was accused of robbing and raping a white
woman in the Belmont Heights area of the town. Tampa detectives subsequently investigated the matter thoroughly and exonerated Johnson. Still,
some white Tampans believed he was guilty of the most heinous crime a
black man could commit, the rape of a white woman. The fact that no
formal charges were ever filed against Johnson for this alleged act failed to
change their minds. In spite of the evidence to the contrary, a group of
white citizens remained convinced that he was getting away with sexually
violating a white woman, an idea they found intolerable.[6]

Lynch-minded Tampans plotted Johnson's execution; police officials
made it easier to plan the black man's demise by the way they mishandled
the case. The Tampa police department of the mid-1930s, plagued by corruption and inefficiency, apparently did not have its heart in the job of
protecting the rights and safety of a black man accused of a lynchable offense.[7] Indeed, there may have been officers on the force who sympathized
with those who wished to punish the suspect in this case. In any event, the
police refused to let Johnson walk away a free man after the detectives'
investigation, and issued a warrant accusing him of stealing chickens and
turkeys. In light of this development, it became necessary to transfer him
from the city jail to the county prison.[8]

The transfer, however, was fatally ill-timed. For some reason, Johnson
was not moved by Tampa policemen or Hillsborough County deputies.
Indeed, the person assigned to pick up and move the black prisoner was
Deputy Constable Thomas Graves, who acted in this matter on the authority of his brother, Constable Hardy Graves. The deputy constable was on
his way home from a routine evening shift when he decided, with his brother's
approval, to transfer Johnson to the county facility. Graves called the police
detective bureau shortly after midnight on 30 January to inform city authorities that he was coming for the black man. Needless to say, it was not
standard procedure to move a prisoner in the middle of the night. The
Tampa police department and sheriff's office could not later explain why
this was allowed to happen. Graves, however, would later defend his actions by stating, "I went to the police station to transfer [Johnson] to the
county jail, thinking with that out of the way, I would not have to get up so
early the next morning."

In the dead of the night, at about 2:30 A.M., detectives delivered Johnson to Graves at city hall. The deputy constable put his prisoner in the front seat of his automobile and drove toward the county jail. Suddenly, three cars appeared on the deserted downtown streets of Tampa and hemmed Graves in. "At first I thought it was a traffic jam and tried to drive out of it," the deputy constable declared subsequently. Men in these cars proceeded to kidnap Johnson from his escort in a dramatic and somewhat acrobatic way, according to Graves:

> By this time there was a car on either side of me, and before I realized what was happening a man got out of either car, jumped on the running board of my car and threw open the front doors at the same time. The man at my left caught me by the mouth and whirled me over the backseat of my car. This man and the other one then got in the back seat and forced me down on the floor board, one holding his foot on my neck.

At this point, one of Graves's assailants promptly disarmed him. They also forced him to lie down in his own car for the entire twenty-minute death ride. Graves later reported that Johnson was resigned to his fate and never begged for mercy or broke down in any way. "I heard the Negro say only one thing," stated the deputy constable. In response to one of the kidnappers who said to Johnson, "You ——, you know you did it," the latter supposedly replied, "Yes, white folks, but I am sorry." Finally, the vigilantes put Graves out of the car and drove off with Johnson to a wooded section of town.

The lynching was a carefully planned and swiftly executed murder. The kidnappers carried the terrified Johnson to the lynching site along the Hillsborough River near Sligh Avenue, where a crowd of about thirty Tampa citizens had gathered to witness the victim's execution. Ironically, the lynchers gunned down Johnson with Graves's own .38 caliber pistol. The killers, making every round count, shot the hapless black man four times in the head and once in the body. Leaving the bloody remains by the side of the road, the crowd of men piled into about fifteen automobiles and drove off. Just about thirty minutes after being kidnapped, Johnson was dead.

As soon as he could, Graves phoned the sheriff's office to report the lynching. He then walked to the home of a nearby justice of the peace, and the two men searched with flashlights for Johnson's body. At daybreak they found it. Later that morning a coroner's jury examined the body, but the inquiry into this lynching would go much farther than a coroner's investigation.

Governor David Sholtz immediately involved himself in this case. He ordered Tampa officials to take meaningful investigative steps to bring the lynchers to justice. The governor's telegrams to state attorney Rex Farrior and sheriff Will Spencer were published in full in the *Tampa Tribune* for all to read. Florida's chief executive ordered the state attorney "to use every agency and function of your office to detect and bring to speedy justice those guilty of the lynching which took place in your county today."[9] He wired the sheriff a similar message:

> I have just been informed of the lynching of Robert Johnson, Negro, in your community today, but have no report from you. We don't condone the crime of lynching in Florida. I am holding you responsible for immediate and diligent investigation of this crime to the end that those persons guilty of this murder shall be brought to speedy justice under the laws of this state.[10]

In reply to Sholtz's demand for a thorough investigation, Tampa officials fashioned their plans. Farrior and other authorities conferred briefly on 31 January, and then announced that the Hillsborough County grand jury, already in session, would look into the lynching at once. The state attorney declared that "lynching is as much a matter for investigation by the grand jury as murder and other capital crimes." He added, "We must not tolerate such a happening that spreads a blot on Tampa's history." In heading up the grand jury inquiry, Farrior revealed a determined attitude, stating, "We expect to dig to the bottom of it, and if the evidence is produced pointing to persons who had part in it, indictments will be returned."[11]

In a marathon all-day session the day after the lynching, Farrior and the grand jury grilled some twelve witnesses. The state attorney immediately ruled out the possibility that the work of the jury was to answer the "question of the guilt or innocence of the Negro as regards the attack on the woman." Rather, he observed, "It is a question of stamping out lynching."[12]

The obvious possibility confronting jurors was that Tom and Hardy Graves had conspired with the lynchers. In a strenuous effort to ascertain this, a determined grand jury questioned Tom Graves for four-and-a-half hours. Under pointed questioning it was revealed that the deputy constable was wholly without authority in transferring the prisoner from the city jail and that he had no more right in that capacity than had any private citizen. In fact, Graves was working as an assistant to his brother on a special police commission that had expired weeks earlier. Other parts of Graves's testimony also dismayed the grand jury. For instance, he claimed that the vigilantes had mishandled and badly bruised him during the kidnapping; yet when jurors examined his body, they found no such bruises. Until 7:35 P.M.

the grand jury put considerable pressure on the deputy constable but failed to uncover evidence of any conspiracy involving Graves or his brother.[13]

Governor Sholtz, outraged over the lynching, demanded that Tom and Hardy Graves be brought before him to explain their actions. He did not even want to wait a day for the Graves brothers to testify before the grand jury. When telephoned by Farrior, however, Sholtz relented, saying, "All right, but have them here by Thursday." And so the governor confronted the two suspected conspirators but failed to persuade them to change their highly suspect story.[14] Sholtz's indignation over the lynching was genuine. He fancied himself a New Deal liberal who abhorred such a gruesome custom as lynching.[15] Indeed, his strong reaction to the Tampa incident earned him praise from unexpected quarters. One black notable wrote him that the "Negroes of Florida commend you for your stand in [the]deplorable Tampa tragedy."[16] "You give encouragement to my people by taking prompt and definite action," declared J. R. E. Lee, president of the Florida Agricultural and Mechanical College for blacks.[17] The Colored Citizen's Committee of Jacksonville stated that it had "voted its unanimous approval of [his] attitude toward the lynching of Robert Johnson."[18] "The colored citizens wish to thank you for your fearless stand and hasty action in upholding the dignity of the law," wired the Key West branch of the NAACP.[19] Several black clergymen also lavished Sholtz with praise, and one in particular observed that the governor "believes in Justice and fair play regardless of race or color."[20]

Not everyone, of course, praised Sholtz for his words and deeds. In fact, a few whites wrote him, criticizing his antilynching stance. One Tampa woman asserted that she could not understand Sholtz's concern and the public stir over the lynching of Johnson when "nothing is done if white women are murdered by blacks."[21] A woman from Minneapolis, Minnesota, declared, "I must say that the Negroes are responsible for all things that happen to them."[22] And a Jacksonville woman observed, "I noticed through the daily press you seem to be much concerned over the recent lynching of that Negro rapist in our state." She added, "The sob sisters are urging you to hunt out and prosecute men who are only endeavoring to protect their children from these beasts in human form. . . . If they let our white girls alone there will be no lynching."[23]

By no means were these harsh sentiments shared by all whites in Tampa. Indeed, many Tampans knew all too well that lynchings were messy affairs that created bad press for their community. The Kiwanis Club, for example, publicly "deplored" the crime because it was concerned about damage to the city's and state's good name. One of its spokesmen stated, "It was not a Negro lynched any more than it was the lynching of Tampa, Hillsborough

County, and Florida. And the publicity going out over the country is the very worst kind we could get."[24] Further, a *Tribune* editorial demanded, "There must be the fullest investigation of the lynching which occurred in this county." And it added, "The Governor should order officers here to continue the inquiry until the responsibility for the act is definitely placed."[25]

Tampans who protested the lynching of Johnson said little in the press about its causes. Nonetheless, almost everyone in the community, white and black, understood why Johnson was murdered by vigilantes. The extralegal execution of this black man was not merely punishment meted out to one individual. Rather, it was a device designed to warn blacks "to stay in their place." To be sure, white Tampa was never uncertain about what place blacks should have in the city's life. During the 1930s they were determined to maintain the city's large black population of some twenty-two thousand residents (about 21 percent of the total) in a socially inferior position.[26] They forced this large minority to endure an existence of harsh segregation and unending racial discrimination. The result was a sharply drawn color line that marked blacks off as a segregated group deemed undesirable for free association with white people in many types of relationships.[27]

It was common at this time to see signs around town pointing "colored" here and "white" there. In the area of transportation, blacks either had to sit at the back or ride in separate streetcars. Unlike the situation in many other southern cities, Tampa blacks did not attend any of the downtown movie houses and theaters because no balconies or other provisions were made for them. A separate waiting room was provided for them at the downtown railroad station. White objections kept blacks out of parks, beaches, and swimming areas in various sections of the city. In addition, blacks had to attend their own schools in their own neighborhoods. Amusement places, such as Ballast Point and public dance halls, had a rigid color line. The city's restaurant and hotel managers, by general agreement, did not permit blacks to use their facilities.[28]

The color line was also tightly drawn in the area of employment. At no time during the 1930s were blacks permitted to compete on equal terms for jobs in the city. Custom relegated the majority of them to service occupations so that the bulk of the black population was concentrated in lower-paid menial and unpleasant jobs.[29] The employment policies of Tampa companies and racial discrimination in training and promotion made it virtually impossible for blacks to find jobs in the skilled trades, in clerical and sales work, or as foremen or managers. Most Tampa industries had what might be described as a "lily white" employment policy; this was especially true of the public utilities and the city banks and offices.[30] Moreover, certain Tampa trade unions constitutionally excluded blacks from membership and thus restricted black job opportunities.[31]

Tampa blacks were confined to certain residential areas of town. Not surprisingly, these regions were the most run-down and deteriorated areas of the city. Most blacks rented housing from white property owners, and the poorest wood-frame quarters were crowded and lacked even indoor plumbing facilities.[32]

It was in the social realm, however, that Tampa blacks were most completely segregated from whites. The web of social relationships among black people was sharply marked off from the corresponding world of white people. The typical white in Tampa did not believe in addressing a black as Mr., Mrs., or Miss. He usually would not permit a black to call him by his first name. He did not approve of shaking hands with blacks or of eating with them or of sharing public sanitary facilities with them. He would not sit next to blacks in public places nor allow them to attend his schools or churches. He vehemently objected to interracial marriage, although he may have overlooked a white man's occasional sexual excursion across the color line.[33]

Economic factors undoubtedly aggravated racial tensions in Tampa. In 1934 this Florida community was still struggling to recover from the Great Depression; in fact, the number of persons employed in wholesale and retail trade at this time was well below pre-Depression levels.[34] In this troubled situation some whites and many blacks vied for the same low-paying jobs provided by the city's numerous enterprises. Job-seeking whites, moreover, were naturally resentful when blacks found employment as laborers, janitors, filling station attendants, cooks, maids, and dishwashers.[35] In addition, unemployed whites were, in all probability, dismayed that some blacks found jobs on public works projects provided by New Deal agencies and that other blacks received federal aid as victims of the Depression.[36]

In spite of their subordinate social position, blacks did not passively accept the Johnson execution; black Tampans urged officials to fix responsibility for the lynching. One black minister declared that the vigilante murder was "particularly unfair because those who took the prisoner from the deputy did not know he was guilty." He added that Johnson was "given no chance to establish his innocence."[37] The Tampa Urban League and local branch of the NAACP protested the lynching to the mayor, chief of police, state attorney, and the governor.[38] The Tampa Negro Ministerial Alliance called on Sholtz and other "officers of the law to use every means to fix responsibility for the act," and then urged white officials "to make life more secure for the Negro citizens of Tampa, Hillsborough County and Florida."[39]

The 1934 Tampa lynching also disturbed the national black community. An acrimonious black press denounced this extralegal execution; black newspapers in Chicago, Baltimore, Pittsburgh, and Atlanta printed the bloody details of the crime on their front pages.[40] The *Pittsburgh Courier* wrote that the Johnson lynching was a "death-dealing orgy" and "cold-blooded murder" that "aroused the ire of the entire nation." The *Courier* also claimed that the Tampa slaying was certain to "help the antilynching bill cause" because it occurred "in the short space of a month since Costigan-Wagner [federal antilynching bill] was introduced" and showed how powerless state authorities "are to deal with lynch murders."[41] Along these same lines, the NAACP magazine, the *Crisis*, argued that the facts of the Johnson killing and other similar outrages invalidated the argument of many southerners that a federal antilynching law was not necessary because state leaders could stop the practice.[42]

The lynching of Johnson did indeed stir antilynching forces. The first such organization to protest the Tampa episode was the ASWPL. As soon as she heard about the Tampa affair, Jessie Daniel Ames sternly lectured Governor Sholtz about his commitment to take action against lynchers. In a telegram she reminded him, "Last Thursday you assured a committee headed by Mrs. William P. Cornell, Chairman of Florida Council of ASWPL, that while you are governor of Florida there would be no lynching if you had two hours to get to the scene of the disturbance and that the law gives you sufficient power to apprehend and punish lynchers, which you would use to the utmost should a lynching occur in Florida during your administration." In explaining his failure to take preventive measures, the governor pointed out, "The deplorable lynching which took place in Tampa early this morning came out of the clear sky without prior warning or knowledge of this office that it was anticipated."[43]

The NAACP also took a special interest in this case. During the 1930s this organization made combating lynching its major goal, and its leaders adopted the strategy of exploiting emotional revulsion over the brutality of lynching. They would, then, publicize findings of their investigations in newspapers and circulate them among liberal organizations. In this way they hoped to stir public opinion in favor of the need for passage of federal antilynching legislation.[44] In this particular instance, Walter White asked Governor Sholtz to support the Costigan-Wagner antilynching bill in light of the Tampa tragedy.[45] White mailed the governor a fresh copy of this proposed legislation, which defined a mob, provided for federal action through federal district courts if states or local agents did not act against lynchers within thirty days, and proposed a fine of ten thousand dollars on counties where lynchings occurred.[46] White's letter accompanying the bill anticipated the governor's objection that the law would certainly "infringe upon the rights of the states," so he assured Sholtz that "it relieves the states of no single responsibility nor deprives them of one iota of any of their rights in that it provides for federal assistance in punishing lynchers only after states shall have failed, neglected, refused, or been unsuccessful in acting." It also cited President Franklin Roosevelt's "unequivocal condemnation of lynching as 'mass murder'" as well as the president's statement at the opening of Congress that lynching "calls on the strong arm of the government for suppression, and calls for an aroused public opinion."[47]

Sholtz had kept abreast of the antilynching law controversy and knew that in January 1934 the NAACP's bill had been introduced into Congress. In spite of the Tampa affair, however, the governor refused White's invitation to support a federal antilynching law. He wrote to the NAACP executive director, "I am unalterably opposed to lynching and shall use the full powers of my office at all times to bring about the proper punishment of those guilty of this unlawful practice."[48] Sholtz had already thrown in his lot with the ASWPL, and decided to work for eradication of extralegal violence at the state level.[49]

Although the Tampa slaying failed to convince Sholtz to support the federal antilynching bill pending in Congress, it did serve as an example of the tragedy of lynching in one Florida community. Tampa lynchers kidnapped Johnson from a deputy constable, passed judgment on his guilt, and summarily executed him on the banks of the Hillsborough River in the middle of the night. They were determined that blacks in Tampa should remain socially subordinate and that no black man should escape even the accusation that he had sexual relations with a white woman.

The vigilantes, of course, were never brought to trial. Yet from the beginning of the grand jury investigation, the Hillsborough County sheriff and even the governor of Florida were certain that Tom Graves knew "every man in the crowd," and they believed he should have been indicted as a conspirator in the lynching.[50] But the grand jury probe, which had initially promised so much, failed to return any indictments. In March 1934 State Attorney Farrior privately explained the outcome to the governor, contending, "I did everything in my power . . . to get an indictment," but the majority of the jurors were in "sympathy with the lynching" and voted by a large majority against removing Tom Graves from office.[51] In the final analysis, the white citizenry of Tampa and Florida officials did not genuinely support vigorous prosecution of lynchers when the victim was black. By failing to apprehend and punish the Tampa lynchers, officials did little to discourage other vigilantes in the state, who were soon to strike again.

THE CLAUDE NEAL LYNCHING

Scottsboro has so successfully preempted the attention of liberals and scholars as the cause célèbre of racism and parochial justice in the 1930s that few remember a second, similar event: the lynching of a black man named Claude Neal in Greenwood, Florida, on 26 October 1934. The grotesque murder of Neal, which NAACP spokesman Walter White condemned as "one of the most bestial crimes ever committed by a mob,"[52] did not, even then, upstage the Scottsboro case. Yet, like Scottsboro, it too produced an outcry from liberal organizations, attracted the attention of President Roosevelt, and received widespread newspaper coverage. Similarities of circumstance united Neal's plight with that of the Scottsboro boys: in both cases, there had been alleged violation of the South's most sacred taboo— sex between a black male and a white female; in retaliation, the persons who determined justice, the Alabama juries and the Florida lynch mob, imposed severe penalties to deter further transgressions.

Though discrimination against blacks characterized American life and was acceptable to most Americans at this time, Scottsboro and the Neal murder produced an outcry against racial injustice. The message was carried principally by the national media, and with it came the threat of deterrence from the more effective national government. Violence toward blacks, whether in a formal court of law in Alabama or under an oak tree in Jackson County, Florida, was increasingly unacceptable.

Jackson County was clearly a lynch-prone area. In fact, six lynchings of blacks had taken place there between 1900 and 1930, the largest number for any Florida county at a time when the state had the highest ratio of lynchings of blacks to its black population of any in America.[53] It was a highly conservative, culturally isolated rural county with a population of 31,969 in 1930.[54] Located on the borders of Alabama and the tip of southwestern Georgia, it was identified by Howard Odum in 1933 as a part of the "southern cotton and tobacco sub-region," one of the poorest in the South.[55] Traditions and values of the Old South still influenced popular thought at that time, and recollections of Reconstruction still produced vivid and unpleasant memories.[56] More than 90 percent of its inhabitants were considered rural population in 1930,[57] and nearly half of Jackson County's farm operators were either tenants or sharecroppers.[58] Circumstances of the Depression heightened social tensions and probably increased the likelihood of violence against blacks, who comprised 40 percent of the county's population. McGovern has argued that economic factors in the Neal lynching were undoubtedly present,[59] along with confidence by whites in their nearly unlimited power over blacks. Perhaps, however, he underestimates the role of "status anxiety" on the part of whites in dictating their use of violence against them.

The murder of pretty nineteen-year-old Lola Cannidy on 18 October 1934 brought instant and unwanted attention to Jackson County. According to local sheriff Flake Chambliss's report, Cannidy, of Greenwood, whose father was a poor farmer with twenty acres of land, left home at noon on 17 October to go to a nearby water pump and did not return.[60] Her body was found at 6:30 the following morning, after a protracted search during the night. A married black, Claude Neal, 23, who lived across the road from the Cannidys, was arrested as a suspect later that morning and jailed in Marianna when Sheriff Chambliss found a piece of cloth that allegedly fit Neal's torn shirt. Although Neal could not be considered as more than a major suspect at the time, the sheriff sensed a lynch spirit and immediately transferred Neal to a jail some distance from Marianna. A coroner's jury impaneled at the time heard from a local physician that Cannidy had been raped, although this contention was denied by a second doctor, who made a special report to the sheriff and the state attorney. Other fragments of evidence served to incriminate Neal with the jury, aside from the fact that the two had been talking together, there were the bloodied piece of torn shirt, a bloody hammer (ownership never identified), cuts on Neal's hands (his employer testified that Neal explained this to him as a consequence of working on a fence), and a ring from the watch stem found near the body (believed incriminating because the ring from Neal's watch was missing when he was taken into custody).[61]

Even before the completion of hearings by the coroner's jury, a large number of whites assumed that Neal had killed or raped Cannidy. On 19 October, the first day of the coroner's jury hearings, and during the two days before that all-white body would actually accuse Neal of murder, a lynch mob was already speeding down adjacent highways, looking for him.[62]

Neal, meanwhile, was spirited from one jail to another in northwest Florida, just steps ahead of the mob. Lawmen hurriedly moved the black youth to jails in Washington County (Chipley), Bay County (Panama City), and then to Escambia County (Pensacola). The Jackson County mob almost caught Neal in Panama City. Comprised of a group of about one hundred men, it arrived in town Friday evening and went directly to the jail, demanding the black suspect be turned over to them. Jailer Will Pledger stood up to the throng. Although he informed them that the Bay County sheriff had just left with Neal for an undisclosed location, he allowed them to search the facility to verify his story. The mob failed to find its prey but decided to wait for the sheriff to return. At length he arrived and apologetically explained to the waiting crowd that Neal had been moved to another town, but he just could not tell them where. Lastly, he asked them to "kindly disperse."[63]

The frustrated mob, however, was not yet ready to call it a night. Returning from Panama City, a large group of these would-be lynchers suddenly appeared at Sheriff Chambliss's home in the middle of the night, demanding to know where Neal had been taken. Chambliss, who endured a great deal of verbal abuse from the crowd, stood firm and refused to accommodate them.[64] The rebuff by the sheriff failed to discourage this determined rabble, who next showed up at the Chipley jail. It called for officials to give up Neal's live-in relatives, Annie and Sallie Smith. The two Smith women apparently had nothing to do with the murder of Cannidy, but in the excitement of the hour, they were threatened by the mob, who wanted to lynch them only because of their close association with Neal. Authorities incarcerated these potential victims for their own protection.[65]

Sheriff John Harrell of Washington County was determined to repel the band of over two hundred men. He boldly exclaimed to the large crowd that he was prepared, if necessary, to protect the two Smith women with tear gas. He doggedly stayed on duty Saturday night through Sunday morning, turning a deaf ear to the waiting throng, who repeatedly begged him to turn over his prisoners to them. At daybreak on Sunday morning a designated group of men came to the jail with acetylene torches, saying the two women were locked in the courthouse vault, and they would cut through it to get at them. Fearing his resources would be insufficient to repulse the crowd, Sheriff Harrell decided to transport his prisoners to Pensacola. The transfer was done carefully; he hid the women on the floor of an automobile and drove circumspectly out of town.[66]

In the meantime, Neal had been transferred to Pensacola. Almost immediately after receiving him, however, Sheriff H. E. Gandy of Escambia County took the prisoner to Brewton, Alabama, and turned him over to Sheriff G. S. Byrne of Escambia County, Alabama. Gandy was obviously reluctant to keep Neal in his jail: "I told Neal he would be locked in the Brewton jail as John Smith of Montgomery on a vagrancy charge." He continued, "I made two visits to Brewton and it was on these occasions that we obtained the confession from him." Sheriff Gandy further stated, "We told Neal not to talk to anyone."[67]

On Monday, 22 October, Gandy phoned Sheriff Chambliss, informing him that Neal had made a complete confession.[68] He coldly told of meeting Lola Cannidy at the hog trough about a quarter of a mile from her home and of beating her to death with a club. He supposedly related to officers how he decided to kill the girl. A printed version of Neal's confession, in the possession of the police, read as follows: "I got to thinking I had done played the devil and she was half dead anyhow, so I went back and killed her."[69] It should be noted that details of the conditions under which Neal made his confession were never made public.

Soon after the confession, Sheriff Byrne hoped to transport Neal back to Pensacola. However, word of Neal's location mysteriously leaked out at this point, because at 12 noon on 25 October the Associated Press called Byrne and asked him to confirm a statement that they had received from Florida that Neal had confessed and was in the Brewton jail.[70] Byrne admitted the confession but denied Neal was in Brewton.

A motorcade consisting of a scout car with three other vehicles, each containing four or five men, descended on Brewton at about 2 A.M. on 26 October. Eyewitnesses attest that the group, which had driven about one hundred miles from Marianna to Brewton, was orderly and that a number of them were well dressed.[71] They flashed guns on the lone jailer and threatened to "blow up" the jail if Neal was not released to them. According to the jailer, "They took the keys from me and being unable to unlock the cell, held their guns on a white trustee in jail and compelled him to unlock the doors." He added, "They might have overlooked the Negro in the death cell if he had not rushed to the door to see what it was all about, but as soon as they saw him they expressed their satisfaction, had the cell unlocked and took him away."[72] Neal's abductors were apparently unconcerned that their action might invoke the death penalty for kidnapping under the Lindbergh Act.[73] They were equally oblivious to their recognizability, making no effort to conceal their faces or their license plates.

The lynch caravan returned to Jackson County on the morning of 26 October. Members of the mob felt sufficiently justified in lynching Neal to make known their determination to do so that evening. Thus, the afternoon edition of the *Dothan Eagle* in Dothan, Alabama, forty miles north of Marianna, stated in headlines: "FLORIDA TO BURN NEGRO AT STAKE: SEX CRIMINAL SEIZED FROM BREWTON JAIL, WILL BE MUTILATED, SET AFIRE IN EXTRA-LEGAL VENGEANCE FOR DEED," and the Dothan radio announced the impending event several times.[74] The mob, or those privy to its affairs, even called the sheriff of adjacent Washington County and notified him of the time for the scheduled lynching.[75] It also spread the word that the place would be the Cannidy property. And, in the words of a *Dothan Eagle* reporter, "for hours . . . the grapevine and telephones of northwest Florida buzzed and grim-faced farmers prepared to make the Cannidy home their rendezvous." The reporter continued: "They knew what was to happen: The mobsmen and the citizens of northwest Florida waited for nightfall when the Negro is destined to pay the extralegal penalty for his crimes—the murder of and the outraging of the white girl. . . . The Negro is to be carried to the spot where he committed the crime a week ago."[76]

Neal's kidnappers may have been surprised to learn that the Associated Press had heard about their "invitational lynching." The AP by 3:00
P.M. made the nation aware of the coming fatal event over its wire services.[77]
Not surprisingly, then, Walter White of the NAACP, Will Alexander of the
CIC, and Jane Cornell of the ASWPL also learned of the impending execution and wired Governor Sholtz, imploring him to intervene in the crisis in Jackson County.[78] Sholtz, in turn, asked Sheriff Chambliss if he wanted
National Guard units sent to the Marianna area. The sheriff, however, turned
down the governor's offer for outside help. He also told Sholtz that he could
handle any situation that might arise and that he had sworn in a force of
thirty-two deputies and a dozen special officers to stop the lynchers.[79] In
spite of these assurances, however, the sheriff was completely ineffectual in
preventing the scheduled crime. Despite the fact that several hundred cars
reached the Cannidy home that night, no deputies were observed in the
crowd. Chambliss later explained his performance saying, "I tried to surround Jackson County with deputies, but we never did see the mob."[80]

While the crowd of several thousand waited in a "good humored and
orderly" way near the site where Lola Cannidy had been killed, leaders of
the vigilantes, including a number of "solid citizen types" who wished to
avoid rabble-rousing, began to have second thoughts about bringing Neal
before it. After several hours wait the crowd grew impatient and most of
their number departed.[81]

Neal, meanwhile, had been tortured for many hours by whites who
held him captive.[82] A man who accompanied the mob declared, "A lot of
boys wanted to get their hands on him so bad they couldn't stand it."[83]
Howard Kester, a young white man who conducted an investigation of the
lynching for the NAACP only a week after it occurred, was "nauseated" by
disclosures from a member of the lynch mob.[84] He reported the story of
"the actual lynching," partly in the words of his informants, as follows:

"After taking the nigger to the woods about four miles from Greenwood,
they cut off his penis. He was made to eat it. They then cut off his testicles
and made him eat them and say he liked it." (I gathered that this barbarous
act consumed considerable time and that other means of torture were used
from time to time on Neal.)

"Then they sliced his sides and stomach with knives and every now and
then somebody would cut off a finger or toe. Red-hot irons were used on the
nigger to burn him from top to bottom." From time to time during the torture a rope would be tied around Neal's neck and he was pulled up over a

limb and held there until he almost choked to death when he would be let down and the torture began all over again.[85]

When Neal was dead, his body was subjected to other indignities in a manner one writer described as a "carnival of sadism."[86] It was tied to a rope and dragged by an auto to the Cannidy property. When the car dragging the corpse stopped in front of the Cannidy home, a man riding the rear bumper cut the rope.[87] A witness present at the scene later recalled, "Old man Cannidy came out and shot him [Neal] around the head."[88] The remainder of the crowd then walked by and kicked the lifeless form. Finally, it was reported that small children, some of them mere tots, poked the body with sharpened sticks.[89]

Neal's body was dragged by car into Marianna from the Cannidy farm, and on the morning of 27 October it was hung, nude, in the courthouse square. Live-wire photographers were on the scene early and took many pictures of the remains. They reckoned their business investment well, because some whites, who assembled after Neal's body was taken down early that Saturday morning, were so disappointed that they quickly bought up photographs for fifty cents.[90] Fingers and toes from the corpse were exhibited as souvenirs in Marianna that morning.[91]

Sheriff Chambliss "discovered" Neal's body about 6:00 A.M. and cut it down. Within the next few hours, however, Marianna was jammed with white people demanding to see the lynch victim's body, and even requesting to have it hung up again.[92] Many in the discontented crowd began drinking, and more than a few were armed.[93] At first, the sheriff refused to accommodate the throng and denied them access to Neal's corpse. Nonetheless, circuit court judge Amos Lewis was on the scene that morning and sensed the powerful restlessness of the crowd; he overruled the sheriff and authorized the rabble to view the body. Scores of aroused, curious people quietly paraded through the tension-filled jail in an orderly fashion to see the remains. Judge Lewis also adjourned court proceedings for the day because of the danger presented by the potentially violent crowd. Finally, at about 10:00 A.M., Claude Neal's body was buried.[94]

The crowd's wrath toward blacks was still unappeased, however. They accused a black man of starting a fight near the courthouse and began to attack the building when police wrested him from a mob intent upon lynching him.[95] Besieged policemen and Mayor Burton hastily called Governor Sholtz and implored him to send the National Guard to assist them.[96] Angry groups of whites meanwhile marauded Marianna's streets, where they sought out blacks and subjected them to beatings for several hours.[97] The crowd even pursued blacks into private houses and businesses. Blacks proved incapable of defending themselves or retaliating during the period of violence; their extreme vulnerability undoubtedly enticed whites to exploit this opportunity for destructiveness.[98] Those blacks not protected by their white employers stayed out of sight. Many of them left Marianna and nearby towns to live with relatives in the country or to sleep in the woods.[99] Blacks who lived as far away as seventy miles remained in their houses to avoid confrontation with whites.[100]

In the meantime the governor was mobilizing units of the National Guard. On the Saturday of the riot, at 1:50 P.M., Sholtz called Adjutant General Vivien Collins, making arrangements to send help to Marianna. The general informed the governor that it would take three or four hours for his men to reach Jackson County; this estimate proved to be correct.[101]

The National Guard arrived in Marianna at about 4:30 that Saturday afternoon. One member of the guard remembered that "The troops were unloaded at the edge of town and marched through the town to intimidate the crowd. There was trouble moving the crowd of perhaps 1,000 people." He continued, "They yelled, 'Soldiers Go Home! What business you got here?' and 'We can take care of ourselves.' We posted at ten to twenty foot intervals around the courthouse with machine guns at each corner of the building." He concluded, "Black people were still being beaten up. Many blacks came to the courthouse for protection. We had a rough situation on the first day [27 October]."[102]

Colonel J. P. Coombs of Apalachicola, commander of the troops, told reporters he did not know how long the guardsmen would need to stay in town to restore order. General Collins had ordered him to use his own best judgment in this matter. The message was clear: the troops would stay as long as necessary. At midnight Saturday, guardsmen patrolled the city streets, flashing their weapons as they rode.[103]

The situation had so calmed on Sunday that Coombs sent home Company B from Panama City, part of the deployed contingent. Nonetheless, the commander cautiously kept Company M from Tallahassee, a machine gun squad, on duty in Marianna until Monday evening, 29 October. By this time, however, peace and order had been restored; the military ended its three-day occupation.[104] On the same night that the troops left town, the city council held an executive meeting to plan the maintenance of order. It was decided to increase the size of the city's police force and to keep the street lights burning all night.[105]

White citizens and officials of the area exhibited neither contrition nor remorse over the two-day outburst that required the National Guard to restore order.[106] By implication, their response demonstrated that whites were not deterred from violence against blacks by accusations of conscience.

One day after the riot, a reporter observed, "Marianna goes on her placid way apparently unaware of the drama that has attracted the attention of a nation." When he asked a waitress what she thought of the excitement of the last two days, she replied, "Well, it has certainly kept us busy with so many strangers here to feed."[107] Howard Kester sensed that both the lynchers and riot had broad support in the population. "Very few people with whom I have talked resent the lynching at all. Most of them think it was not only justified but that those doing the lynching should be congratulated."[108] No churches or ministers took a public stand against what had happened, and neither did the newspapers in Marianna. Furthermore, local officials accepted events as if they were inevitable. That they were not censured by Governor Sholtz probably contributed to this attitude.[109]

The response to the Neal lynching by individuals in the criminal justice system in Jackson County was typical of rural southern counties at this time. The Jackson County grand jury investigating Neal's death commended Sheriff Chambliss and declared that Lola Cannidy was in fact "brutally murdered and raped in the county . . . by Claude Neal." About Neal's lynching, however, it simply stated, "We have not been able to get much direct or positive evidence with reference to this matter," and it dismissed all information in its possession as "hearsay and rumors."[110] John H. Carter, the state attorney in Marianna, made a public statement declaring that "lynch law is deplorable" but then downplayed its practice and stated, "If the Scottsboro case is a living example of the law taking its course, the outlook for the suppression of the lynch law any time soon is dismal."[111] Mayor Burton never expressed regret over the violence inflicted on blacks but did blame outsiders for the riots.[112] Sheriff Chambliss, who was unable to get the details on the Neal lynching, was able to determine for the edification of the press corps, "The men who lynched that Negro ain't the men who tried to take one of my prisoners."[113]

At the state level, Governor Sholtz called upon State Attorney Carter and Sheriff Chambliss to make "thorough and searching investigations" into the lynching and report back to him promptly.[114] After receiving pointed criticism from across the nation for his failure to send the National Guard to Jackson County to prevent the Neal lynching, the governor defended himself as best he could. He declared that "under the circumstances it would have been futile to call out the militia." Then he pointed out that Jackson County officers had refused his offer to send the guard and repeatedly assured him that they could handle the situation. Sholtz went on to say, "It was not a case of calling out the militia to protect a jail or prisoner in the custody of an officer. The Negro was held in the hands of a mob out in the woods where he was killed."[115] These statements may have deflected criticism of his conduct in this affair, but they failed to condemn lynching or to censure Jackson County officials; indeed, the governor's final comment was that "lynching is unnecessary in this state under the present administration where crimes of this character are so speedily and summarily dealt with."[116]

This exercise of untroubled, unlimited authority by whites over blacks in rural Florida produced a national reaction that could not have been anticipated by the group that seized Neal from the Brewton jail. Their planned execution of Neal, as previously noted, made instant national news via Associated Press, which began disseminating details at 3:00 P.M. on 26 October, perhaps eight hours before Neal was executed. And the nation remained in contact with Jackson County as the AP filed its stories by placing calls on Greenwood's solitary telephone. A large number of papers and at least one New York radio station carried to different parts of the country the story of the mob's plans.[117]

The Neal episode galvanized antilynching forces. At the national level, civil rights leaders called on the Department of Justice to apply to the Neal case the federal kidnapping law known as the "Lindbergh Act."[118] United States Attorney General Homer S. Cummings, however, flatly refused to cooperate; he maintained that the Lindbergh Law did not apply to the Neal affair because the kidnapping of Neal did not involve "ransom or reward."[119] Not surprisingly, though, Walter White and the NAACP took a different point of view. White, who argued that the Department of Justice's interpretation was in error, pointed out that in May 1934 the Lindbergh kidnapping law had been amended to read, "ransom, reward, or otherwise."[120] White also obtained confirmation from the amendment's authors, Senators Royal Copeland (New York), Arthur Vandenberg (Michigan), and Lewis Murphy (Iowa), that they had indeed intended the amendment to give the federal government power to act in any interstate kidnapping.[121] Nevertheless, White's argument failed to change the Justice Department's decision not to involve itself in the Neal case.

Walter White sought to use the Neal lynching to promote the national antilynching cause. Although he was sickened by details of this gruesome execution, he knew that its macabre aspects might bring the lynching problem to the nation's attention.[122] The NAACP leader sent the courageous liberal Howard Kester, a white southerner, to investigate the Neal case at the scene in Jackson County. Kester's powerful report about the affair, which included the grisly story of torture, mutilation, and castration of Neal, proved to be a valuable asset in White's effort to shock the nation into awareness of the need for a federal antilynching law.[123] He and the NAACP circulated one series of five thousand copies of the Kester Report, then a second series of ten thousand copies as hundreds of requests came into the association's offices.[124]

The Neal episode stimulated the national antilynching movement and its allies in Congress. The day after the Jackson County slaying, White wired President Roosevelt to put the Costigan-Wagner antilynching bill on his "must program" for the country."[125] And on the same day, Senator Robert Wagner announced that he would reintroduce an antilynching bill in the next session of Congress and that he was confident it would pass this time.[126]

White exerted great pressure on the White House over the Neal incident. He accomplished this largely through Eleanor Roosevelt, with whom he communicated eleven times between 5 November and 27 December 1934.[127] On 8 November he pointedly asked her if she or the president would make a public statement denouncing lynchings in light of the recent horrible instance "involving Neal."[128] Roosevelt conveyed the message to her husband, adding her inscription at the bottom, "I would like to, but will do whatever you say." A return note from Miss Lehand with the statement, "Pres. says this is dynamite," led Eleanor Roosevelt to reply to White, "I do not feel it is wise to speak on pending legislation."[129] After receiving a preliminary copy of the Kester Report, which White sent to her on 20 November, she replied, giving White some hope: "I talked to the President yesterday about your letter and he said that he hoped very much to get the Costigan-Wagner Bill passed in the coming session. The Marianna lynching was a horrible thing."[130] And in response to White's request that Attorney General Cummings prosecute members of the lynch mob who kidnapped Neal across the Alabama-Florida state line in seeming violation of the Lindbergh Act, she declared, "I wish very much the Department of Justice might come to a different point of view and I think possibly they will."[131]

In his *Anatomy of a Lynching: The Killing of Claude Neal,* James R. McGovern clearly apologizes for President Roosevelt's weak, ineffectual response to the Neal lynching in particular and to the civil rights issue in general. He points out that whatever FDR's hopes for Costigan-Wagner, he would not personally come to its defense when he needed the support of southern congressmen for such vital measures as the Works Progress Administration, the National Labor Relations Act, and the Social Security Act.[132] Perhaps Roosevelt would not take the political risks to lead the country to a firm commitment to racial justice for black citizens because he was overly sensitive to southern congressional leaders. It appears that FDR was all too willing to sacrifice black rights in order to appease these men. Indeed, the president may have missed several opportunities during the thirties to push at least one major piece of civil rights legislation, an antilynching bill, through Congress.

Even without any meaningful presidential support, Walter White and the NAACP made a strong effort on behalf of a federal antilynching bill. He personally gave testimony at Senate Judiciary Committee hearings and discussed at length the horror of the Neal lynching under questioning from Senator Costigan.[133] He also presented the full text of the Kester Report to the committee. He later informed Eleanor Roosevelt that he had "written pledges" from 43 senators and 123 congressmen in support of the bill.[134] But the Costigan-Wagner Bill once again failed when southern congressmen filibustered the measure and White failed in a last-minute bid to obtain Roosevelt's support to break the filibuster.

In spite of this setback, White kept interest in the Neal episode alive. He devoted the entire January 1935 issue of the *Crisis* to the subject of lynching, and he was also instrumental in arranging the "Art Commentary on Lynching" at the Arthur V. Newton Gallery in New York City from 15 February to 2 March 1935.[135] The display exhibited the work of thirty-nine artists (black and white) and attracted about two thousand people in its first two weeks, including Eleanor Roosevelt.[136] Some of the remarkable paintings on exhibit included the work of major American artists, such as George Bellow's "The Law is Too Slow."[137] White was pleased that the entire artistic exercise, inspired in large part by the Neal case, made a powerful antilynching statement. These efforts encouraged the NAACP leader to continue the antilynching struggle with resolve and purpose for the rest of the decade.

The lynching of Claude Neal. Reproduced courtesy of the Schomburg Center.

Account of the lynching of John Hodaz. Reproduced courtesy of the *Tampa Tribune.*

Governor Doyle Carlton, who unsuccessfully tried to have lynchers indicted in Calhoun County. Photo courtesy of the Florida State Archives.

Governor David Sholtz, center, and President Franklin D. Roosevelt, left, declined to back antilynching legislation during the 1930s. With them at right is Mayor John J. Alsop of Jacksonville. Photo courtesy of the Florida State Archives.

Governor Fred P. Cone, who once declared, "I think a man ought to be hung on a tree if he advocates overthrow of the government." Photo courtesy of the Florida State Archives.

Sheriff Frank Soutamire pulled the switch on Robert Hinds and was nearly suspended over the 1937 Tallahassee double lynching. Photo courtesy of the Florida State Archives.

Raiford Prison electric chair. Robert Hinds was executed in "Old Sparky" in 1937. Photo courtesy of the Florida State Archives.

3

Florida Vigilantism
at Mid-decade

THE FT. LAUDERDALE LYNCHING

DURING his last three years in office, Governor David Sholtz endured the worst years of lynching and vigilantism in the entire decade. In these years (1934–36) there were six lynchings in Florida. The second of these tragedies, the Neal execution, was by far the most damaging to the governor's reputation, and Sholtz certainly hoped to avoid any further extralegal incidents. This wish, however, came to nothing. Nevertheless, in 1935 Florida's governor was offered an opportunity to avert a lynching. His determination to respond forcefully to vigilante threats was reflected in his actions in the Levy County crisis, which occurred six months after Neal's demise in northwest Florida. On 22 March 1935 Jane Cornell of the ASWLP, representatives of the CIC, and Mrs. O. O. McCullom of the Methodist Women in Jacksonville all urgently telegrammed the governor, imploring him to prevent the lynching of a black man threatened by a mob in Levy County. Jane Cornell raised the painful memory of Claude Neal, asking the governor to "prevent a repetition of the failure of the law such as occurred in Marianna."[1]

Sholtz acted resolutely in this instance. He promptly wired the Levy County sheriff the following telegram: "I am depending upon you to take every precautionary measure to prevent mob violence upon the Negro whom you are seeking when he is apprehended. . . . By all means you should transport him directly when captured to Raiford [Florida's maximum security prison] for safe-keeping."[2] Moreover, the governor was not willing this time to rely solely on the judgment of a local county sheriff as to whether troops should be dispatched to prevent a lynching. Sholtz contacted General Vivien Collins of the Florida National Guard, a veteran of the Marianna riot, and asked him to send a trusted representative to Levy County to monitor the crisis. The governor wanted the monitor to advise him "suffi-ciently in advance of any possible need of the militia to prevent a reoccur-rence of mob violence in our state."[3]

In part because of the governor's actions, no lynching took place in Levy County. In early April, Jane Cornell praised Sholtz for aiding in the prevention of a possible tragedy; he replied, "I fully appreciate the circum-stance which developed in the Marianna lynching and nothing has been left undone to avoid a repetition of this occurrence."[4] The ASWPL was so pleased with the governor's actions that Jessie Daniel Ames herself followed up the Levy County success with a congratulatory message and a request that Sholtz work for a state antilynching law for Florida.[5]

Whatever satisfaction Sholtz felt over the averted lynching in Levy County was short-lived; on 19 July 1935 a black man was unexpectedly lynched in Ft. Lauderdale. Reuben Stacey, alias "Guff," was accused of attacking a white woman with a knife. The local press described him as a man in his late thirties, about six feet tall, and weighing about 180 pounds. He was arrested after a one-day manhunt and then charged with attempt to commit murder, not with attempt to rape.[6]

He was apprehended on 18 July by Constable W. D. Dougald of Deerfield, Florida. The arrest took place after a chase on foot in which Stacey fled for his life, ducking the constable's poorly aimed bullets. At the time of the arrest a revealing dialogue transpired between the officer and the suspect.

Holding a weapon on Stacey, Dougald asked, "What is your name, boy?"

"Fred Austin," replied the out-of-breath black man.

"You are right sure that is your name?" inquired the skeptical con-stable.

"Yes," he said.

The reply came back, "What are you running for?"

Stacey tried to explain, "Well, you know, Cap, Negroes can't stand to see white folks after them; they just run."

Dougald declared, "Well, nobody was after you when I was driving down the road."

The black man asked, "Well, what you got me for?"

"Well, in the first place, you haven't told me your right name. Boy, why don't you tell me your right name," retorted the constable.

Stacey finally gave his correct name, and the constable again asked why he ran.

"Well," replied the suspect, "I just can't stand it. You know how Ne-groes are. They just can't stand for anyone to chase them."

Dougald pressed the issue. "Oh," he said, "you know what it is, alright; you may just as well tell me."

In response to these provocative questions, Stacey claimed that he had had trouble with his wife and was leaving her to travel to Jacksonville. The skeptical constable turned Stacey over to the Broward County Sheriff's Department, headed up by Sheriff Walter Clark.[7]

On the morning of 19 July, Sheriff Clark's office promptly began an investigation into the black man's alleged attack on the white woman. The suspect was not placed in a police lineup for the alleged victim of his attack to identify. Instead, sheriff's deputies and the arresting constable took Stacey by car out to the small wood-frame home of Marian Hill Jones, the alleged white female victim. This action created a scene of chaos and panic as the police car pulled up; the Jones children ran excitedly to inform their mother of the black man's arrival. One little girl reportedly exclaimed to her mother, "There he is!" and all of the other small children began screaming as they scurried from one window to another.[8]

In that tension-filled environment, Jones positively identified Stacey as the man who had attacked her with a knife. According to the woman's story, she had admitted the stranger into her home for a glass of water when suddenly he seized her by the throat and flourished a small knife. She maintained that he kept stating, "Don't holler, don't holler," but did not do any thing else. "I fought him as hard as I could, cutting my hands on his knife. . . . I ran through the back door and he followed me, succeeding in throwing me to the ground while I continued to fight him," declared the distraught woman. "It seemed to me that from the look in his eye he was intent on cutting my throat." Jones stated that her frantic cries for help probably scared the attacker away.[9] Having acquired this positive identification from the victim, the law officers returned Stacey to the county jail. During this visit sheriff's deputies paid Jones a twenty-five dollar reward that had been put up for information leading to the black suspect's apprehension.[10]

As soon as they returned to town, Sheriff Clark and his officers immediately observed signs of a rising lynch spirit in the community. Ft. Lauderdale is not a city one usually associates with lynchings and interracial violence; however, during the decade of the 1930s this rapidly growing tourist town felt the need to rely on extralegal justice to punish this alleged black criminal and to keep blacks in their place. In 1935 Ft. Lauderdale was a modern-looking city of paved streets and many new buildings and homes.[11] The modernization of this town, however, did little to weaken the strong anti-black views of its white inhabitants.

Blacks moved into Ft. Lauderdale during the twenties and thirties at a slightly higher rate than did whites. As the population boomed from 1,870 residents in 1920 to some 8,666 in 1930, then to 15,000 in 1935, the black proportion of the population increased from 23 percent in 1930 to about 26 percent in 1935.[12] The city's blacks were victims of discrimination and racial exclusions of all kinds. In such a racially stratified community black men risked their very lives if they attacked a white woman, sexually or otherwise.[13]

Local law officers were well aware of this risk to their suspect. They also did not consider the small county jail where Stacey was being held as mob-proof, and that troubled them. They worried about its adequacy when they observed that the jail was under constant surveillance by men who kept "riding continuously around the courthouse." This city's law officers learned, to their consternation, that a move on the jail to obtain Stacey was planned for nighttime. In light of this, Sheriff Clark consulted with his deputies and state attorney Louis F. Maire about the possibility of moving their prisoner to the Dade County jail, some miles away in the Miami area of the state. The sheriff asked Maire if they should wire the governor's office in Tallahassee to obtain permission for the move. The state attorney, however, quickly vetoed this idea because Governor Sholtz was away from the capital, and the crisis was just too acute to wait for word from so far away. Subsequently, these two local officials conferred with circuit court judge George W. Tedder, who concurred with the plans to move Stacey to a safer jail.[14]

The transfer of Stacey was an ill-fated exercise. In an effort to safely move the black man from jail, Deputy Virgil Wright had someone drive his car away from the back of the courthouse and then park it out in front of the county facility. After checking to see if all was clear, a group of five men walked out of the courthouse with Stacey to the deputy's waiting car. They put the prisoner in the right-hand corner of the backseat and hurriedly drove off. What they soon discovered, however, was that well-organized bands of men had blocked several major highways and roads leading out of Ft. Lauderdale. After steering clear of several blockades, Wright finally ran through one of the roadblocks. When he evaded this barrier, men at the roadblock piled into their cars and followed him. In the ensuing high-speed chase, officers claimed that they were driving at times up to eighty miles per hour but were still overtaken by one of the pursuing autos.[15]

Deputy Wright described the chase in the following manner. "The road was mighty rough and I seen the fellow [in the chase car] was going to outstrip me anyway; he had a better motor than I had; and he pulled [up to the] side of me and said something to me; I kind of glanced around, [but I] was scared to look and see what he said or pay attention to who he was."

The officer continued, "It was about all I could do to stay in the road and keep going. First news I know he was right up into me and another car right up beside him, and it was either to wreck or take to the woods. . . . I decided I would rather take to the woods and take a chance of being turned over rather than to wreck the car and maybe kill somebody." He went on, "I had taken out to the woods off the shoulder of the highway there and I guess I must have skidded my tires a little before I hit the dirt, I must have skidded my tires probably 70 to 75 feet before I went into the dirt" (6).

As Wright's car lay stuck in the sandy dirt off of the highway, his assailants descended upon him. Twenty to thirty men, from about five or six automobiles, were out of their cars and all around Wright's. He stated, "They had pistols, the ones I seen." The deputy said that when he tried to get out of his car, an armed man pushed him back into his vehicle, slammed the door, and screamed, "You son-of-a-bitch, set still!" These men then took Stacey from the officers and drove off toward the south. However, in just a few minutes they drove back past the immobile lawmen in the opposite direction. The original kidnapping vehicles were followed by what Deputy Wright would later describe as a "mob of automobiles" (6-7).

This large lynch caravan drove perhaps ten to fifteen miles down the county's deserted roads to a spot near the Jones place. It is difficult to estimate the exact size of the throng who had possession of Stacey, but there may have been some fifty to one hundred men in it. The precise actions of the mob may never be known, but they apparently strung their victim up with thin wire to a pine sapling and riddled his body with bullets. It was never determined with certainty whether he was hung first and then shot, or if he was shot first and then strung up. The result was the same, for the lynchers took their victim away from law officers and executed him without trial.[16]

In the meantime, Stacey's former escorts were busy extricating themselves from the ditch into which Wright had driven the car. It took about ten to fifteen minutes to get their vehicle out of the sand and rock, and they immediately followed the trail of the kidnappers. About fifteen to twenty minutes later they found Stacey "hanging to that tree."[17]

This lynching occurred at about 4:30 P.M., and within several hours word of the incident had spread throughout the county and adjoining communities. Thousands of curious onlookers gathered to view the ghastly scene. It was unofficially reported that there were perhaps sixteen bullet wounds in the victim's body. The corpse was cut down on orders from Sheriff Clark and handed over to a black undertaker at about 7:15 P.M. The roads in the vicinity of the death spot were jammed with traffic that evening. Morbid souvenir seekers cut pieces of the black man's overalls, picked up slugs as they fell from the body, cut pieces of the wire by which he was hanging, and even took pieces of the bark from the hanging tree. The body was viewed by the coroner's jury before it was cut down. At the coroner's inquest, justice of the peace Hugh Lester called eleven witnesses, who revealed the details of the tragedy. The jury deliberated about forty minutes and concluded that Stacey had met his death at the hands of "a person or persons unknown," and that this murder was the result of a willful and malicious plot. However, it left the manner of death, which was either strangulation or bullet wounds, an open question.[18]

Reporters asked Sheriff Clark to comment on the lynching. He told the local press that he deeply regretted the illegal execution, and that he had acted in accordance with his own best judgment (and that of Judge Tedder's and State Attorney Maire's) in moving the prisoner from the Broward County jail. "We wanted to safeguard the Negro and prevent violence," declared Clark, "but when our plans became known to the mob it was impossible for five deputies to do anything about it without running the risk of being injured or killed in the melee which would have followed an outburst of shooting."[19]

Word of the lynching spread almost instantly to the outside world. In fact, on 19 July, the day of the slaying, Jane Cornell wired the governor's office about the incident. Her blunt telegram read in part as follows: "Ft. Lauderdale lynching this afternoon again brings Florida into nation's limelight as state where passion and mob violence take precedent over personal control and respect for law and order."[20] Since Sholtz was away from the capital at this time, his trusted executive secretary, J. P. Newell, handled the situation as best he could. He promptly wired the ASWPL, stating that it could "depend"' upon the governor to thoroughly investigate the matter.[21] On 24 July, Mrs. O. O. McCullom, chairwoman of the Methodist Interracial Committee in Jacksonville, wired Sholtz, stating that her organization "deplore[d]" the Ft. Lauderdale lynching.[22] Newell replied that he had been in contact with the governor, who had ordered an inquiry into the affair, and that a special session of the Broward County grand jury had been called to deal with it.[23]

The day after the lynching, the governor's office addressed this illegal execution. Newell at that time sent a telegram to State Attorney Maire, ordering him to initiate an "immediate and searching investigation," and wired Sheriff Clark, stating, "Governor Sholtz directs you to cooperate with the state attorney in the investigation of this lynching."[24] To answer the governor's order, Maire replied that he would call the grand jury into special session and look into the matter.[25]

The Broward County grand jury convened on 23 July 1935 and conducted a one-day inquiry into the execution. A total of twenty-nine witnesses were called to testify, but after the proceedings, the state attorney concluded that no witness was able to "shed any light as to the guilty parties participating in the lynching." All five law officers who comprised Stacey's escort on the fatal day testified that they did not recognize anyone in the lynch band; they further swore that the kidnappers wore masks and that their license tags were "covered up with paper or some kind of cloth that was turned up so we couldn't see the numbers."[26] As expected, the grand jury inquiry led to no indictments and no arrests. This futile effort frustrated both Maire and Governor Sholtz; they had genuinely hoped for firm evidence leading to prosecution and punishment of the Ft. Lauderdale lynchers.

In a letter to the governor, Maire summed up his thoughts about the incident. He stated that Stacey should have been moved to another jail, and that the five officers in the escort party "used all reasonable diligence and did all possible to safely conduct him to the Miami jail." He was "convinced that there was a leak somewhere as to the sheriff's plans" to take Stacey out of Broward County, "but there has not been produced the slightest evidence that such a leak occurred and who might have been responsible for such."[27] More importantly, however, he ignored the fatal error in judgment he and the sheriff made in not calling the governor's office to ask Newell to call out National Guard units to protect Stacey.

This lynching provoked a weak attack in the local press on the very idea of lynch law vengeance. In a front-page editorial in the *Ft. Lauderdale Daily News* titled, "The Law Must Say," the writer began by declaring, "There is no question but that the avengers 'got the right man.' The crime he attempted [rape] though he was futile, was one that has ever stirred men to personal vengeance, and probably, always will." He continued, "The Law moves slow and ponderously. That is admitted. Evidence of the fact that too frequently are the courts of justice obstructed by technicalities of the Law and subterfuge of those who live by its manipulation exists in Broward County today. . . . But two wrongs have never made right, and disregard of the Law has never served to strengthen it." He then added, "A crime was committed here. It is for the Law to move, to determine facts, to itself uphold its majesty. It's not for the individual or a newspaper to assume authority in fixing blame, in determining responsibility. That's the Law's job." The writer then concluded, "The execution here yesterday wiped out a menace to society. That is pretty certain. But it accomplished that achievement at the expense of law and order. The Law has been violated and its majesty belittled. It is for the Law to have the final word."[28]

Editorial opinion throughout the state weighed against the lynching.

Without any direct references to the Stacey affair, the *Tampa Tribune*, in a Sunday editorial, discussed the Old Testament story of Saul, who "desired to take the law into his own hands" by wanting to slay David because of jealousy. It concluded, "He would not take the law into his own hands. He did right and left the results to Providence."[29] Also, the *Tallahassee Democrat* offered an interesting analysis that began by declaring, "The lynching near Ft. Lauderdale at least demonstrated that mob violence is not confined to north Florida." It continued, "Mobs go into action in thinly populated sections and less frequently in cities to take the law into their own hands when a group of men become aroused over a crime." It then stated that "lynch law is inadvisable for two reasons: It encourages a disrespect and disregard for the law; and, since it is hasty, it sometimes punishes the innocent." The editorial next tried to put the matter in a historical perspective. "In this country lynch law is the survival of a necessary frontier institution; enforcement of personal and property rights through vigilante committees and the Klan of Reconstruction days. Unquestionably, law-abiding citizens should work to eliminate the vestiges of an outgrown institution that now is a handicap." It added, "And it would be helpful for the bar . . . to eliminate the practice of lawyers working to free guilty criminals through technical loopholes." Finally, it concluded that "the powerful primitive instincts aroused in the mob should be first understood and then opposed with the certainty of legal punishment of the guilty."[30]

The black press throughout the nation was, not surprisingly, more critical of the execution in this case than were the Florida editors. The *Atlanta Daily World* put the entire affair in a broad perspective, pointing out that the Stacey slaying was the third such crime within one week (two blacks had been lynched in Mississippi just a few days before the Ft. Lauderdale tragedy), "which according to available evidence will go down in history as a week with the greatest number of blots against it in the entire annals of the country." It also reported that the Stacey execution was the seventh recorded lynching of 1935, and the first in Florida since "the gruesome lynching at Marianna" in October of 1934.[31] The *Pittsburgh Courier* ran an editorial titled "Judge Lynch Marches On," which declared that "had the Costigan-Wagner antilynching bill been passed, the offending counties could have been fined, and the guilty officers tried and jailed." This piece then concluded by chiding blacks for not pushing hard enough for passage of antilynching legislation when so many freely talked about aiding Ethiopia in its struggle against Mussolini, the "Italian lyncher."[32] The *New York Age* carried a front-page picture of an unidentified black man hanging from a lone pine tree, an obvious dramatic likeness of the Stacey lynching.[33]

THE SHOEMAKER LYNCHING

Although Stacey had allegedly committed some act that aroused the ire of the white community, the victim in Florida's next lynching, some four months later, was a white man marked for punishment because of his radical political beliefs. The vicious flogging death of Joseph Shoemaker, in fact, stands apart from all the rest of the decade's vigilante murders. First of all, Shoemaker and his two radical associates—Eugene Poulnot and Sam Rogers, who were also flogged—were guilty only of being socialists and activists. They were leftists involved in Tampa politics in 1935, and for this reason Tampa policemen and Klansmen assaulted them in a shocking way.[34]

A recent arrival in Tampa, Shoemaker was alarmed over the corruption of city politics as revealed in the divisive 1935 municipal primary. He was so concerned, in fact, that he organized the Modern Democrats, a new left wing party, that prepared to run a slate of candidates in the November general election. This new party reflected the views of its founder, who was a moderate social democrat who sympathized with FDR's New Deal policies and the outlook of the liberal wing of the Democratic Party. Moreover, the Modern Democrats were committed to the classical socialist principle that production should be for human use rather than profit. Shoemaker fearlessly argued his case in a series of letters that appeared in the editorial pages of the *Tampa Tribune*. He advocated such innovations as "public ownership of utilities, free hospital care for the needy, monthly investigations of city departments, an effective referendum law, and a system whereby the unemployed could produce goods for their use."[35] Unfortunately for Shoemaker, he was not particularly careful in distinguishing his views from the dreaded and hated doctrine of Communism. This serious error in judgment was reflected in his bold, provocative statement that "the biggest cooperative enterprise in the United States is our post office. Is this communism? If so, we want more of it" (20). This bold indiscretion inflamed the passions of unsympathetic readers.

The Modern Democrats prepared to run a slate of candidates in the fall elections. Miller A. Stephen, a local mechanic, was picked to run for the mayor's office; the party also chose men to run for tax assessor and the board of aldermen. These candidates and their party were not completely isolated in their community. Indeed, the Modern Democrats were supported by the American Federation of Labor, local socialists, and the Tampa branch of the Workers' Alliance (a national organization of relief workers closely allied to the Socialist Party). This group in Florida was led by an out-of-work pressman named Eugene Poulnot. Tampa officials saw him as a rabble-rouser who had organized the Unemployed Brotherhood of Hillsborough

County and had led a number of demonstrations by the unemployed against low relief payments. In fact, he had been arrested at a protest meeting in 1934 for disturbing the peace when the police believed he was attempting to incite a riot with the following remark: "If they don't give us the relief we want, let's go open a warehouse and take what we need" (20).[36] When these charges were finally dropped, Poulnot pressed on with new vigor in his efforts on behalf of the unemployed. He was aided in this endeavor by Sam Rogers, another socialist who worked as hard as Poulnot on behalf of the Modern Democrats' candidates.[37]

Shoemaker, Poulnot, Rogers, and other members of the party were not at all discouraged by the overwhelming defeat of their candidates in the November general election. Indeed, they resolutely responded to the defeat by undertaking the task of preparing for upcoming county and state elections. Their various activities included rallies, the formation of a permanent organization, and the continued presentation of their socialist ideas in the *Tribune*. In fact, Shoemaker's last letter to the editor appeared just four days before he was abducted and flogged.[38]

Six Modern Democrats, including Shoemaker, Poulnot, and Rogers, were holding a political meeting on 30 November 1935, at 307 East Palm Avenue, when tragedy struck. Meeting in executive session, they were seated around a living-room table in a private home, debating the form their constitution should take. Suddenly, at approximately 9:00 P.M., seven policemen stepped inside the house without warrants and abruptly broke up the meeting. With guns drawn, three officers came in the front door and four in the back door; they proceeded to grab papers, frisk the surprised suspects, and arrest everyone. The detained men were taken to police headquarters, where authorities grilled them for some time about their so-called communist activities. As the interrogations ended, the men were released one at a time, and three of them—Shoemaker, Poulnot, and Rogers—were picked up by kidnappers right in front of the police station.[39]

The three captives were taken by their abductors to a secluded area in the woods more than ten miles to the east of Tampa. There the kidnappers took off their victims' clothes and proceeded to administer a severe flogging to all three men. After Rogers was stripped, he was placed over a log, and his hands and feet were held while he was beaten, and then boiling hot tar was administered to his abdomen, genitals, and thighs. Poulnot was flogged with a chain and a rawhide, then he was tarred and feathered. Shoemaker received the severest beating of all, to the point of mutilation. Finally, the victims were warned, "Get out of town in twenty-four hours or we'll kill you."[40] Poulnot and Rogers somehow returned to town, but a severely injured Shoemaker fell unconscious into a ditch somewhere east of Tampa, where he lay for about seven hours during a cold night. Concerned friends located Shoemaker the following morning and immediately took him to a local hospital. The attending physician who examined him commented on the extent of his injuries: "He was horribly mutilated. I wouldn't beat a hog the way he was whipped. . . . He was beaten until he is paralyzed on one side, probably from blows to the head . . . I doubt if three square feet would cover the total area of bloodshot bruises on his body, not counting the parts injured only by tar."[41] Surgery was performed in a failed attempt to save Shoemaker's life, but on 9 December he died.

This fatally violent incident focused instant national attention on Tampa. The Socialist Party of America, under the leadership of Norman Thomas, led the effort to protest this outrage. Thomas promptly wired Tampa mayor R. E. L. Chancey and Hillsborough County sheriff J. R. McLeod to denounce the crime and to demand that the vigilantes be apprehended and punished. Furthermore, New York socialists put together the Committee for the Defense of Civil Liberties in Tampa, which carried out a "fund-raising drive" and "letter-writing campaign" in order to "bring down upon the heads of government in Tampa the full force of public indignation everywhere" (15). A thousand-dollar reward "for information leading to the arrest and conviction" of the floggers was offered by the American Civil Liberties Union. Additionally, the American Federation of Labor publicly decried the beatings and threatened to move its 1936 convention, planned for Tampa, to another location if the vigilantes were not found and put on trial. Finally, about one thousand labor unions, socialist organizations, and concerned citizens throughout the entire nation telegrammed the governor's office, the mayor's office, and the sheriff's department to protest the affair (14–15).[42]

Many observers in Florida deplored the beatings, and as pointed out in one careful study of this affair, editors in one community after another denounced the incident on their editorial pages. The *Miami Herald*, for example, angrily observed that the brutal floggers were "as venomous as a mad dog, and its [the mob's] leaders should be dealt with just as we would a rabid animal" (15). One historian has noted that "numerous editorials argued that the city must ferret out and punish the perpetrators of this outrage" (15). In addition to this, numerous Tampa groups such as local labor unions, the Junior Chamber of Commerce, the American Legion, and the Hillsborough County Bar Association protested the floggings and demanded action against the vigilantes. Further, several religious leaders responded to the beatings by holding a mass memorial service on the first Sunday after Shoemaker died. The social gospel minister of the activist First Congregational Church, Walter Metcalf, was so moved by outrage that he helped organize the Committee for the Defense of Civil Liberties in Tampa, and then became its chairman.[43] This group expressed its determination to work with other organizations to find and punish the vigilantes.[44]

Metcalf and his organization lived in a Tampa that was an expanding urban community during the mid-1930s, with a population of over one hundred thousand residents. Its growing economy, slowly recovering from the Great Depression, was based on its busy port trade of citrus and phosphate, and especially on the profitable cigar-making industry. Still another major industry was gambling. A middecade study conducted by the Junior Chamber of Commerce estimated that the so-called numbers racket alone usually grossed over one million dollars a month. Interests that controlled gambling in Tampa apparently protected their illegal operations by paying off corrupt local officials. Not surprisingly, then, public office was often quite lucrative and Tampa politics was plagued by severe factional conflicts over who would win access to this graft. This view of Tampa as a Florida gambling center was so widely held that the *Tribune*, with a sense of sad irony, called it "our Biggest Business."[45]

The corrupt nature of the city's politics was clearly reflected in the 1935 municipal primary. Two opposing political groups battled for the spoils of office in Tampa: Pat Whitaker, a prominent local attorney, led one faction, and D. B. McKay, one-time owner of a local newspaper and former mayor, led the other. In this bitterly contested election both the Whitaker faction candidate (incumbent mayor Robert E. Lee Chancey) and challenger McKay tried to portray the other as no more than a stooge controlled by gambling interests. This circumstance was further complicated by the fact that the Whitaker group "controlled the Tampa police department," while its opponents controlled the county government and the sheriff's office. Because both sides were to monitor the elections, a tension-filled situation was bound to develop.[46]

As election day rolled around in early September, each side beefed up its manpower to the tune of over one thousand additional policemen and about six hundred new deputies. The tension between these two armed camps mounted to the point that Governor Sholtz felt it necessary to send some three hundred National Guardsmen to Tampa in the fall of 1935 to keep the peace. This outside show of force, however, was unsuccessful in preventing outbreaks of violence and election fraud. After the election it came to light that two individuals had been shot in one confrontational incident, and that about fifty people were arrested for "stuffing ballot boxes." These happenings undoubtedly tarnished the victory of the incumbent Whitaker faction that sponsored Mayor Chancey (19). The day after the election the *Tribune* lamented the sad state of local politics: "Tampa must get away from this sort of thing ... when, with no important issue or interest at stake, the selfish rivalry of competing factions of politicians and of grasping gambling syndicates, each fighting for control of the offices and the law-breaking privileges, can involve the city in a heated, disrupting, and discreditable fight such as we experienced yesterday" (19).

It was in response to this state of political affairs that Shoemaker had decided to organize the Modern Democrats and participate in the November elections. As events proved, this challenge cost Shoemaker his life. Reverend Metcalf recognized this fact at the memorial services. "These victims did not like the looks of our infamous primary election with hundreds of armed men at the polls. They did not like to think of nearly half the population of Tampa on relief rolls. Such men were branded as 'reds'" (21). The local Committee for the Defense of Civil Liberties in Tampa struck a similar note in their statement:

> The man who was murdered and his friends who were tortured and kidnapped were marked for only one reason: they had the courage to organize workers and to oppose a corrupt and tyrannical political machine. They took seriously their rights as workers and citizens and by their activity became undesirable to certain persons in the community of Tampa. (21)

After these initial protests, observers began to call for an investigation into the possibility of police complicity in the crime. The issue first surfaced when Poulnot related to newspaper reporters that he had recognized a policeman in the mob. This charge elicited an immediate response from Tampa's chief of police, R. G. Tittsworth, who, of course, denied the accusation, stating that "no member of the police department has any participation directly or indirectly with the flogging" (21). In spite of this denial, however, Governor Sholtz ordered local authorities to investigate the charge of police involvement in this crime.[47]

The governor specifically called on Sheriff McLeod and state attorney Rex Farrior to conduct a thorough inquiry into the matter. Working with the state attorney, McLeod had begun to gather evidence when he first heard of the flogging. This joint investigation soon led to the inescapable conclusion that the entire affair was a well-planned lynching. The crucial figure in this revelation was John A. McCaskill, a city fireman and the son of a Tampa policeman, who had joined the Modern Democrats to spy on them for the police. Investigating officials learned that on the fateful night of 30 November, McCaskill had left the meeting under false pretenses and called Tampa police, tipping them off on the location of the meeting. They also discovered that when the names of the Modern Democrats were logged in at police headquarters, McCaskill's name was mysteriously missing.[48]

In mid-December 1935, the state attorney and sheriff went before the grand jury with their findings. At this point in the investigation the mayor felt obliged to suspend McCaskill from his job with the fire department for working undercover for the police. The city officers who, without a warrant, had broken up the 30 November meeting were also suspended by the mayor. Furthermore, authorities arrested five of these officers and "charged them with premeditated murder of Joseph Shoemaker," as well as with the kidnapping and assault of Poulnot and Rogers. The list of those charged expanded to six when still another policeman was indicted on 19 December. Chief Tittsworth told the press he was taking "an indefinite leave of absence." A few weeks later the chief was indicted as an accessory after the fact for attempting a coverup to obstruct justice in the case (22–23).

Against the background of these events, evidence came to light indicating Ku Klux Klan involvement in this affair. According to one of Shoemaker's relatives, the Klan had called him with this warning: "This is the Ku Klux Klan. We object to your brother's activities. They are communistic. Tell him to leave town. We will take care of the other radicals too" (23). A copy of a Klan circular that had suddenly appeared in Tampa right after the flogging was printed in the *Tribune;* it declared that "Communism Must Go" and announced, "THE KU KLUX KLAN RIDES AGAIN." This circular asked for white Tampans' aid and support, and even gave a local address where they could be contacted (23).

Just a few days after this circular appeared in the press, the sheriff took two alleged Klansmen from Orlando into custody. They were accused of participating in the beating of Shoemaker; soon afterward, another suspected Orlando Klansman was also arrested and charged with taking part in the brutal attack. Sheriff McLeod declared that all three Orlando men were Klansmen who had been deputized for duty in the September primary in Tampa. The last man indicted in this case was a police stenographer who was charged with being an accessory after the fact. In all, eleven men had been indicted in the Tampa flogging crime, and as noted in one study, they all had worked at some point in time for the Tampa police department (24).

According to all available historical records, the eight men who were still working for the police department at the time of their arrest might be classified as "part of the local establishment," but only Chief Tittsworth "could be considered a member of the city's elite" (24). This distinction may be critical for an understanding of this vigilante crime. Recent studies by political scientists have described vigilantism as "establishment violence," or illegitimate or illegal coercion by "certain groups that believe they possess a vested interest in preservation of the current distribution of values." Apparently the vigilante violence of Tampa policemen and Klansmen was aimed at maintaining the existing sociopolitical order in Tampa. This kind of violence is different from "revolutionary" or "reactionary" violence, both of which are directed at change. Vigilantes, according to the theory, "compose an establishment though not necessarily an elite"; that is, whether prominent or not, vigilantes are people who identify with the existing order and use violence to maintain it. Circumstances of the Tampa case clearly reveal that it was an example of this kind of vigilantism (17). This sort of analysis fits well with Robert P. Ingall's thesis in *Urban Vigilantes in the New South* that class may be a more important factor than race in vigilante crimes and lynchings. Further, some elite members of the Tampa establishment offered crucial support for the accused floggers. For example, Pat Whitaker, the mayor's brother-in-law, headed up the defense team. Moreover, a number of prominent local businessmen posted bail for the defendants, which totaled about one hundred thousand dollars (24).

As the time for the trial neared, Norman Thomas journeyed to Tampa and stayed at the home of Reverend Metcalf.[49] Arriving in town on Sunday, 19 January 1936, he spoke before a supportive throng of several thousand. The socialist leader sharply criticized the powers that be while lavishing praise on Sheriff McLeod and the local press.[50] Trial began for the seven accused policemen in March of 1936 in the community of Bartow, in adjoining Polk County.[51] Six of the seven men were tried for the kidnapping and assault of Eugene Poulnot (not Shoemaker), because the prosecution felt it had a good chance of winning convictions based on the testimony of the victim (25). Five defendants were identified by law officers as those who kidnapped the victims in front of the police station. When asked why they withheld this information for so long, the prosecution witnesses asserted they acted on the assumption that telling the truth would have cost them their jobs. It also came to light that they made a full disclosure of the facts as soon as Chief Tittsworth was removed from office. Lawyers for the accused policemen tried to portray the prosecution's witnesses as "liars or Communists." In response, the state produced convincing evidence that showed the Modern Democrats operated legally and believed in democracy (25).[52]

Observers were stunned when the six-man jury returned a guilty verdict. No one, including the prosecution, had expected a rural Polk County jury to make such a decision. Jurors, when asked by reporters about their deliberations, flatly declared there were no doubts in any of their minds. "Communism and all that stuff had nothing to with the case," observed one juror. Ingalls has pointed out that another juror boldly stated: "What got us was the way those policemen, supposed to be law enforcement officers, went right out and participated in an unlawful act."[53] Finally, Judge Robert T. Dewell handed out four-year prison sentences to the convicted policemen (who were immediately released on bail while they appealed their case) (26).

Many were pleased with this turn of events. According to the American Civil Liberties Union, the conviction in this case was "a victory in the fight for civil rights in Florida and the beginning of a drive against the Ku Klux Klan" (26). One leftist newspaper called the verdict "the most stunning blow against vigilantism ever struck in Florida," but then warned that "the convicted kidnappers may still be cleared by legal maneuvers in the Florida Supreme Court" (26).

As events proved, there was indeed reason for concern about this possibility. About one year after the trial, the state supreme court overturned the convictions, arguing that Judge Dewell erred by not informing the jury that "it could not consider evidence related to the charges of conspiracy to kidnap which the judge had dismissed" (26). A new trial, therefore, was ordered by the state's highest tribunal for the five policemen who had been convicted of kidnapping Poulnot (26).

As the defendants waited for this new trial, they were pulled into court in October of 1937 for the murder of Joseph Shoemaker. This time around Judge Dewell took charge. At first he sharply curtailed what evidence could be introduced in the case, then he took matters out of hands of the jury by directing from the bench verdicts of acquittal (27). This action alarmed and outraged observers all over the country, so that when Governor Fred Cone visited the New York's World Fair in 1937 in the wake of the acquittals, he was blasted by various groups, publicly embarrassed by Mayor Fiorello LaGuardia, and attacked by the New York press.[54] Pressure continued to be applied to the governor, most of it aimed at getting him to disqualify Dewell from these cases. Rex Farrior, counsel for the prosecution, even asked Cone to take Dewell off the case.[55] Finally, feeling the pressure in Bartow, the judge requested the governor to allow him to disqualify himself.[56] After Dewell stepped aside, all legal proceedings came to an end in June of 1938, when a new judge retried the policemen on kidnapping charges only to have a jury find them not guilty.[57]

THE MADISON COUNTY LYNCHING

Less than a year after Tampa floggers killed Shoemaker, Florida vigilantes struck again, this time in the northern part of the state, in Madison County.

In decline since the late-nineteenth century, this "old plantation belt" county had been "economically and demographically stagnant" long before the Great Depression of the thirties. Farming, the chief industry, employed almost half of the male workforce by the 1930s, as many of the old plantations had been subdivided again and again into plots worked by numerous sharecroppers and tenants. Madison, the county seat, and Greenville were the only sizable towns in those days; one recent study has noted that "from 1900 to 1945, the Madison county population grew 60 percent while the state population increased 325.7 percent," and "in 1940, the per capita income in Madison County was $203, compared with $498 for the rest of the state, excluding the old plantation belt counties." Moreover, Old South and antiblack values persisted long after the Civil War and Reconstruction and well into the twentieth century, contributing in large part to the lynch-prone history of this county. Indeed, one historian has observed that "with thirteen lynchings from 1889 to 1918, Madison County experienced the third highest number of lynchings of Florida counties, behind Alachua with eighteen and Marion with twenty-one."[58]

Sparsely settled in the thirties, Madison County had a population of only 16,190 residents in 1940. It was classified by the federal census as 100 percent rural, with a high rate of tenancy. It was also a poor county with a large black population; in fact, in 1930 blacks comprised about 52 percent of the total population.[59] In an area where black people were so numerous, whites were particularly careful to keep the upper hand by closely controlling their social subordinates. This meant that any individual black who violated the caste code was subject to dire consequences. And in September of 1936 Madison County whites readily made an example of Theodore "Buckie" Young in Greenville, Florida.

Buckie Young allegedly attacked a white woman in the Greenville area. This accusation was more than enough to stir mob fever in Madison County, and a lynching band soon organized itself and began to search for the thirty-six-year-old suspect. They found him at home on Friday evening, 11 September 1936, with his mother. The vigilantes apparently stormed the home and forcibly removed Young; they took him out and unleashed a barrage of gunfire that instantly killed the hapless black man. The mob reportedly kept the body in its custody for two days before it was finally turned over to a local black funeral home. Finally, on 14 September, Buckie Young was unceremoniously buried in a segregated cemetery.[60]

Although Young was the eighth American lynch victim of 1936, his murder received little attention from the press and concerned groups. Governor Sholtz, who had just lost in the recent primaries, must have known about this lynching, but he ordered no inquiries, nor did he issue a public

statement deploring the lynching. Sholtz may have been indifferent because he had only a few weeks left in office before the November general
elections, and in any case he was probably weary of dealing with these
affairs. The Associated Press carried a very short story about this incident
that appeared in only a few of the state's larger papers.[61]

The most detailed account of this lynching can be found not in any
Florida newspaper but in the *Atlanta Daily World* of 15 September 1936.
The local newspaper, the *Madison Enterprise-Recorder*, ignored the incident.
In the first issue after the lynching, space on the front page was devoted to
stories about school news in the county, a new ladies' shop, a local man who
built a new shop, church news, and a local woman who almost had an
accident on her way to town. There was no mention of the Young slaying,
just as if it never happened.[62] Apparently no Florida papers bothered to
write editorials about the Madison County tragedy; they devoted their editorial space to speculation about the upcoming state and national elections
in November. Because papers in Florida and the rest of the country paid
little attention to this affair, there were no protest letters or telegrams sent
to the governor's office. Indeed, this tragic crime was ignored by a lame-
duck governor and overlooked by the preoccupied press and public in their
anticipation of the 1936 elections.

Moreover, the black press and the NAACP were unusually quiet after
this lynching, perhaps because the national black community was distracted
by election-year concerns, particularly the Roosevelt-Landon race for the
presidency. Walter White had also momentarily relaxed his efforts on behalf of an antilynching bill and so did not respond as vigorously as he might
have if the NAACP antilynching proposal had been up for a vote before
Congress. Indeed, in 1937, when White and the association renewed their
antilynching drive, every Florida lynching became an object of intense scru-
tiny by an outraged national black community.[63]

4

Mob Spirit in the Panhandle

THE ROBERT HINDS CASE

T HE compelling drama of Scottsboro overshadows similar, though less well-known, occurrences of racial injustice in the South during the 1930s. One such incident was the trial and execution of a black Apalachicola teenager named Robert Hinds in July of 1937. Like the Scottsboro boys, Hinds was accused of breaking the South's most sacred rule: no sex between a black man and a white woman. In both instances a southern governor tried to avert lynching by handing the youths over to parochial jurists, who tried them in haste in the prejudicial atmosphere of a small town. The plight of Hinds and the Scottsboro defendants also attracted the attention of civil rights organizations and received widespread newspaper coverage in their respective states of Florida and Alabama. However, the crucial difference between the two tragedies was that only Hinds was sent to the electric chair and executed as a black youth charged with a lynchable offense. Florida officials acted so that chroniclers would not add Hinds's name to the long list of lynch victims murdered over the years by Floridians. As events surrounding the Hinds case would prove, one reason for this was the obvious substitution of "official" for extralegal justice.

Florida governor Fred P. Cone signed Robert Hinds's death warrant and watched over proceedings leading to the young man's subsequent electrocution. Cone involved himself in this case from beginning to end. An elderly (he was an "old" sixty-one when he took office in 1937) conservative southern governor who came of age in the Old South region of north Florida in the 1880s and 1890s, he was undoubtedly not the most qualified chief executive to deal with crisis situations in which a black man was accused of a lynchable crime. His slave-owning father and grandfather had served with distinction in the army of the Confederate States of America; the governor

fell heir to their antiblack racial views as well as to their frontier spirit of
rugged individualism. In fact, young Fred Cone himself, in the late 1880s,
committed a vigilante act when he shot and wounded a carpetbag Republican in an act of political vengeance.[1] In spite of all this he was not reckless
enough to give public support to mob murder of blacks, no matter what his
private feelings were on the issue.

Indeed, Cone was forced by circumstances to adopt a public antilynching posture all during his administration. He clearly wished to avert such
tragedies whenever possible, perhaps to avoid the adverse national criticism that invariably accompanied these crimes. In this regard he worked
closely with the most influential antilynching organization in his state, the
Florida Council of the ASWPL, and gladly accepted its help in combating
this abuse at the state level.[2] More than anything else, however, his first
experience as governor in handling a lynching threat forced him to come to
grips with this problem and set the pattern of how he would deal with these
crises thereafter.[3]

Governor Cone confronted the lynching issue after only five months in
office. On 16 May 1937, Sheriff Charles L. Robbins of Franklin County
arrested Robert Hinds, a sixteen-year-old black, for allegedly assaulting and
raping Mae Polous, a white woman. A wary Sheriff Robbins temporarily
lodged Hinds in the Apalachicola jail. He sensed a threat of mob violence,
stating that "feeling is running high against the Negro." He was indeed
correct, for within an hour of the suspect's arrest, an angry white mob had
gathered in front of the county courthouse. It loudly demanded that the
black youth be turned over immediately. However, the sheriff had already
moved Hinds to the Panama City jail in Bay County on the Gulf coast.[4]

When they heard that the prisoner had been moved, the vigilantes
crowded into their automobiles and hurriedly drove the sixty-five miles to
Panama City. Just before the motorized caravan arrived, however, Sheriff
Robbins and his charge had escaped to Pensacola. Holding their ground,
Panama City law enforcement officials refused to tell the mob where Hinds
had been taken. Nonetheless, as a concession, authorities allowed four of its
representatives to search through the Bay County jail facility for the suspect. Finding nothing, the frustrated whites reluctantly dispersed.[5]

Word of Hinds's arrest and the persisting threat of lynch violence stirred
the Florida branch of the ASWPL and its leader, Jane Cornell, into action.
She saw in the crisis an opportunity to use her organization's influence to
prevent an extralegal execution. In her book on Jessie Daniel Ames and the
ASWPL, Jacquelyn Dowd Hall portrayed the Hinds case as "a vivid example of the ASWPL system at work." Furthermore, she revealed in no

uncertain terms how many southern white women, including rank-and-file as well as association leadership, rejected the patriarchal assumption of protecting white women as justification of lynching. Moreover, she was entirely accurate in detailing the steps that Jane Cornell took in the case. The ASWPL leader promptly contacted the governor, the sheriff of Franklin County, and circuit court judge John Johnson, urging them all to protect their prisoner from the lynch mob.[6]

Other concerned groups also contacted the governor. The Women's Missionary Council of Florida and the Jacksonville Ministerial Alliance wired Cone, exhorting him to take steps to ensure Hinds's safety. The governor promptly responded to their telegrams: "I have taken necessary precautions through proper authorities and feel sure that the law will be allowed to take its course in this case."[7]

Governor Cone had indeed taken precautionary steps. Although Sheriff Robbins had already moved Hinds to Pensacola, where he was relatively safe, the governor wasted no time in writing an urgent letter to the lawman. In it he related, "I have been informed that there is an attempt to lynch a Negro prisoner and I am requesting you to use every precaution to prevent this unlawful act and let the law take its course."[8] Several weeks later, as the danger of mob violence persisted, Cone promised two companies of National Guardsmen for Hinds's protection when he came to trial. In fact, the Franklin County sheriff had traveled to Tallahassee to inform the governor in person that he had only two deputies in Apalachicola, the county seat, and they certainly could not adequately protect the young black man if he stood trial there.[9]

Sheriff Robbins acted decisively and courageously to prevent a tragedy that would have disgraced his county in the eyes of the state and nation. He wished to protect the reputation of Franklin County, a part of Florida that lies on the Gulf coast around the mouth of the Apalachicola River. This waterway extends inland into southern Georgia. During the antebellum period it sustained a golden age of trade and commerce centered around cotton exports through the busy port of Apalachicola. By the fourth decade of the twentieth century, however, that era had long passed into history.[10]

On the eve of Hinds's trial, Franklin County could best be described as small, sparsely settled, poor, and isolated. Yet it was by no means a typical southern farming county of large planters, tenants, and sharecroppers. In fact, federal census records show that in 1930 fewer than 1 percent of the population of 6,283 residents engaged in commercial farming. About half of the county's residents lived in or around Apalachicola, where they worked in small enterprises in the port town. It was a county of fishermen, cannery laborers, dock hands, sawmill laborers, and workers in the forest products industry. This was also an area where few people owned cars or had electricity, telephones, or radios. Census data indicate a high illiteracy rate, and throughout the 1930s about one-third of the county's children between the ages of seven and thirteen did not even attend school. Additionally, the Depression brought unemployment and hard times to many of the county's citizens.[11] This may have increased racial tensions as whites and blacks competed for employment in the local labor market.

Blacks comprised about 40 percent of the county's population in the 1930s. They worked at the same kind of jobs as they had in the 1880s and 1890s; most of them lived in Apalachicola and worked on the docks, on fishing boats, in nearby turpentine camps and sawmills, or in white people's homes as domestic servants.[12]

There can be little doubt that this county was still affected by attitudes and standards of the Old South. In Franklin County, as throughout the South, whites enforced segregation and racial discrimination, and the greatest prohibition was for a black male to make any physical or sexual contact with a white woman. In light of this, few observers were surprised when Franklin County whites threatened extralegal violence against Hinds.[13]

Surmising that it was not safe to deal with the accused in Apalachicola, judicial officers made the decision to seek a change of venue so that the young black man would be tried in Tallahassee. The averted lynching and change of venue pleased the ASWPL. Eager to cooperate with this group, the governor and other officials still worried about the possibility of a lynching and the damaging media publicity that would undoubtedly accompany such an incident. Naturally, they anticipated a quick trial, a guilty verdict, and swift execution. State attorney Orion C. Parker, who was to be the prosecutor, openly speculated that the trial could be completed in one day.[14] Officials in this instance acted on the premise, widely accepted by southern leaders, that a fast trial and prompt legal execution of a black man in such a case would show white southerners that lynching was unnecessary; Governor Cone undoubtedly hoped that speedy judicial action would tend to discourage mob action in similar cases in the future. Cone had promised the ASWPL, "There will be no lynchings in Florida if I can prevent it."[15]

In early June 1937 the Franklin County grand jury indicted Hinds; soon afterward, authorities made plans to transport him to Tallahassee, in Leon County, to stand trial. This county was a southern farming area, and almost half of the population lived in Tallahassee. As they did in Franklin County, most people in the rural areas around the state capital went without many of the trappings of modern life such as electricity, automobiles, telephones, and radios. The Great Depression had hit hard, resulting in unemployment, mortgage foreclosures, and difficult times for many.[16] These economic conditions in all likelihood increased job competition in the lower-class labor market, exacerbating racial tensions.

Unlike Franklin, Leon County had a black majority. In fact, 60 percent of this rural county's population of 9,454 in 1930 was black. Nonetheless, whites were determined to keep the black majority in a subordinate position by enforcing all the harsh restrictions of the racial caste system that had been fashioned in the South during the late-nineteenth century.[17] Likewise, the judicial system in this county served the interest of maintaining these racial arrangements.

On 30 June Governor Cone made good on his promise to provide armed protection at Hinds's trial by calling out the National Guard.[18] Branch Cone, the governor's brother and executive secretary, announced that Colonel Percy Coombs of Apalachicola would command one unit. He had previously commanded this same guard outfit when it had been sent to riot-torn Marianna in the fall of 1934, in the aftermath of the Claude Neal lynching. Learning from mistakes of his predecessor, Governor Sholtz, who had been slow to deploy guardsmen in the Neal lynching case, Cone saw to it that troops were in place before anything could happen. Adjutant General Vivien B. Collins, another veteran of the Marianna disturbance, was chosen to command the National Guard unit from Live Oak. In charge of the entire operation, General Collins reported to the governor that these two companies, numbering 132 men, would be stationed around the Leon County courthouse throughout the trial. He also informed Cone that both companies would be armed with sawed-off shotguns, tear gas, machine guns, and other riot-suppressing equipment.[19]

Authorities kept Hinds's whereabouts in Pensacola secret until time for his trial. On 30 June, Judge Johnson wrote the Escambia County Sheriff's Office, ordering it to transfer the prisoner to the legal custody of the Leon County sheriff, Frank Stoutamire.[20] Authorities carefully arranged to move the black defendant, with a minimum of publicity, to his trial site. They flew him to Tallahassee in a privately chartered airplane.

Hinds went on trial on 6 July 1937, and guardsmen surrounded the courthouse throughout the proceedings. This impressive show of force may have thwarted any lynching plans, but the tense atmosphere in Tallahassee was hardly conducive to a fair trial.[21] In Florida courts, a black male accused of raping a white woman had little chance of obtaining impartial justice and by "letting the law take its course," the system could legally carry out the mob's demand for vengeance.[22]

Hinds's trial stands as a clear example of this. It began on a sweltering
July morning with the selection of a jury of twelve white men. A court-ap-
pointed attorney, William Hopkins, represented the black teenager, who
lacked the money to retain a private lawyer. Hinds's attorney decided on
the strategy of pleading his hapless client not guilty by reason of insanity.[23]
This was a safe tactic for everyone concerned except for the defendant
himself. Hopkins must have known that to plead not guilty and go into
court aggressively refuting the testimony of a white woman who had accused a black man of rape would certainly stir passions in the community
that perhaps even the guardsmen could not control. On the other hand, an
insanity plea guaranteed the appearance of a fair trial while also assuring
the outcome of a conviction. An all-white male jury in Tallahassee would,
of course, view an insanity plea as a sham, and find the defendant guilty of
the capital offense.[24]

State Attorney Parker came prepared to refute the insanity plea. He
indicated that the state would base its case on an admission of guilt by the
defendant and on the testimony of several key witnesses. Most important,
he planned to offer psychiatric testimony that Hinds was not insane when
he committed this crime.[25]

The prosecution's star witness, however, was not its psychiatrist but the
alleged victim, Mae Polous, a twenty-six-year-old Apalachicola woman who
gave the damning testimony. She claimed that Hinds had followed her and
her sister-in-law down a road to a berry patch. They ran, and the black
teenager pursued them. She described in vivid detail how the defendant
caught her, threw her to the ground, tore off her clothes, and raped her.
The white woman also told the jury that Hinds had choked her while she
desperately attempted to call for help. Finally, Polous related to the court
how she called on God to "save" her soul while the sister-in-law ran to a
nearby house for aid.

Hopkins revealed some interesting details in his cross-examination and
did so without being aggressive or belligerent. Polous admitted that no doctor had examined her after the attack, and she shed some more light on her
encounter with the black youth. She stated that when they passed Hinds on
the road to the berry patch, he had asked them for directions to a nearby
farm. After the women walked farther down the road, they noticed that the
black youth was following them. They hid in a swamp near the berry patch.
Sometime later the two women were picking berries when he came up
again, and after speaking a few words he started to run at them.

Other prosecution witnesses called that morning also offered damaging testimony. A white man who lived in the area of the crime scene testified that Hinds had come to his house asking for food on the morning of

the alleged assault. The next witness was the arresting officer, who claimed that the defendant had admitted to him that he had indeed attacked and raped the white woman. Hinds, he swore, had told him that he woke up in the morning with the idea of sexually assaulting a white woman.

Hinds sat despondent during the day's proceedings. Several times during the testimony of the state's witnesses he would shake his head as if to deny their statements. However, he never uttered a sound and remained virtually motionless, wearing a poker face. The only testimony that might have offered him a hint of encouragement was given by the arresting officer on cross-examination. He told the jury that when he took the defendant to Polous's house and asked her if this was her attacker, she replied only, "He looks like the one, but I am not sure."

At noon the jury was excused for lunch. When court reconvened, Hopkins presented evidence in an effort to prove that Hinds was mentally impaired at the time of the attack. He offered testimony from family members and friends in a vain attempt to prove this claim. However, the critical flaw in the defense's case was that no psychiatrist gave expert testimony to substantiate the insanity plea. Neither the defendant nor his family could afford to hire a private physician for this purpose.

The prosecution, on the other hand, called in a psychiatrist at the state's expense. Dr. J. C. Robertson from the state mental hospital examined Hinds in his Pensacola jail cell. Testifying as an expert witness, he told the jury that he had detected no signs of insanity in the defendant. This testimony undermined the defense's case and was not challenged by any other medical opinions.

The trial ended the same day it started. Hopkins pled for mercy for Hinds, but the prosecutor demanded a guilty verdict and then recommended the death penalty. The jurors took the case into deliberation at 5:12 P.M. Only one hour and five minutes later, they returned to their box with the request that the judge read them his instructions a second time. Seven minutes later they trooped single file back into the jury box and took their chairs. To no one's surprise, they returned a verdict of guilty. Three jurors recommended mercy, four short of what was required for a sentence of life imprisonment. Thus, the court sentenced Hinds to death in Florida's electric chair.

Authorities sent the convicted man to Raiford prison to await execution. His attorney routinely appealed the case "in order that the [appeals] court might review the trial in this capital case before punishment is meted out." The higher court turned down the appeal for a new trial, and on 17 July 1937 Governor Cone signed Hinds's death warrant. The governor set 23 July 1937 as the date of execution; Sheriff Stoutamire was assigned to pull the switch.[26]

   This case made history in Leon County. It was the first death sentence handed down there since 1901, and the first time in the county's history that the electric chair was the means of execution. The story behind Florida's electric chair is an interesting one. Convicts built it in the spring of 1924 in the prison carpentry shop at Raiford. It was bolted to the floor in a special room, a thick black rubber pad covered a broad seat, and leather straps dangled about the chair. It had but three legs—two back legs and a brace-styled front leg. Hinds would see this device only once, on the morning of 23 July 1937.[27]

   On the appointed day, Hinds went through a kind of "ritual of death" that all condemned prisoners must submit to. Prison officers placed him in the chair at 10:28 A.M. and quickly strapped his legs in place. Next, guards strapped his chest and waist, immobilizing his torso. They secured his hands in the same fashion, and the prison electrician attached an electrical jack to a metal plate fastened tightly to Hinds's right ankle by a leather strap. He then proceeded to scoop a sponge from a bucket of water, squeeze it, and set it inside the death cap. After his head was strapped in, Hinds was helpless, able only to move his fingers a few inches. Someone asked the teenager if he had any last words. He did not speak; onlookers said that he appeared to be resigned to his fate. About thirty witnesses were present, most of them from Apalachicola, and all were white. A guard pulled the black leather mask over Hinds's face, which was as much for the witnesses' benefit as it was for the prisoner's. Someone nodded, and the executioner, Sheriff Stoutamire, threw the switch. The surge of electricity stopped the prisoner's heart, and after one or two minutes he died. The entire process took about five minutes. A doctor pronounced him dead at 10:32 A.M.[28]

   Hinds died in Florida's electric chair without his case becoming a cause célèbre. Neither the NAACP nor the ASWPL offered any legal aid to this young man. Jane Cornell of the ASWPL was satisfied just to play a part in preventing a lynching prior to the trial. The time and resources of the NAACP were tied up in other activities, especially the fight for an anti-lynching bill in Congress.[29]

   While this case would clearly not become another Scottsboro, it resembled the Alabama tragedy in several important respects. Local white juries convicted Hinds and the Scottsboro boys of sexual assaults on white women and then handed down the death sentence. The respective trials were conducted in haste in a tension-filled atmosphere. The legal drama surrounding both incidents was played out in a southern small-town setting where the accused were at a distinct disadvantage. Finally, the persistent threat of mob violence was an element in both trials.[30]

   In spite of these similarities, however, there were important differences between the two cases. Hinds died in the electric chair, but none of the Scottsboro boys was ever executed. The Florida youth received no outside legal help from civil rights organizations, and his plight never attracted the national or international attention focused on the Alabama incident. In addition, Hinds may have indeed been guilty of rape. By way of contrast, the facts surrounding the Scottsboro affair strongly indicated the defendants' innocence.[31]

Still, Hinds deserved more competent legal representation than that offered by the lackluster Hopkins. One can only imagine that had someone like Samuel S. Leibowitz (the aggressive New York attorney who defended the Scottsboro boys in 1936 and 1937) directed Hinds's defense, the Tallahassee trial would have been handled differently. He would have undoubtedly exploited the weaknesses in the prosecution's case. He might have dwelled on the fact that the victim was unable to identify Hinds as the man who had raped her when she saw him in police custody only hours after the attack. Furthermore, he could have brought it to the jury's attention that, except for the two white women, there were no other eyewitnesses to the sexual assault. Finally, a competent and committed attorney like Leibowitz would have arranged for an independent psychiatrist to examine Hinds, then testify on the black youth's behalf to rebut the state's expert witness.[32]

The criminal justice apparatus in this rural county made no allowances for the special circumstances of the case. In the first place, there was no juvenile justice system or social welfare institution to handle this sixteen-year-old's problems. A professional psychological probe might have uncovered mental retardation or some other serious impairment. The court, however, did not consider Hinds's possible psychopathology as a mitigating circumstance. Possible medical factors were just not as important as racial considerations in deciding the black teenager's fate.

Most white Floridians at the time probably believed that Hinds and other blacks received adequate justice in their courts. They would have strongly objected to the contrary claim that the South's legal system, including Florida's, operated in such a way to "keep blacks in their place." Yet, in this instance, and in many others during the 1930s, this was essentially what it did.[33]

Hinds's guilt was taken for granted. There was an obvious informality in the proceedings, and the court's admitted goal was a speedy verdict. The strategy of Governor Cone and other Florida officials in the Hinds case was obvious: they wished to thwart lynchings by rushing through the legal formalities of trial, sentencing, and execution.[34] Authorities tried Hinds under adverse conditions and in a hostile, prejudicial atmosphere. It was the most sensational trial in the twentieth century (up to that time) in Leon County.

National Guardsmen armed with bayonets, tear gas, and machine guns surrounded the courthouse during its course; nothing in the proceedings hinted at enlightened racial views on the part of the court. A fair trial under those circumstances was highly unlikely, and the outcome of the proceedings was the execution of a black victim. Just as in a lynching, community pressure dictated this final end.

THE TALLAHASSEE DOUBLE LYNCHING

Governor Cone was seriously mistaken if he believed official action in the Hinds episode pointed the way to ending lynching in Florida. Indeed, in this instance it proved futile to demonstrate to the state's white citizenry that the judicial system would hastily dispose of blacks who had committed so-called lynchable offenses. In fact, while Hinds awaited certain death in his jail cell at Raiford, a small band of vigilantes in Tallahassee lynched two black teenagers accused of assaulting a white policeman. The swift and sure execution of Hinds apparently had negligible influence on Florida lynchers; in fact, Florida led the nation in lynchings in 1937.[35]

The series of events leading up to the Tallahassee double lynching began on 19 July 1937, shortly after midnight, when two black youths, Richard Ponder and Ernest Hawkins, both eighteen and unemployed, forcibly broke into a local business establishment on South Adams Street, in the downtown area. In the midst of the robbery, city patrolman J. V. Kelley surprised and captured them. With his suspects in custody, the police officer was en route to jail when one of the prisoners attacked him with a knife. Fortunately, the wound was not fatal.[36] The attackers left the seriously injured Kelley at the scene and they fled into the darkness. Within the hour, however, Ponder and Hawkins were back in police custody.[37]

City, county, and state law officers expressed an immediate interest in the case. Tallahassee police chief Gid Powledge, Leon County sheriff Frank Stoutamire, and state attorney Orion C. Parker questioned the youths for several hours. The two suspects finally admitted to breaking and entering, but each accused the other of stabbing the police officer. Officials charged both with assault with intent to murder, as well as with breaking and entering. Ponder and Hawkins were locked up in the Leon County jail, recently constructed by the Public Works Administration.[38]

The two prisoners' stay in jail was brief. On 20 July at about 3:30 A.M., night guard Harry Fairbanks sat quietly reading a newspaper, with his back to the door, at the Tallahassee city jail. Suddenly, four masked men entered the station, captured him, and drove four blocks to the county facility.[39]

There was no night guard on duty. Knowing that Fairbanks had the keys to the county prison, they ordered him to open the main entrance. Inside they told him, "We want the keys and we don't want any damn foolishness." Following these instructions, he opened the gun case that contained the county jail's keys. To reach the prisoners hidden in various areas of the jail, the gunmen used Fairbanks's knowledge of the key system. They forced him to unlock eight different doors, enabling them to seize Ponder and Hawkins. Holding their terrified captives at gunpoint, the small group of kidnappers sped away in their automobile.[40]

Ponder and Hawkins were quickly lynched. At about 4:00 A.M. the kidnappers and their victims arrived at a destination just outside the city limits. There the men stopped the car and pulled the two youths out of the vehicle. They readied their small firearms, .32 and .38 caliber handguns. At this point, they turned one of the blacks loose and urged him to flee for his life. After only a few steps, however, the gunmen cut him down with about fifteen or twenty rounds. As he lay bleeding from his multiple fatal wounds, the killers turned on the other captive and riddled his body with about fifteen or twenty shots. Then, as the bodies lay on the ground, the vigilantes lingered at the scene to paint threatening signs. These warnings admonished other blacks to "stay in their place" or they might be lynched also. Their task completed, the gunmen then drove away, leaving the remains of Ponder and Hawkins by the side of the road.[41]

About four hours after the abduction, a Leon County resident telephoned the sheriff's office, reporting that he had come across the bodies of two men shot to death near his home. Responding to the call, Powledge, Stoutamire, and Parker proceeded out the Jacksonville highway to where the informant resided. There they spotted the bodies of Ponder and Hawkins, three miles east of Tallahassee on the edge of the right-of-way of State Road Number 1. Ironically, the remains were located only yards from the home of a Florida state supreme court justice.[42]

Local authorities in Tallahassee took the first investigative steps in the case. Upon official discovery of the bodies, the county judge convened a six-man coroner's jury and took testimony from several witnesses. Chief Powledge raised the possibility of police complicity in the lynching when he testified that only policemen and county law officers knew that Fairbanks, at the city jail, had a set of keys to the county facility.[43]

The testimony coming out of the coroner's inquest cast a shadow over Sheriff Stoutamire and his deputies. Some observers asked why the sheriff's office had not provided adequate security measures for its prisoners in this case. Others questioned the sheriff's judgment because he had failed to foresee the possibility of vigilante action and because he did not move

Ponder and Hawkins to a safer jail in another town or at least provide them with adequate armed protection.[44]

In an effort to answer persistent charges that the police might be implicated in the lynching, Tallahassee officials exhumed the bodies, removing several slugs for evidence. Test bullets fired from the guns of every city and county officer were also collected for comparison with those removed from the victims. In addition, the sheriff picked up four bullets near the remains of Ponder and Hawkins. On 21 July, authorities sent all of their evidence to the Department of Justice in Washington, D.C., for examination. Explaining these steps, State Attorney Parker declared: "If policemen are implicated we can establish it, and if they are not implicated the evidence will clearly exonerate."[45]

Meanwhile, allegations of police complicity and negligence in his case moved state leaders to act. Circuit court judge John Johnson wrote Governor Fred Cone, stating that "there is something rotten in Denmark." He added that he and the governor should "try to find that rottenness," even if it implicated law officers.[46]

Under pressure to take some steps, the governor considered disciplinary action against Sheriff Stoutamire. However, when rumors circulated around Tallahassee that Cone might suspend the sheriff, prominent officials came to his defense. L. A. Wesson, mayor-commissioner of Tallahassee, wrote the governor: "The action of the persons responsible for the perpetration of this unwarranted and inexcusable act have caused the sheriff of Leon County considerable embarrassment." He also noted, "The government of this city has always considered and looked upon Mr. Stoutamire as one of the most efficient law enforcement officers in the state of Florida."[47] Judge Johnson also wrote Governor Cone in support of the sheriff: "I have been officially associated with Mr. Stoutamire for more than ten years. I can assure you that he is one of the best, most efficient and straightest sheriffs in the state of Florida."[48] In view of these strong recommendations, the governor decided not to suspend Stoutamire.

His fate settled, the sheriff tightened security at the county facility. He arranged for a full-time night guard to work as a deputy sheriff at the jail and to be paid by the city so long as it kept prisoners there. Stoutamire also organized a security system in which only employees of his office would have keys to the county prison.[49] The sheriff asked the city police to return their set of keys, then sought to explain this step in a letter to the mayor-commissioner. He tactfully stated that he meant no criticism of the police, and he added, "I am responsible for all prisoners in the jail, and these developments have proven it is not wise and safe to permit any division of this responsibility."[50] Finally, a federal prison inspector examined the Leon County jail and certified it as a safe place to lodge federal prisoners.[51]

On 1 August 1937 test results from the U.S. Department of Justice arrived in Tallahassee. The Federal Bureau of Investigation reported in a telegram to Sheriff Stoutamire that sample bullets from the guns of Tallahassee policemen and Leon County deputies bore no connection to those that killed the lynch victims. Obviously eager to close the case, a relieved Stoutamire stated, "In my opinion there isn't much more we can do." Called back into session on 3 August, the coroner's jury examined the FBI's report but heard no additional evidence. The jury, as expected, concluded its proceedings and returned a verdict that Ponder and Hawkins had died by "gunshot wounds inflicted by person or persons unknown."[52]

The utilization of the FBI's facilities by Tallahassee officials was laudatory because local law enforcement in the South rarely sought federal aid in a lynching inquiry. Nevertheless, the probe into the murder of Ponder and Hawkins was limited in scope. The evidence indicates that investigators had not questioned in any great depth law officers suspected of complicity. Moreover, no one pursued the possibility that several policemen or deputies, using personal weapons, might have committed the crime and then fabricated convincing alibis. In addition, law officers could have informed third parties that Fairbanks had the keys to the county jail. Needless to say, investigating authorities did not aggressively explore these possibilities.[53]

Indeed, these possibilities were not even mentioned in the public discussion of the murders in the local press. The *Tallahassee Democrat* addressed the lynching in an editorial titled "An Unfortunate Incident in the City's Record," which appeared 20 July 1937. This editorial articulated the community's embarrassment: "It does not promote the city's prestige in the eyes of the state and nation to adopt extralegal means for the enforcement of justice." Tallahassee whites obviously were aware that their community had attracted national attention because of the double slaying. Nonetheless, the editorial appeared to excuse the lynching as understandable because vigilantes had acted in response to an unsatisfactory criminal justice system. In fact, this point of view reflected the prevailing view in the local white community that the execution was a reaction to the "law's delay in dealing with Ponder and Hawkins." Furthermore, the editors even speculated that the Tallahassee lynchers may have been justice-seeking southerners acting out their frustrations over what they considered to be the legal system's failure to convict and execute the black defendants in the Scottsboro cases being tried in Alabama courts.[54]

Tallahassee, the capital of Florida, the seat of government in Leon

County and an educational center, seemed an unlikely setting for a lynching. Nevertheless, Tallahassee was still a small southern town of some twelve thousand residents in 1937, and was perhaps the most isolated of all state capitals in the South in its proximity to heavily populated areas.[55] It was also a very conservative community, still influenced by its Old South historical experience. The slave pews in the city's antebellum Presbyterian and Episcopalian churches called attention to the community's experience with slavery.[56]

The execution of Ponder and Hawkins was more than just simple vengeance; indeed, it was a mechanism contrived to control the town's blacks. During the 1930s whites in Tallahassee firmly resolved to preserve white supremacy in their community by holding five thousand black residents (about 41 percent of the total) in a socially subordinate position.[57] They forced this large minority to submit to racial exclusions and discriminatory laws and customs. Needless to say, Tallahassee was a rigidly segregated community with a well-defined color line in all areas of social life: education, religion, public accommodations, recreation, and employment.[58] Furthermore, the city's blacks were crowded into certain residential areas of town such as Frenchtown, around the Florida Agricultural and Mechanical College, and Smokey Hollow.[59] Moreover, one way whites in this community sought to maintain the inferior social position of blacks was to limit physical contact between the two races. Thus, any black who assaulted a white man broke one of the strongest taboos of prescribed interracial conduct and risked terrible punishment.

The lynching of Ponder and Hawkins carried an unmistakable message to Tallahassee's black community. White Tallahasseeans would not tolerate an assault by two black men on a white police officer, the uniformed representative of white authority. To make this clear, the lynchers left at the lynch scene a line of placards, hastily lettered in green paint on the side of pasteboard packing boxes. They read: "His last crime." "This is the beginning, who is next?" "This is your warning negros [sic], remember you might be next." "Warning, this is what will happen to all negroes who harm white people."[60]

These intimidating threats and the execution itself embarrassed state leaders. Governor Cone, in particular, was surprised by this extralegal murder because only one month earlier he had helped prevent a similar crime, the Hinds case. Yet he had taken no steps to guarantee the safety of Ponder and Hawkins. Indeed, this incident surprised other state officials as well. A local judge who had collaborated with the governor in keeping Hinds out of mob hands wrote Cone a letter explaining that he had not seen the need for providing the two black prisoners with any extra protection.[61]

The immediate, widespread reaction to the Tallahassee killings impressed

Governor Cone. As soon as the papers carried the news of the lynching, letters and telegrams poured into his office. These messages, condemning the slaying, came from as far away as Chicago and New York.[62] One Jacksonville minister wrote a perceptive letter comparing the Tallahassee incident to the two most dramatic vigilante murders of the decade in Florida: the Claude Neal lynching near Marianna and the flogging of Joseph Shoemaker in Tampa. He wrote that Marianna "and Tampa and other places [Tallahassee] have permitted things to occur which have certainly blackened the name of our fair state of Florida."[63]

Florida editors also expressed concern about damage to the state's good name. The editors of the *St. Petersburg Times* seemed to feel that their community might be viewed as guilty by association in the eyes of the nation because of the Tallahassee incident: "Florida was disgraced again early Tuesday when an armed mob of masked men took two accused Negroes from the county jail at Tallahassee and riddled their bodies with bullets. Publicity attendant upon this incident will do the city [St. Petersburg] irreparable harm everywhere throughout the North in areas St. Petersburg is so dependent upon the good will and respect of the people for its continued growth."[64] A *Tampa Tribune* editorial titled "Murder in Tallahassee" declared: "We had hoped Florida might get through 1937 with a clean lynching record. Whatever the charge, they were entitled to a fair trial."[65] The *Miami Herald* stated, "All intelligent and loyal citizens of Florida deplore the lynching that took place in Tallahassee a day or two ago."[66] The *Miami Daily Times* called on the governor to prosecute the vigilantes because that would be "the only way of salvaging the reputation of the state."[67]

The public outcry over this lynching stirred the governor to announce, "I am going to do everything I can to get whoever did this!"[68] He ordered the state attorney and county sheriff to make a prompt and thorough investigation into the matter. However, he claimed that the slaying of Ponder and Hawkins was not actually a lynching; he referred to it as a simple "murder." This curious statement puzzled many observers. The governor knew that lynchings were bloody incidents leading to sharp criticism of Florida; he may have wished to downplay the importance of this event by mislabeling it. His attempt to do so, however, was counterproductive and reflected the belief that he had not given much thought to the lynching issue. In light of what he had observed in Florida as a young man in the 1880s and 1890s, he apparently understood lynchings as ceremonial racial murders characterized by white mobs, manhunts, chases, torture, mutilation, and the public display of the victim's remains. The Tallahassee double slaying was not that kind of ceremonial lynching. In this particular case a small group of armed men kidnapped Ponder and Hawkins from jail and shot them to death in a vigilante-style execution conducted wholly outside the authority of the law. This kind of extralegal murder met all the criteria of a "lynching" as defined by antilynching organizations of the day and the proposed federal antilynching legislation.

Governor Cone was well known for his frequent intemperate remarks, and in this instance he committed one of his most damaging and controversial blunders. Indeed, national press coverage of the affair centered around his statement denying that the double slaying constituted a lynching. Newspapers in several large cities across the country, including New York, Washington, Chicago, Boston, St. Louis, and Atlanta, carried the governor's remarks, as well as the salient details of the incident.[69] The *St. Louis Post-Dispatch* struck a skeptical note in an editorial that read as follows: "Governor Cone says, 'I'm going to do everything I can to get whoever did this! This looks like a lot of carelessness here by somebody.' Those are brave words, but if developments run true to form for the Deep South, nobody will be convicted of the lynching and nobody will lose his job at the jail."[70] Finally, on a national broadcast over NBC radio, socialist Norman Thomas questioned Cone's ability to control the lynching problem when he was unable even to recognize this specific crime when it occurred.[71]

Cone's handling of this episode greatly disturbed the national black community. In this particular instance the NAACP promptly corrected the governor's erroneous definition of the crime when the assistant secretary, Roy Wilkins, sent a telegram to Cone. In it he stated, "*New York Times* today quotes you saying lynching of two Negroes in Tallahassee yesterday by masked men who took them from city jail four blocks from state capital was not lynching but murder. This double killing [is] clearly a lynching since a group took over functions of government and meted out punishment without due process of law. NAACP urges you to use all forces at your command to speed apprehension, trial, and conviction of lynchers. Failure to act or perfunctory action will constitute additional proof states are unable or unwilling to punish these crimes and federal government must act."[72] A number of black newspapers, including the *Chicago Defender, Baltimore Afro-American, Norfolk Journal and Guide,* and the *Atlanta Daily World* derided the governor's irresponsible labeling of the double slaying and lamented the fact that he had failed to prevent this lynching in the state capital.[73] A sharp attack by the *Norfolk Journal and Guide* declared that "to Governor Cone, this state's 'Negro-baiting executive,' the year's fifth and sixth lynchings were not lynchings but 'plain murder'."[74] Finally, the *Crisis* asserted that Cone's inability to apprehend and try the Tallahassee vigilantes invalidated the argument of many southerners that a federal antilynching law was unnecessary because state leaders could deter lynchings.[75]

In contrast to the strident tones of the NAACP and the black press, the Association of Southern Women for the Prevention of Lynching responded rather mildly to Cone's blunder. Jane Cornell wrote the governor: "We have experienced your handling of the threatened lynching of Robert Hinds and find ourselves convinced that you will carry out your determination to thoroughly investigate and punish the crime which has shocked the citizenry of the state. We noted that you said 'this is a murder, not a lynching.' We presume you mean this only in the sense that all lynchings are 'murders'. The Tuskegee Institute and the Association of which I am an officer have both listed the death of these Negroes as 'Lynchings'. We would respectfully call your attention also to the fact that under either the Gavigan or Wagner-Van Nuys Bills, now pending in Congress, the Tallahassee deaths would be attributed to 'lynchings'."[76] Even in response to Cornell's tactful prodding, Cone never admitted his mistake.

Meanwhile, the governor was aware of events in Washington. Ponder and Hawkins had been executed just a few weeks after the Wagner-Van Nuys antilynching bill had been introduced in the Senate.[77] The Tallahassee lynching provided Walter White and the NAACP with an opportunity to apply additional pressure on supporters in the Congress. He called the attention of his chief ally, New York senator Robert Wagner, to the tragic event. Just days after the death of Ponder and Hawkins, Wagner promised to renew efforts on the bill's behalf.[78] On 27 July the bill came before the Senate.[79]

Some onlookers hoped that the Tallahassee lynching, along with other notorious southern executions, would prompt national and Florida officials to support federal antilynching legislation. This was not to be the case. In the summer of 1937, Walter White, as he had done through the 1930s, urged President Roosevelt to endorse the NAACP bill.[80] The administration, however, would lend no more support to the Wagner-Van Nuys bill than it had to earlier proposed antilynching legislation.[81] The president, overly sensitive to southern sensibilities about race, had not supported this kind of legislation. Moreover, in July 1937, Roosevelt was too deeply involved in the controversy surrounding his ill-advised Supreme Court reform bill to consider endorsing the antilynching law.[82]

Florida's U.S. senators, Claude Pepper and Charles Andrews, were no more disposed to embrace the antilynching cause than was President Roosevelt. Senator Pepper knew about the Tallahassee tragedy but spoke forcefully against Wagner-Van Nuys. In a brief speech from the Senate floor on 12 August 1937, he cited a few statistics showing that the number of lynchings had steadily declined every decade since the 1890s, and he asserted that with the return of prosperity, this undesirable custom would die off on its own.[83] Pepper and Andrews both took a stand against the measure late in 1937, during a special session of Congress.[84]

When southerners filibustered Wagner-Van Nuys early in 1938, Senator Pepper fully participated in this effort. Indeed, he even read into the *Congressional Record* a protest telegram from Governor Cone. It began, "Wired Senator McKellar today people of Florida composed of citizens from every state in the Union bitterly opposed to antilynching law. We do not think it wise at this time of international unrest to pass a sectional bill like this, which can do nothing but cause bitter sectional feeling, as everyone knows it is aimed at Southern people." He continued, "You can state to the Senate that Florida as always will be loyal to our country and our flag, but we do not want a return to the shackles of Reconstruction days upon the backs of our people, and we appeal to you Senators, as loyal American citizens, not to pass this bill."[85] In the end Pepper and Cone were probably not surprised when, in late February 1938, the Senate became tired of southern obstructionism and buried the proposed legislation.[86]

Although the 1937 Tallahassee double lynching failed to convince Senator Pepper and Governor Cone to support the antilynching bill, it did reveal something of the social dynamics behind one particular Florida tragedy. Tallahassee lynchers kidnapped Ponder and Hawkins from jail in the state capital, passed immediate judgment on their guilt, and summarily executed them on the outskirts of town. They were determined to demonstrate that blacks in Tallahassee should remain socially subordinate, and that no black men should escape white wrath if they attacked a white police officer.

THE J. C. EVANS LYNCHING

Pending federal antilynching legislation did not deter Tallahassee lynchers, who took the law into their own hands. Moreover, the authorities' failure to apprehend and punish the executioners did little to discourage other Florida lynchers, who were soon to strike again. Their victim this time was a young black man named J. C. Evans.[87] There can be no doubt that Evans was an unsavory character; he was wanted by Bay County police for a robbery he had allegedly committed there in the summer of 1937. But more importantly, he was wanted in Santa Rosa County for a sexual crime of an unspecified nature against a "white boy." That the exact nature of this alleged attack was never explained in detail by officials only served to encourage the spread of wild rumors around the county among the white citizenry. No one knew with any degree of certainty whether Evans may have just fondled the child or if he had attempted a more serious act. Whites in this locality,

who already believed black men were a threat to their women, likely re-
coiled in horror when they learned that a black man might attack even
their male children.[88]

The effect of all this unsettling speculation was a rising mob spirit in
Santa Rosa County.[89] This region of the state, in the Florida panhandle
between Pensacola and Panama City, suffered a degree of commercial, social, and cultural isolation that made it a relatively backward area. Further,
it was thinly settled and listed in the 1930 federal census as 100 percent
rural.[90] In addition, this was a poor county during the thirties; by 1937
farm income and retail and wholesale trade were still below the levels of the
more prosperous 1920s.[91] These harsh economic circumstances, one can
easily imagine, adversely affected race relations in Santa Rosa County.

Blacks, who comprised about 16 percent of the population, found themselves at a distinct disadvantage.[92] In this county whites viewed blacks as
inferior people and expected them to stay in their place in accordance with
the South's racial caste system. And, not surprisingly, whites were willing to
use violence to maintain these racial arrangements. In light of this state of
affairs, it seemed likely that a black man suspected of being a sexual deviant
was a ready target for outraged whites. Add to this situation that Santa
Rosa County displayed many of the characteristics of a frontier society,
such as inadequate police protection and men carrying guns, and the stage
was set for a lynching.[93]

J. C. Evans had been arrested in Bay County on 12 July 1937 for suspected armed robbery. For this crime he was tried, found guilty, sentenced
to prison, and lodged in the Panama City jail. He was then supposed to
stand trial in Santa Rosa County for the alleged molestation of the white
child, but not until it was safe to transport him to the county seat at Milton.[94]
On 3 October 1937 Santa Rosa County sheriff Joe Allen reckoned it safe to
make his move. On this day, soon after dark, he and his deputy, Aubrey
Martin, drove from Milton to Panama City to pick up Evans. The sheriff
claimed that he kept this trip a closely guarded secret. Allen declared, "I
didn't even tell my office force I was going to Panama City." He added,
"The deputy sheriff who went with me didn't know until we had left Milton
where we were going."[95]

The return trip to Milton was ill-fated, premature, and a fatal error. In
some unexplained way, a well-organized band of vigilantes found out about
this move and plotted to intercept the sheriff and his deputy on the return
leg of the trip. Sheriff Allen's car was nearing Ft. Walton when a lone vehicle pulled up in front of him, forcing him to stop. At this point, four men
jumped out of their auto and covered the officers with shotguns. The sheriff later stated that these assailants were careful enough to keep outside the

range of his headlights to prevent him from seeing their features. They shouted, "We want the nigger!" These unmasked men knew exactly what they were doing, and they met little resistance from either Allen or Martin, who were unwilling to risk their lives to fight off the kidnappers. They put the sheriff and Evans in their car, leaving the deputy behind, and drove on for about a mile or two down the road; there the sheriff was put out of the vehicle and given his car keys.[96]

The kidnappers, who at last had sole possession of the terrified Evans, proceeded to execute him. Apparently they drove just a few more miles down the road, pulled the black man out of their car, and riddled his body with buckshot and pistol fire. The wounds were so numerous and severe that the victim, in all probability, died quickly. His lynchers, however, did not linger at the scene long enough to verify this; after the shooting, they quickly drove off, leaving Evans in a ditch by the side of the road.[97]

The two lawmen, meanwhile, had recovered their bearings. They immediately drove to Milton and telephoned the appropriate authority, Sheriff John Steel, because the lynching had occurred in Okaloosa County. Early Monday morning, 4 October, Sheriff Steel informed the county judge of the incident so he could convene a coroner's jury. Hastily summoned, the jury visited the lynch scene, where they found Evans's body by the side of the road about three to five miles from where the mob had stopped the sheriff's car.[98] In view of the facts of this case, the coroner's jury probed first into the issue of how the killers knew when Sheriff Allen was to pick up Evans, and how they knew what roads he would travel over. As the only witness to testify, Allen swore he had kept his plans for the trip a well-guarded secret. This story was accepted without challenge. Further, he also testified that he was unable to identify any of the lynchers. Predictably, the jury found that very day that J. C. Evans had come to his death at the hands of "parties unknown."[99]

This was by no means the end of the matter, however. When news of the lynching was made public, many asked the still unanswered question of how the kidnappers and executioners knew about Allen's trip to and from Panama City. Sheriff Steel, in his comments to the press, did what he could to cover for his colleague. "Sheriff Allen didn't think anybody knew he was going after the prisoner," declared Steel. He added, "He told me a week ago he thought he was being watched by somebody, but he didn't connect it with the Evans case." Finally, the sheriff concluded, "We don't have a thing to go on. It must have been somebody from Santa Rosa County who knew all about the case and what Sheriff Allen was doing."[100] These explanations were unsatisfactory to Governor Cone, who promised, "I will do all I can to straighten this thing out and run down the guilty parties." Taking action that was by now routine, he ordered the appropriate state attorney and local officials to thoroughly investigate the crime and do everything possible to apprehend the lynchers.[101]

Delivered so soon after the Tallahassee lynching, these hollow-sounding declarations by the governor failed to impress skeptical observers. Florida editors wasted no time in registering their displeasure with Cone and the lynching problem. A *Miami Herald* editorial cynically stated, "As usual Governor Cone is aroused and orders an investigation and punishment, and again a jury hands down the usual verdict of the crime being committed by parties unknown . . . this meaning the officials have no desire to know, at least I publicly," who lynched Evans.[102] The *St. Petersburg Times* bluntly reported, "Governor Cone has ordered a thorough investigation of the crime, but the rest of the state will be none too optimistic over the chances of the guilty parties being brought to trial."[103]

A lynch-hardened NAACP immediately focused its attention on Florida as soon as it received word of the affair. Its leaders expressed alarm to Governor Cone over the possible collusion between Sheriff Allen's office and the lynch band. Roy Wilkins, assistant secretary of the NAACP, wrote: "It should be noted further that this prisoner was in the hands of only two officers and this despite the well-known fact that feeling was high in the community." He continued, "It would seem to be elementary that were extraordinary precautions taken . . . more than two officers would have been protecting the prisoner." He finished, "It should be noted further that no effort whatsoever was made by the officers to protect their prisoner, the latter being surrendered on demand."[104] A telegram from Walter White expressed a similar concern, "It is apparent that Allen's story is most open to question. If he [Allen] is not guilty [of] taking the prisoner directly to the hands of the mob he is certainly guilty of extreme stupidity."[105]

The Florida press also raised the issue of collusion between law officers and lynchers. The *Miami Herald* observed, "One naturally wonders how the lynchers knew that the two officers were going after the Negro unless they were tipped off, how they knew what route the sheriff was following, which car he occupied, and where he could be halted. Men do not know these things by chance."[106] The *Miami Daily News* echoed these sentiments and compared the Evans tragedy to the Tallahassee double lynching. "In each case [Tallahassee and Santa Rosa County], prisoners have been seized from what have appeared to be careless and inadequately manned guards. The circumstances in more than one case even left room for hints of collusion between mobsters and officers of the law. In each case a 'thorough' investigation has been promised and in each case, up to the present, the investigators were quite unable to 'establish the identity' of the murderers." It also

remarked, "This sort of performance has gone on now to the point of dragging Florida's reputation in the blackest mire. It has also gone to the point
where the next session of Congress can hardly resist growing pressure in
the North to curb Southern mob murders by antilynching legislation of
such an extreme nature as to be thoroughly unpalatable, if not unjust, to
the South." It finally asked, "When will hotheads in Florida and other states
wake up and realize that the only way to avoid this onerous federal control
is to clear up the lynching disgrace between themselves?"[107]

If Florida editors and black leaders were critical of Cone's response to
the Evans lynching, others were kinder.[108] For example, Mrs. O. O. McCollum
of the Women's Missionary Society sided with Cone, stating, "As you have
done in the past, we feel sure you will do all in your power to bring to justice
the lynchers" in this case.[109] In reply to the uproar over the entire matter,
the governor defended himself in a letter to the NAACP in which he wrote,
in a vain attempt at silencing criticism, that "this crime was committed
without any knowledge of the facts until after it was too late to take any
action. I have been opposed to lynching . . . since I have been in office and
expect to have this investigated and use every means to bring the guilty
party to justice."[110]

Such a perfunctory reply failed to win sympathy from Walter White,
Roy Wilkins, or the black press. More than one black newspaper lashed out
at Cone and Florida over the Evans execution. For example, the *Norfolk
Journal and Guide* ran headlines that read, "FIVE HOODED MEN LYNCH
FLORIDIAN," and referred to the Evans lynching as "the third bloody
blot of the year on Florida's scroll of Justice."[111] The *Baltimore Afro-American*
was most indignant about this extralegal killing, running a headline that
exclaimed, "FLORIDA MOB GETS PREY." It also reported the bloody
details of the incident and expressed chagrin that nothing happened to the
killers. It also carried the following pointed editorial titled: "Florida Lynching Quota," which declared: "Last week Florida staged its third lynching of
the year, when a sheriff in the customary manner turned over J. C. Evans
. . . to a mob which riddled his body with bullets. No doubt the Florida
mobs are making a strenuous effort to get their yearly quota of lynchings
before the passage of the federal antilynching bill."[112]

Evans, Ponder, and Hawkins were only three of eight blacks lynched in
the South that year. Indeed, it bears repeating that Florida led the nation in
lynchings in 1937; this prompted the *Christian Century* to assert about lynch
law in the Sunshine State that the "most ominous item" about the slayings
of its three victims was that "there was no single arrest, indictment, or conviction."[113]

5

Kidnapped from the Police

THE three lynchings of 1937 in the Florida panhandle placed Governor Cone under considerable pressure, and that evoked certain aspects of his character. In the course of governing Florida during the late thirties, circumstances forced "Old Suwannee," as he was nicknamed, to confront time and again the issues of race and extralegal violence. Moreover, his handling of these matters was unmistakably characterized by bigotry and intolerance.

Several of the governor's statements during his first months in office revealed that he had problems dealing with the race issue. At a cabinet meeting early in his administration, he and Florida's secretary of state, Robert A. Gray, argued about the salary of the president of the Florida Agricultural and Mechanical College for blacks. Cone bluntly asserted, "There's no Negro on earth worth four thousand dollars a year salary." In reply Gray asked him, "What is Joe Louis worth?" The governor retorted, "Not worth a damn, at least by the time he gets tied up with two or three more Schmellings, he won't be worth a damn." At this point Gray informed him that Thomas Edison had once offered a black man fifty thousand dollars a year. Cone replied, "Well, but Mr. Edison also said that there is no God, but just a sort of spiritual something, and a man like that might make that kind of offer."[1]

The headstrong Cone was, in many respects, a disappointment as governor. A small-town banker and lawyer from rural Columbia County, he vainly sought to cultivate an image of himself as a man of the people. Yet his numerous critics scoffed at this idea; one detractor even called him "a cracker from his head to his toes."[2] The widely circulated rumor that he and Branch Cone, his brother and executive secretary, worked barefooted in their offices did little to discourage these critics.[3] Back in the 1936 campaign, the pleasing southern drawl and colorful homespun mannerisms of "Old Suwanee" had charmed many Florida voters. During his first year in office, however, the new governor showed he was a difficult man to work

113

with; likewise, his overbearing manner often made cabinet meetings unproductive scenes of bitter debate and controversy.[4]

Worse still, the governor displayed a special talent for intemperate, impulsive verbal eruptions; what is more, some of his most reckless remarks dealt with lynching and vigilantism. In New York City in October of 1937—soon after the executions of Ponder, Hawkins, and Evans, and during the well-publicized trial of the Tampa floggers—Cone committed his most harmful and embarrassing gaffe. Indeed, his timing could not have been worse. On 27 October a delegation of representatives from liberal and religious organizations went to the Waldorf-Astoria Hotel, where the governor was staying, to question him about the trial of Tampa policemen and Klan members accused of flogging Shoemaker to death. The discussion was heated, and Cone lost his composure and lashed out with a blanket threat to all political radicals who might come to Florida. He bluntly declared, "You go down there [Florida] and violate state laws and you'll be punished. You go down there advocating overthrow of the American government and you'll be rode out on a rail. I think a man ought to be hung on a tree if he advocates overthrow of the government." A Workers' Defense League lawyer pressed the irate Cone and asked him if he "wouldn't go to the law" before resorting to rail-riding and hanging. The governor snapped back, "I'd go to you first if you came into my home and were trying to take something."[5]

Not surprisingly, Cone's remarks that clearly sanctioned a lynch-law ethic were national news, and drew an immediate, hostile response from many quarters. The American Civil Liberties Union (ACLU) promptly challenged him to a public debate on his views. Explaining in a telegram that such an exercise could be arranged while he was in the city, it promised that a man prominent in public life would be his opponent. When the stunned governor curtly declined this offer, the ACLU charged that his inciting comments encouraged lawlessness in his state.[6] In addition, the *Daily Worker* accused Cone of "lynching the Constitution," and called him an "open apostle of the rope and faggot."[7] Further, a religion professor from Smith College wrote a letter to the governor stating, "There was a time, was there not, when people in Florida did attempt to overthrow the duly established government? Would you have treated them so?"[8]

Cone's provocative indiscretion in this instance received widespread national newspaper coverage. For instance, the *New York Times* reported that the governor came to the city to visit the Florida exhibit at the World's Fair and publicly humiliated himself and his state. According to the *Times* story, Mayor Fiorello La Guardia was so unhappy over the governor's rash words that he snubbed him and the Florida delegation when they came to visit.

The mayor sent a message to the group that he was too busy to see them, so the Floridians left a basket of grapefruit and returned to the Waldorf-Astoria. However, as soon as they left, La Guardia received the Texas Christian University football team and donned a ten-gallon hat for the benefit of photographers.[9]

In addition to this scathing attack by editors of the *Times*, the *New York Post* also blasted Cone. It eagerly resurrected the ghost of Joseph Shoemaker so that it could exact a measure of revenge at the governor's expense. In a blistering and sarcastic editorial titled, "To His Excellency," it stated: "We welcome you to New York City. We welcome you because it gives us a chance to express our disgust with the enforcement of law in the state of Florida, of which you are governor." It continued, "We don't know how you feel about it, but we would be ashamed to be governor of a state in which police can arrest men without warrants, beat them without mercy, leave one of them to die and go unpunished." Next, it bluntly asked, "What are you going to do about it? What are you going to do about the Tampa floggings and murders? . . . The murderers of Joseph Shoemaker go unpunished, because the Florida cracker judge you appointed to hear the case barred out [*sic*] most of the state's evidence. The kidnappers and floggers of Shoemaker and his two companions, Eugene F. Poulnot and Dr. Samuel J. Rogers, go unpunished because the same judge refuses to set a date for their trial." It concluded, "Are you going to play ball with the Ku Klux Klan and the other anti-labor forces in the state of Florida and let the case slide? The blood of Shoemaker cries out for your answer."[10]

Cone and the Shoemaker saga painfully embarrassed the state of Florida, and press spokesmen let the governor know it. Leading the way, the *St. Petersburg Times* probably spoke for many thoughtful Floridians when it disassociated itself from Cone's injudicious remarks in New York City. It carried the entire *Post* editorial and added that "such publicity as the above editorial does not make this state any more attractive for visitors. The Tampa situation has already brought Florida into sufficient disrepute. Governor Cone's greatest kindness would be to take the first train homeward bound and entrust his good-will missions hereafter to those gifted with greater tact and considerably greater clarity in expressing themselves."[11]

Black spokesmen all over the country were outraged by the governor's remarks that clearly sanctioned lynching. Walter White wrote that this "was the first time that a governor, even of a southern state, within the last ten or fifteen years, had openly condoned lynching." He added that "Governor Cone has advocated hanging by mobs. In recent years, no governor has made a statement so bold and vicious."[12] The headlines of the *Chicago Defender* on 30 October stated, "FLORIDA GOVERNOR APPROVES LYNCHING," and the *Baltimore Afro-American* wrote that "Governor Fred P. Cone has put his approval upon lynching." The *Norfolk Journal and Guide* ran a headline that read, "FLORIDA GOVERNOR OKAYS LYNCHING."[13]

It appears that Cone himself merely shrugged off the sharp, blistering attacks leveled at him over his New York gaffe. By his calculations, it was by far more important to support measures suppressing radicalism than to protect the civil liberties of political radicals who might become vigilante targets in Florida. Throughout his tenure in office he fully supported House Concurrent Resolution 13, which had been approved by the state legislature on 12 May 1937 and set up a formal government project to obtain and compile information concerning "Communist activities" in Florida.[14] Furthermore, he turned a deaf ear to protests over civil liberties violations, such as occurred on 28 April 1938 in Ft. Lauderdale, when local police acting without a warrant arrested alleged Communist Party members meeting in a private home.[15]

By 1938 Governor Cone braced himself to deal with a harsh dilemma: on the national scene he had spoken out in defense of a vigilante ethic, but he still had to deal with lynching problems in his own state. How he would handle this and other problems was made much more problematic by his failing health; in July 1938 he was struck down by a nearly fatal heart attack. And as he recovered his strength over the next two years, he uncomfortably witnessed the last three lynchings of the decade. Otis Price and Lee Snell (two blacks), as well as Miles Brown (a white man), died violently at the hands of men who kidnapped them from the police and shot them to death. Understandably, these three lynch-law episodes greatly disappointed many concerned Floridians, state officials, the Florida press, the black press, and antilynching groups. By the end of the decade it was all too clear that Florida had failed to bring a halt to the lynching evil.[16]

THE OTIS PRICE LYNCHING

News of the 9 August 1938 Otis Price lynching caught the governor's office completely by surprise. Governor Cone was too weak to deal with the crisis himself, so it fell to his brother and executive secretary, Branch Cone, to handle this affair, but only after agents outside the state called it to his attention. Acting on instructions from her national office of the International Labor Defense (ILD), Margaret Bailey on 24 September protested to the governor's office the lynching of a black, Otis Price, in Perry, Florida, as well as suppression of the news about the affair by local authorities.[17] Two days later Branch Cone received a telegram from Roger Baldwin, director of the American Civil Liberties Union, urging an immediate investigation of the Price lynching, which had been kept secret since early August.[18] And on the same day, he also received protests from the NAACP and the Modern American Youth Club of Jacksonville that denounced the lynching and subsequent coverup.[19]

ILD and ACLU protests prompted the governor's office to act. Branch Cone responded in the same fashion to all correspondents: "I have just been apprised of this act within the last few days and I am having the case investigated. I stand for law and order and do not condone any unlawful act, as justice should be sought in the courts."[20] In addition, on the governor's behalf, he wrote to Sheriff S. L. Wilson of Taylor County, asking for a "report on this case and [to] advise [him] if there is any chance of apprehending the guilty parties."[21] The sheriff complied with his request, and the governor's secretary received Wilson's report on 6 October.

This document spelled out the details of the incident. In it the sheriff told how on the day of the lynching, while he was in Gainesville on official business, his deputy and brother, Napoleon Wilson, traveled to a turpentine camp about fourteen or fifteen miles from Perry. There he learned that a black man named Otis Price, who may have attempted to sexually violate a white woman, was hiding in the woods from angry white men. Deputy Wilson had the suspect's wife go into the thicket and coax him into giving himself up, the assumption being that he would be safer with the lawman whose sworn duty it was to protect him from harm. The deputy took Price into custody (although it was not clear if he was formally arrested at this point), put him in the car, and proceeded to drive back toward Perry. Suddenly, a motorized mob of unspecified number and strength overtook the lawman, forced him to stop his vehicle, and kidnapped the prisoner. Soon afterward, the kidnappers gunned down Price by the side of the road and then simply drove off and left him.[22]

Local authorities investigated this crime with predictable swiftness. The day after the execution they promptly convened a coroner's jury that viewed the remains and took in an afternoon of testimony. The jury, as expected, concluded that the black victim had "come to his death by gunshot wounds inflicted by parties unknown."[23] As far as Taylor County officials were concerned, this was the end of the matter, and somehow news of the incident was kept out of the state's newspapers for over a month. Eventually, however, word of the lynching leaked out of the county. And, in fact, American Communists were the first to make the extralegal killing known to the public; ILD activists led the effort to publicize the episode. Next, news of the illegal execution in Florida appeared in the *Daily Worker* on 19 September, over a week before it made the state papers.[24] The ILD was also the first organization to bring this particular matter to the governor's attention, and shortly afterward the ACLU followed suit.

This lynch-law murder also appeared in several black newspapers before surfacing in the Florida press. The *Chicago Defender* and the *Norfolk Journal and Guide* on 24 September reported that an unidentified man from Macon, Georgia, who had seen Price's body and knew about circumstances preceding the murder, wrote a letter to the national office of the NAACP, informing them about the lynching.[25] Based on this dramatic revelation, the association reported in the *Crisis* that Price had been on his way to a well to draw water when he unintentionally walked by the rural cabin of a white farmer whose wife was bathing in the open doorway. She may have seen the black man, panicked, and screamed rape.[26] These curious circumstances prompted the *Baltimore Afro-American* to run headlines on 24 September that declared, "MODERN BATHSHEBA CAUSES LYNCHING," followed by a story of how the NAACP was informed of this tragedy.[27]

Not until late September did news of the Price lynching finally appear in the state's newspapers. The Associated Press version of the story was carried in the 28 September editions of the *St. Petersburg Times*, the *Tampa Tribune*, the *Jacksonville Times-Union*, and the *Tallahassee Democrat*.[28] Pleased with the AP story, the ILD pressed local and state officials to act. Margaret Bailey, working out of Jacksonville, revealed to news reporters that Price's execution "was the first of its kind in Florida since the defeat of the anti-lynching bill in the last session of Congress." The ILD representative also sent a telegram to state attorney A. L. Black of Lake City, demanding a full investigation and maintaining that racial conditions in Taylor County were "a disgrace to all Florida." When approached for a response to this sharp criticism, the state attorney flatly declined to discuss any aspect of his office's investigation of this matter.[29]

Taylor County officials referred the matter of the Price slaying to the grand jury that was already in session. Onlookers outside the county hoped that possibly this inquiry might yield some positive results in light of widespread publicity about the crime; perhaps a few lynchers might even be identified and indicted. This was not how developments unfolded, however. After a three-day superficial inquiry, the Taylor County grand jury recessed on 1 October without returning any indictments after concluding that Price had been killed by unknown persons.[30]

In the meantime, Sheriff Wilson felt obliged to explain his office's actions in this case, especially the charge that it may have suppressed information about the lynching for some six weeks. He frankly told reporters that he and other Taylor County officials did not, in fact, view this particular killing as a lynching, nor was it in any way unusual enough to merit a special report to the governor's office. "There wasn't much to report. We haven't been reporting deaths to the governor's office, and I don't know of any reason to report this one." What agitated the sheriff most, however, were persistent questions about the precise nature of the arresting charges and about whether there was a formal arrest made at the turpentine camp on the day of the execution. Wilson could not tell the press if Price had been accused of insulting, attacking, or actually trying to rape the white woman.[31] Apparently, the unspoken understanding was that these distinctions made little difference to the vigilante killers; all in their eyes were lynchable offenses.

Sheriff Wilson did not even try to conceal his chagrin over being placed on the defensive by what he assuredly thought of as "outsiders." He and other Taylor County whites were surprised and annoyed that public opinion held them accountable for the lynching of a black man. They undoubtedly wondered what all the fuss was about; but circumstances were changing, and they could no longer allow lynchers to execute black victims and hide it from the outside world. Moreover, the fact that American Communists were the first to raise the issue of a coverup only reinforced the sheriff's indignant attitude. Nonetheless, not everyone in Taylor County agreed with Wilson; in fact, one unnamed Perry minister stated he believed news of the lynching was indeed hidden because the county was ashamed of it.[32]

What kind of place was Taylor County, and how did it treat black people? On the west coast of the Florida peninsula and far enough north to be part of the Old South region of the state, it was a culturally isolated area in the 1930s. About 80 percent rural during the decade, its sparse population numbered only 11,565 by 1940, and Perry, the county seat, was the only town of any size, with 2,668 residents.[33] At this time nearly one-third of the county's population was black, and a good number of them, like Otis Price, lived and worked in turpentine camps.[34] In these camps they were subjected to unfair treatment, including long hours, low wages, and harsh living conditions. Moreover, in the county as a whole, equality for blacks was denied in all areas of social life; members of this minority were, of course, not admitted to white schools, white neighborhoods, white restaurants, or white churches. This strict separation of the races in Taylor County was firmly established by the 1930s in order to save white people from having to tolerate black company. These whites naturally embraced "white supremacy" and the conviction that blacks must stay in their place, and above all, they believed that no black man should sexually offend a white woman, even unintentionally. Evidently, then, the Price lynching was motivated in large part by white determination to maintain the county's racial caste arrangements.[35]

Some onlookers hoped that something would be done by the governor's office to keep this case open until some of the lynchers were identified and punished. In fact, several concerned groups pressured the governor to reject the findings of the Taylor County grand jury; the ILD, the American League of Peace and Democracy, the International Workers' Order Local 142 of Miami and the Interdenominational Ministerial Alliance of Miami urged Cone to stand firm and force local authorities to make a more genuine attempt to find and punish the lynchers.[36] The governor's office, however, honored tradition and once again let the matter die locally.

THE PANAMA CITY LYNCHING

Before the memory of Otis Price had time to fade from the minds of Governor Cone and antilynching activists, they witnessed still another extralegal execution in their state. Less than six months after the Taylor County incident, Florida vigilantes lynched Miles Brown, a twenty-five-year-old white man and a convicted murderer, in Panama City, in the panhandle. On 16 January 1939, after a violent argument with his former employer, Roy Van Kleeck, Brown apparently flew into a rage and shot the Panama City hardware store owner to death. Subsequently, he stole the victim's money and fled to Jacksonville. Police investigations of this prominent and well-respected businessman's murder immediately led to a statewide manhunt for Brown, and on 18 January so-called special detectives arrested him in his Jacksonville hotel room with $1,363 on his person.[37]

Lynching threats prompted Bay County sheriff John Scott to keep the incarcerated Brown out of Panama City. This town, located on the Gulf coast in the Florida panhandle, was a rapidly growing community; its population boomed from a mere 1,090 residents in 1920 to 11,610 inhabitants in 1940.[38] To some extent, the community had modernized in the 1920s, when the city fathers had paved the streets and automobile ownership became fairly widespread. During the thirties Panama City's economic well-being was in large part based on the traditionally profitable fishing industry and an all-important paper mill that provided employment for hundreds of residents. Although the town had modernized in the twenties and the local economy had a solid base, many of its residents still embraced traditional attitudes about law and order. These attitudes fostered the belief that they could not really count on the formal criminal justice system to punish offenders with timely severity. Moreover, if the legal system would not dispose of criminals by administering the kind of sure and swift punishment they expected, then extralegal action was a justified remedy.[39]

The murder of Van Kleeck aroused strong desires for vengeance against Brown that were slow to recede. Understandably, then, wary officials wisely kept the defendant in a secret and "safe" jail somewhere in northwest Florida. On 21 January Brown made a full confession of the murder to Bay County authorities, who, in reply, turned it over to the local newspaper, the *News-Herald*, to print in full. The public confession, of course, further inflamed local passion against this young man. Soon after this, the Bay County grand jury returned an indictment against the suspect for the first-degree murder of Roy Van Kleeck.[40]

On 29 March 1939 Brown went on trial in Panama City, where feeling still ran high against him. On this day, a carnival atmosphere settled over the town and the courtroom was packed to overflowing; even though this was hardly a situation conducive to a fair trial, officials proceeded without hesitation. With his mother and father seated near him, young Brown faced the court with no show of emotion. As the trial opened prosecutor John H. Carter—the same Carter of the Neal and Smoaks lynchings—called on the jury to find the defendant guilty and invoke the death penalty. J. M. and Herbert Sapp, two local lawyers who served as defense attorneys in this trial, hoped that since they could not possibly win an acquittal, they might be able to convince the jury to hand down the sentence of life imprisonment instead of death in the state's electric chair. In this three-day event, the prosecution presented an airtight case that the defendant was indeed guilty of killing Van Kleeck. After a brief presentation of its case, the defense pleaded to the jury for mercy in its sentencing for this young man. On the afternoon of 31 March the jury began deliberations that lasted only a few hours; they returned a guilty verdict but recommended mercy, automatically fixing Brown's sentence as life imprisonment.[41]

This verdict stirred a group of lynch-minded citizens into action; they would not accept any punishment short of the death penalty. On 1 April, at about 3:00 A.M., four men came to the Bay County jail to kidnap Brown. Quietly entering the jail in the early morning, the intruders made their way to the jailer's room on the second floor. There they bound him, took his keys, and warned him that if he came out of the room, he would never go back in alive. According to a later report by the jailer, these assailants declared, "We waited for the law, now we are going to get justice." The bound-and-gagged lawman heard nothing more until one of the men came back upstairs and threw his keys into the room with a warning not to come out.

Obeying this order, he waited until daybreak in the belief that if the kidnappers had left a lookout, he would be gone. Finally, he worked himself free, confirmed that Brown was missing, and called Sheriff Scott.[42]

Before a search could be organized, a local newspaper boy found Brown's pajama-clad body. Vigilantes had lynched him fewer than five miles from the downtown area in an obviously well-planned and carefully executed murder. They were indeed efficient: one shot to the head did the job. Investigators on the crime scene that morning reported finding no tracks leading to the body except those made by the victim's bedroom slippers; the killers had covered their trail from the scene.[43]

Word of this extralegal slaying of a white man spread through the state and nation. Governor Cone's office responded with indignant denunciations followed by the demand for an immediate, thorough inquiry. On this occasion, however, there was a novelty: a special investigator, appointed by Cone, aided Panama City and Bay County officials in looking into the matter.[44] In light of his earlier experiences with lynching, the governor apparently decided to make a special effort in a genuine attempt to find the lynchers. The special investigator's involvement led to the arrest of three blacks and one white as the suspected vigilante killers of Brown. These men, however, were soon released. Further investigative efforts led nowhere, and on 17 April the grand jury formally labeled the killing an unsolved mystery.[45]

Local authorities on this occasion honored two traditions—failing to identify the lynchers and holding up the so-called shortcomings of the legal system as the real cause of this lynching. State Attorney Carter presented an argument widely accepted in the community that it was the jury's "mercy" recommendation that had led directly to this illegal, but understandable, execution. Indeed, there can be little doubt that many Panama City residents approved of the vigilantes meting out fatal, informal justice. *Panama City News-Herald* editors fully agreed with this view; the jury had failed to do the right thing, namely, sentence Brown to death, so what other choice, it earnestly asked, did justice-seeking citizens have in this matter?[46]

Editors throughout the state vigorously rejected this view. In fact, they expressed outrage that Floridians were still, even in 1939, lynching fellow citizens. Remembering that Florida had led the nation in lynchings in 1937, they wondered if the state might repeat this dubious distinction in 1939. In an editorial titled "Florida's Shame," the *Miami Herald* declared: "Again the name of Florida is blackened with a lynching, and this time it was no rising of racial hatred, no sudden emotional outbursts. . . . This was a direct assault upon the courts, a reversion to the primitive, where force only prevailed." This editor also took issue with Carter's argument, which seemed to excuse the lynching as justified. He wrote that "there is often reason to criticize the course of legal justice, but that is no defense of lawlessness." And finally, he called for "action, not a whitewash."[47] The *St. Petersburg Times* simply exclaimed that "lynching is murder, vicious, and savage. It is inexcusable . . . lynching is damnable!"[48]

An editorial in the *Miami Daily News* was thoughtful and reflective. Referring to an ASWPL survey of lynchings for the 1930s, it noted that "There is one striking thing about the survey, however. That is, that during the nine years covered in the survey, Florida is the state which seems to have the most difficulty in foregoing its annual outbreak of mob violence. During only one of the nine years (1933) was Florida totally free of lynching."[49] The *Tampa Tribune* gave the story front-page coverage with a pictorial: a large, imposing man with a smoking gun in one hand and a rope in the other. He stood in a menacing fashion over the victim lying prostrate before him, and the smoke that curled up from the gun read, "Lynch Law." The caption under the picture stated, "It's Still Murder."[50]

This lynching of a white man did not escape the notice of the national press. The *New York Times*, *St. Louis Post-Dispatch*, *Washington Post*, and *Richmond Times-Dispatch* carried details of the incident, as well as the words of the lynchers: "The law didn't do justice, but we will."[51] The black press did not ignore the story either; newspapers in Chicago, Baltimore, Norfolk, Pittsburgh, and Atlanta wrote about the story in terms of its influence on the pending federal antilynching bill in Congress.[52] The *Chicago Defender*, for example, wrote that "Brown's lynching was acclaimed a godsend by many backers of the antilynching bill, because it has naturally silenced much of the southern opposition."[53] An editor for the *Norfolk Journal and Guide* stated that "Florida is now responsible in the eyes of the nation for two lynchings within 8 months. We urge Congressional representatives to support passage of the federal antilynching bill as the only means of ending forever this recurrent disgrace."[54]

Antilynching groups protested this tragedy just as vigorously as if a black man had been killed. Mrs. Henry Hovers, new chairwoman of the Florida Council of the ASWPL, wired Cone, asking him to bring the lynchers to justice.[55] In addition to this, the Florida branch of the ILD called for an investigation and sent telegrams to U.S. senators Claude Pepper and Charles Andrews, asking them to support passage of a federal antilynching bill.[56] The *Crisis* reported that "The mob took the position that Brown should have been electrocuted, and therefore, proceeded to carry out its own sentence upon him." The NAACP also criticized Carter's statements, which seemed to justify the lynching, and wired Senator Pepper, asking if "this and other similar instances did not prove conclusively the need for a federal antilynching law."[57]

THE DAYTONA BEACH LYNCHING

Less than one month after antilynching voices had registered their protests over the Panama City tragedy, the final lynching of the decade occurred in Florida. Saturday, 29 April 1939, was a tragic day in Daytona Beach for Benny Blackwelder, a twelve-year-old white boy, and Lee Snell, a black taxi driver. At about 7:29 A.M., Benny was riding his bicycle down the street when he was accidentally struck by Snell's taxi at the intersection of Second Avenue and Keech Street. This unfortunate mishap proved fatal for the Blackwelder child. According to a police report, the boy had been thrown about twenty-five feet through the air by Snell's car, and the right front fender, bearing paint markings from the bicycle, was bent. Also, the impact of the body shattered the windshield. Before police arrived, Harvey Blackwelder, brother of the injured child, rushed Benny to the hospital about five minutes after the accident. The child, however, was pronounced dead on arrival.[58]

A shaken Snell stopped his car within thirty-five feet of the accident. As soon as the police arrived, they promptly arrested the black taxi diver, escorted him to a city jail, and charged him with manslaughter. Feelings were running high against Snell in the white community, so officials decided to move the black prisoner to county jail in Deland, where they believed he would be safe from mob threats. Assigned to move Snell, a lone constable, James Durden, started to the county seat with his charge when at about 2:15 P.M., four miles west of Daytona Beach, a coupe passed his car at a high speed. It abruptly stopped ahead of him, swinging across the road to block the way. Durden halted his vehicle. Everett Blackwelder, one of the deceased child's brothers, jumped out of the car with a double-barreled shotgun in his hands. Earl Blackwelder, another brother, climbed out from under the steering wheel with a .30-.30 high-powered rifle. When the officer tried to drive his vehicle around the obstacle, both Blackwelders thrust their weapons into his face, ordering him to stop.[59]

Durden immediately complied with this command. As he climbed out of his side of the car, he saw Everett pounding Snell on the head with the butt of his shotgun. The terrified prisoner quickly slid across the front seat and jumped out with Durden, clinging tightly for his life to the officer's arm. Everett ran up to the pair, waving his gun in the air; Durden grabbed the barrel of his shotgun, which went off in the air. Almost simultaneously, Earl shot Snell with his rifle. The injured man fled in panic. Everett shot him in the left knee, and as he fell, Earl shot him twice in the upper body. The lynch victim lay dying on the street while these two brothers covered a shocked Durden with their guns. As they drove away from the murder scene, one of the lynchers called to the constable, "I'll see you after the funeral."

A coroner's jury began an inquest that Saturday evening. Testifying without hesitation at this judicial hearing, Durden publicly accused Earl and Everett Blackwelder of executing Snell. In addition, three blacks who witnessed this extralegal murder testified about the details of the murder, but out of fear for their own safety, they did not go so far as to identify the Blackwelders as the lynchers. After hearing this testimony, the jury journeyed to a black undertaker's funeral parlor to see Snell's body; jurors saw that he had been shot through the left knee with a shotgun and that two rifle bullets had pierced his body.

Clearly, the police showed outward sympathy to the lynchers. On Sunday morning, 30 April, the father of the two suspects send word to the Volusia County Sheriff's Office that his sons would give themselves up to authorities immediately after the funeral for Benny Blackwelder. Ignoring police procedures, a compliant sheriff waited patiently for the two brothers to turn themselves in.

In the meantime, the coroner's jury, for the first time in any lynching case during the decade, conducted an inquiry into an extralegal murder that lasted for more than one day. At length, the presiding justice of the peace informed the press that the Snell lynching was the first such illegal execution in Volusia County since the early 1880s—when whites had lynched a black man accused of murder. On the final day of its proceedings, the jury formally accused the Blackwelders of murdering Lee Snell. The two brothers, who had surrendered after their brother's funeral, were present at the inquest to hear the verdict. At the request of state attorney Murray Sams, Durden publicly repeated his accusatory testimony. But already the constable was having second thoughts about his original statement. On this occasion, he stated that he was now uncertain as to which brother carried a shotgun and which a rifle. Nonetheless, he still pointed to the Blackwelders as Snell's lynchers.[60] The state attorney, hoping to avoid a whitewash, apparently wanted to have his key witness go on the record once again with his crucial testimony. He knew that people outside the county and state were closely watching how local officials prosecuted this matter.

Local officials in Daytona Beach were indeed aware that the Snell lynching focused instant and unwanted national attention on their community. Observers all over the country read about this case and undoubtedly wondered what kind of Florida community they were reading about. Daytona Beach was one of the fastest developing cities in Florida. Indeed, its rate of growth was phenomenal, as the population mushroomed from a mere 825 residents in 1920 to 16,598 in 1930, and finally to over 20,000 inhabitants in 1940. A healthy tourist trade, a flourishing construction industry, and an expanding manufacturing base spurred this rapid growth, even through the difficult Depression years of the 1930s. To be sure, by 1939—the year of this lynching—the city had almost completely recovered from the Great Depression. Furthermore, well-paved streets, new office and commercial buildings, and widespread use of automobiles and electricity reflected this town's modern appearance. An excellent school system, a high literacy rate, and the well-edited local newspaper all called attention to progressive achievement in Daytona Beach.[61] However modern a community, though, white residents still embraced the traditionally hostile attitudes toward blacks that would make a lynching possible.

During the 1930s blacks, in search of economic opportunities, moved into Daytona Beach at about the same rate as whites. In fact, throughout the decade blacks comprised slightly less than one-third of the expanding population. In the community's racial configuration, whites undeniably forced most blacks into a socially disadvantaged position in all areas of life, especially when it came to employment and housing. Further, segregation and discrimination persistently plagued blacks as they strived to improve their lot in this Jim Crow city. Indeed, even in its courtrooms white authorities arbitrarily assigned blacks to special, separate balcony seats. It may have been true that blacks asserting themselves in competition for economic opportunities—like a working black taxi driver—aroused more apprehension than admiration among many whites.[62]

Undoubtedly, negative white racial attitudes, in more than one respect, played a role in the Snell lynching. In this personal act of private vengeance by the Blackwelders, the aggrieved duo may have felt more justified in unleashing their murderous rage on a black, rather than a white, target. Likewise, owing to the victim's race, police officials may have been less troubled about allowing the lynchers to remain in the community until they surrendered at a time of their own choosing. And finally, it was probably less difficult, because Snell was black, for the prosecution's key witness, Constable Durden, to suffer predictable memory lapses about the crime to which he was an eyewitness.

These racial factors, along with the likelihood of a local whitewash, concerned onlookers across the nation. The Associated Press quoted a Tuskegee Institute spokesman who stated that the Snell lynching was the second such incident of the year in the United States, and that both had occurred in Florida. More alarming to locals, the *Daytona Beach Evening News* carried on its front page an ILD telegram sent to several different officials—including Governor Fred Cone, U.S. senators Claude Pepper and Charles Andrews, and U.S. attorney Frank Murphy—that boldly proclaimed: "Second Florida lynching in one month marks complete breakdown of civil rights in this state." It also demanded Governor Cone's "intervention to ensure constitutional guarantees to residents of Florida."[63] In another communication, the Southern Workers' Defense League wrote the governor, urging him to send a "special representative" to Volusia County to aid prosecutors in the upcoming Blackwelder trial. And they boldly threatened that if immediate compliance with this demand was not forthcoming, they would formally request a U.S. Justice Department investigation.[64]

This demand and threat rankled the governor, who flatly refused to comply. For the moment, he had decided to leave the prosecution of this case entirely in the hands of local authorities; he stated, "I always leave those matters to the attorney general and prosecuting attorney." In Daytona Beach the prosecutor, S. A. Sams, attempted to reassure skeptics that there would be no whitewash in this instance. Indeed, he pledged to proceed in the case "just like any other criminal investigation."[65]

Early action in the local court, however, called the pledge into question. On 4 May the Volusia County grand jury indicted Earl and Everett Blackwelder for murder, but in an obvious show of sympathy for the accused recommended that "under the circumstances, the defendants should be granted bail in a reasonable amount pending trial." Realizing that the inappropriate display of special treatment implied by the words "under the circumstances" would draw unwanted criticism, the presiding judge, W. Frederick, summoned the jury into the courtroom and spoke frankly: "In the pressure of this trial going on, the court did not first grasp the significance of the jury's special communication, especially the phrase 'under the circumstances'." Accordingly, the jury retired briefly and returned the recommendation with the phrase "under the circumstances" deleted.[66]

After being released on bail, the Blackwelder brothers took this exchange between the judge and jury as a signal that they might receive special favor from the court. At their arraignment on 5 May, the defendants confidently pleaded "not guilty." The local press noted that as police escorted them into court they were well dressed and appeared to be under no mental or physical strain.[67]

This disturbing, though predictable, turn of events in Volusia County concerned watchful national groups. Expecting the worse in local court, the NAACP, ILD, and ACLU combined their efforts to lobby for a federal trial of the Blackwelders. A delegation representing these organizations appealed to the U.S. district attorney in Tampa, Herbert Phillips, to take over prosecution of the case. Its legal spokesman cited a 1904 precedent for this action. He argued that the earlier decision held that anyone "who forcefully takes a prisoner from an officer deprives that prisoner of the officer's protection under the due process of law clause of the federal constitution." In response, Phillips took the matter under consideration and consulted with the Justice Department in Washington.[68]

In the meantime, the ILD's activists descended on the community of Daytona Beach, agitating for racial justice in the Snell lynching. The high-profile tactics of these radicals alarmed the local press and the citizenry. That communist-sponsored "outsiders" would come to their city and pass around handbills demanding federal intervention in their affairs was a source of great consternation to them. Worse still, they also read in the newspapers that in Washington, liberal congressman Vito Marcantonio had involved himself in this case, asking U.S. Attorney General Frank Murphy for a federal investigation into the Daytona Beach lynching and for a federal trial of the Blackwelders, and giving him the lynching report compiled by ILD officials in Florida.[69] The people of this Florida community were learning a lesson that was becoming increasingly clear as the decade progressed: their local sovereignty in matters of violence toward blacks would no longer go unchallenged.

The local paper reflected community apprehension over what it considered outside agitation. The *Daytona Beach Evening News* ran an editorial charging the ILD with misrepresenting Daytona Beach to the nation. Exercising restraint by showing no hint of red-baiting, it began: "By an unfortunate misconstruction of an act of violence which no thinking person condones, the International Labor Defense has given the nation the impression that the city in the case of the vengeance-slaying of Lee Snell, a Negro whose car accidentally killed little Benny Blackwelder, has fallen into the clutches of mob law. Nothing could be farther from the facts." It went on to say that "two hot-tempered young men took the unfortunate Negro from an officer and slew him. In their blind rage they risked punishment as murderers by taking the law into their own hands. By dictionary definition the act constituted a lynching. But what the International Labor Defense has to gain by dispatching an appeal for aid to Attorney General Murphy in Washington referring to the Snell slaying as the 'third mob murder' in Florida this year it is difficult to understand." It continued: "Any murder may be regarded as a disgrace to the community in which it happens, but the ILD action in broadcasting to the country that the slaying of Snell was the result of community agitation, 'mob action,' is resented by every loyal Daytona Beach citizen." It concluded by trying to turn the tables on the ILD: "Two men

have been jailed and promptly indicted for first-degree murder in this affair, and will be duly tried. There is something significantly like mob spirit
in the anxiety of an organization which seeks to excite the whole nation
and railroad to a climax, a case which Volusia authorities should be competent to handle."[70]

The public furor surrounding this case forced Governor Cone to reas-
sess his role in this matter. Fearing that things might get out of hand in
Volusia County—perhaps the governor remembered the troublesome liti-
gation in the Tampa flogging trials—he reversed his earlier decision about
noninvolvement. He promptly dispatched a high-ranking state official, assistant attorney general Tyrus A. Norwood, to assist state attorney Sams in
prosecuting the lynchers when they came to trial.[71]

Meanwhile, Judge Frederick bided his time while federal authorities
decided who had jurisdiction in the Blackwelder lynching trial. This was a
crucial decision because it was so rare to actually indict and try lynchers;
the entire nation turned its eyes to Florida. In light of this situation, the
judge exercised patience and ignored all distractions when he delayed proceedings three times. He stated to reporters, "This court is not concerned
with public clamor and criticism." At last, on 20 May U.S. district attorney
Phillips informed everyone that the federal government would not prosecute the Blackwelders. A study of the Alabama case, he stated, disclosed
that although the judge had held that the federal courts could act, he reversed his ruling in a later companion case. Phillips, however, held out the
weak hope of future appeals when he declared that "the remedy for wrongs
committed by individuals on persons of African descent is through state
action and state tribunals, subject to supervision of the Supreme Court."[72]

This decision set the stage for the trial to begin. And on 26 May in the
highly charged atmosphere in Volusia County, attorneys selected a jury
with great care. Determined to prevent a whitewash, if possible, prosecutors, led by Assistant Attorney General Norwood, placed special emphasis
on the racial angle. They asked all prospective jurors if they could convict a
white man for killing a "Negro." All of those placed on the jury—who were,
of course, white—publicly assured the court, for the record, that neither
the defendants' nor the victim's color would influence their decision. The
Blackwelders' lawyer, on the other hand, pursued a different tack in his
questioning of jury candidates. He focused on the issue of "outside agitation," calculating that the best chance for an acquittal would come from a
jury with provincial attitudes. His strategy apparently assumed that he could
detect sympathy for his clients by gauging potential jurors' hostility to outside influence. In spite of objections from the prosecution that were overruled by the judge, he asked all prospects if they had talked with anyone

connected with the ILD, NAACP, or the Workers' Alliance of America. All denied any contact with representatives of such organizations.[73]

Understandably, Daytona Beach blacks expressed keen interest in this trial. In fact, more than 150 black spectators turned out for preliminaries, flooding into the courtroom's segregated balconies. In obvious fear of possible black retaliation, sheriffs' deputies searched black observers but found no weapons.[74]

On Saturday, 27 May, the Blackwelder lynching trial began and ended. What many skeptics expected, happened: Constable Durden, the prosecution's chief witness, dropped a bombshell. When, at the climactic moment, State Attorney Sams asked him to identify Snell's murderers, he wavered: "I won't be positive, but I think it was him." At once a mild demonstration among blacks in the balconies, packed to double capacity, spontaneously broke out. One black observer wailed, "Jesus have mercy," a split second after Durden's answer, and further remarks were lost in the general rumbling that followed. Judge Frederick promptly demanded order and scolded onlookers in the balcony for their outburst.[75]

The prosecution now had only one remote chance to obtain a conviction. Would the three black witnesses to the lynch shooting of Snell identify the Blackwelders as the killers? Obviously fearing white retaliation if they did so, they reluctantly declined to place themselves and their families in jeopardy by pointing an accusing finger at the white defendants. Chances of a conviction now dimmed; Durden's equivocation had undermined the prosecution's case. When Judge Frederick asked the defense if it wished to call any witnesses, counsel simply rose and announced, "The defense rests."

Closing remarks to the jury were passionate, lasting some one hour and forty minutes. The defense attorney's final statement was little more than a ludicrous attempt to justify lynch law. He resorted to the ploy of holding up what he called "the unwritten law" in defense of the slaying of Snell, but only after making a guarded statement to the effect that he was not admitting his clients' guilt, "but just in case they did kill Lee Snell." At the end of this remarkable presentation, he virtually clinched an acquittal by pointing out the undeniable truth: the state's evidence was insufficient to warrant a verdict of guilty.

Owing to the weakness of its case following Durden's devastating testimony, the prosecution's closing statements were understandably weak and unconvincing. Speaking first, Norwood attacked the idea of lynch law itself by warning the jury that "we are not living under a principle of 'an eye for an eye and a tooth and a tooth' and we can not afford to let sympathy affect justice." Sams, who spoke next, was apologetic. He first obligatorily observed that "Lee Snell was entitled to the right of trial by jury." He added,

"If they are not guilty, turn them loose, but don't do it through sympathy." The prosecutor then explained that, in fact, he too was in full sympathy with the defendants and their family, but it was his sworn duty to prosecute every indictment handed down by the grand jury to the best of his ability. In a weak conclusion he stated: "There is no blood in the eye of the state; the state does not want you to be any more vicious in your deliberation than necessary. . . . But the weight of evidence is against these defendants and they should be punished." Needless to say, neither prosecutor asked for the death penalty.

Finally, in his charge to the jury, Judge Frederick made provisions for any one of four verdicts: guilty as charged, second-degree murder, manslaughter, or acquittal. He added that upon a majority opinion, a recommendation of mercy could be attached to a first-degree murder verdict. The court further warned that the jury should not be swayed by prejudice or sympathy, and that the jurors should use "commonsense judgment" in their deliberations of the facts.

The jury retired at 5:00 P.M., after Judge Frederick read his charge. After deliberating for about one hour and six minutes, the jury returned a verdict of not guilty. The Blackwelder family wept with joy and embraced Everett and Earl. State Attorney Sams slipped quietly away immediately after the verdict. Although disappointed over the verdict, a packed gallery of blacks listened quietly with a sense of resignation as the clerk read the judgment of the jury. There were no demonstrations of race feeling, as rumors had predicted, and ILD representatives issued a statement asserting that it was not "surprised" at the verdict.

The jury's decision raised an immediate outcry from observers all over the country. The editors of most large papers in Florida denounced the acquittal as an embarrassment; the *Miami Daily News* even called it "a black crime."[76] The national black press was, not surprisingly, acrimonious. The *Chicago Defender*, for example, ran a story under the headlines, "FLORIDA FREES LYNCHERS: CASE WHITE-WASHED," stating that "two white youths were freed of murder because of no positive identification" from an "extremely nervous" constable."[77] The *Norfolk Journal and Guide* declared that "justice was perverted in a Florida court . . . because 12 'good and true' men, sitting in the Circuit Court, deliberated for one hour and six minutes last week and returned the most amazing verdict in the bloody history of 'justice' Florida-style."[78]

In retrospect, the historical verdict on the dramatic Blackwelder lynch trial must be characterized as ambiguous. That white lynchers were identified, indicted, and tried for first-degree murder reflected progressive aspects of the affair. Furthermore, in no other lynching of the 1930s did a

Florida governor involve the state so deeply in an attempt to punish vigilante killers. Sending the assistant attorney general to Volusia County to aid local prosecutors revealed a determined effort on Governor Cone's part to avoid a whitewash, an outcome that would clearly damage the state's reputation outside the South. Finally, even the Justice Department gave serious consideration to claiming jurisdiction in this lynching crime, something altogether new in the chronicles of Florida lynch law.

However hopeful many were for convictions, it was not to be. This case exemplifies the weakness of southern courts in regard to race. Volusia County's Jim Crow court—where blacks were consigned to the balconies—functioned within a deeply prejudiced region and was enormously influenced by white community pressure. Unquestionably, Constable Durden gave in to this community pressure when the crucial moment came in his testimony; he could not point at the Blackwelders, knowing what might happen to them: the electric chair or, more likely, prison. Also, the heavy weight of fear bore down on the three black eyewitnesses to the lynching, motivating them to falter when placed on the witness stand. Finally, the implication of the jury's verdict transcends the exoneration of two murderers; it reaffirmed to whites that since there was a deficiency in legal protection for blacks, they could deal unfairly with this minority group, even to the point of fatal violence, and then go unpunished. Whites in Florida had indeed dealt unfairly and violently with blacks all through the 1930s, making their state the most lynch-prone region in the South during the decade.

6

Trends and Patterns of
a Fading Tradition

THE geography of Florida lynchings in the thirties reveals the patterns of extralegal violence in the Sunshine State during the years that mob law was passing from the southern scene. Traditional historical accounts depict lynching as basically a rural and small-town phenomenon of the South; according to this criteria, the decade's seven rural lynch-law episodes clearly occurred in what can be characterized as "typical" rural lynching areas.[1] As table 6.1 indicates, Florida lynch counties at this time were sparsely populated and overwhelmingly rural, with a high rate of tenancy. In addition, bank deposits, tax returns, and automobile registration were at some of the lowest levels in the state. In spite of the number of rural executions, however, slightly fewer than half of Florida lynch killings in the 1930s took place in what could be called typical lynching communities. Indeed, by the fourth decade of the twentieth century, much of the white vigilante action against blacks (and against whites as well) in this southern state had moved to the city. More specifically, at this time five black men (and three white men) were killed by mobs in what could be called urban areas. The extralegal executions of John Hodaz in Plant City, Robert Johnson in Tampa, Reuben Stacey in Ft. Lauderdale, Joseph Shoemaker in Tampa, Ernest Hawkins and Richard Ponder in Tallahassee, Miles Brown in Panama City, and Lee Snell in Daytona Beach were certainly not rural or small-town affairs.

Lynch activities shifted in some degree from rural areas to the towns and cities as the state modernized. Most Florida cities grew rapidly during the first three decades of the century, with the greatest expansion coming in the 1920s. In 1900 Florida was predominantly rural and agricultural, with only 20 percent of its population classified as urban; further, by 1920 only about 37 percent of the state's total population of 355,825 was urban. During the rapid growth of the twenties, however, when the state was seized by

TABLE 6.1
Characteristics of Rural Lynching Counties in Florida

County	Population in 1930	% Rural in 1930	Tenancy[a]	Bank Deposits[b]	Tax Returns[c]	Auto Registration[d]
Calhoun	7,298	100	39.1	$267,000	67	600
Hamilton	9,454	100	47.6	$266,000	61	620
Jackson	31,969	89.5	49.2	$1,774,000	214	2,040
Madison	15,614	100	52.0	$700	90	1,000
Santa Rosa	14,083	100	40.8	$417,000	124	1,300
Taylor	13,136	79.1	31.2	$740,000	151	1,200

Source: Data in this table were gathered from Florida State Planning Board, *Statistical Abstract of Florida Counties,* n.p., n.d. [Jacksonville, 1944]

[a] Percentage of all farm operators in county who were tenants.

[b] Amounts of deposits made in 1937.

[c] Number of people in county who filed federal income tax returns in 1937.

[d] All cars registered in county in 1937.

"New South fever," the urban population outstripped the rural for the first time in Florida history.[2] Many lynchings in the 1930s, as illustrated in table 6.2, occurred in some of the fastest growing cities and towns in the state.

TABLE 6.2
Population Growth of Florida Lynching Cities

City	1910	1920	1930	1940
Daytona Beach	331	825	16,598	22,584
Ft. Lauderdale	175	1,870	8,666	17,888
Plant City	2,481	3,729	6,800	7,491
Panama City	422	1,090	5,402	11,610
Tallahassee	5,018	5,637,	10,700	16,240
Tampa	37,782	51,608	101,161	108,391

Source: U.S. Department of Commerce, *Fourteenth Census, Fifteenth Census,* and *Sixteenth Census of the United States: Population.*

Communities such as Tampa, Daytona Beach, Ft. Lauderdale, Tallahassee, and Panama City, all with populations in excess of 10,000 people, were hardly the small southern towns usually associated with extralegal violence. There was more to these urban sites than the quaint country stores, unpaved streets, sawmills, cotton gins, parochial Baptist and Methodist churches, and small, corner gasoline stations of the quintessential lynch villages of the South. Indeed, these busy places were some of the larger and more progressive urban regions of the state. Most of them contained large and diversified populations, sizable business enterprises, libraries, colleges, and even the state legislature in the case of Tallahassee.

In these rapidly modernizing Florida communities, racial attitudes lagged behind economic changes. It was obvious to all who cared to notice that many white residents in these localities were burdened by rural and small-town mentalities regarding blacks. Somewhat disoriented by the experience of moving to urban areas where the black percentage of the population was substantially high, as shown in table 6.3, they uncomfortably competed with African Americans for jobs and housing. Reacting to these distressing new urban conditions, whites embraced the old idea that the rope and faggot was sometimes necessary to keep blacks in their place. Likewise, in the thirties many new city dwellers possessed little or no confidence in the established criminal justice system, which they considered woefully slow and inadequate when it came to dealing with both black and white law violators. In fact, it was urban lynchers who killed all three white victims of the 1930s.

TABLE 6.3

Black Percentage of Population in
Florida Lynching Cities, 1920–40

City	1920	1930	1940
Daytona Beach	—	32.7	30.6
Ft. Lauderdale	—	23.0	28.8
Tallahassee	50.0	41.1	39.9
Tampa	22.3	20.9	21.9

Source: U. S. Department of Commerce, *Fourteenth Census, Fifteenth Census, Sixteenth Census of the United States: Population.*

If circumstances called for it, Florida lynchers would execute a white man, showing that they sometimes acted for reasons that had nothing to do with race. Still, the motivations for both kinds of extralegal violence were not dissimilar, especially if whites committed a heinous crime like murder (Hodaz and Brown), or stepped too far out of line politically (Shoemaker) in a way that outraged the self-appointed guardians of community values and honor. Lynchers and their defenders embraced a set of attitudes and beliefs about crime and punishment in which the guiding imperative was quick, sure punishment, and by calling the effectiveness of the criminal justice system into question, they hoped to excuse taking the law into their own hands. They also hoped to direct criticism away from race as the motivating factor in most fatal acts of extralegal vengeance. In the words of one historian, "By ignoring the differences between the lynchings of whites and blacks, defenders of mob violence overlooked just how central race was to most lynchings. Indeed, they convinced themselves that the lynching of whites was the consequence of the failings of the criminal justice system."[3] Moreover, even as they self-righteously employed their attacks on the criminal justice system as justification for this kind of violence, they counted on the ineffectiveness of the criminal justice apparatus. Indeed, local law enforcement and local courts failed without exception to take swift and sure action to prosecute lynchers in Florida during the 1930s; even in the two cases of the Smoaks and Johnson killings, where investigating grand juries knew the identities of several lynchers, there were no indictments. In addition to this, Florida enacted no antilynching statutes despite pressure to do so. Lastly, no governor ever took disciplinary action against any law officer who might have behaved inappropriately in a vigilante crisis.

Three Florida governors during the decade unsuccessfully attempted to control the lynching problem. Doyle Carlton (1928–32), David Sholtz (1932–36), and Fred Cone (1936–40) responded in basically the same fashion to vigilante murders. First, they expressed outrage, and then they ordered the proper authorities to "thoroughly investigate" the crime in order to bring the guilty parties to justice; but then, in almost every instance, they let the matter die locally when the grand jury or state attorney failed to indict any suspects. Nonetheless, pressure mounted on these politicians to strengthen their antilynching stance and actions as the decade progressed and Florida lynch statistics grew. National and local antilynching groups, religious organizations, and concerned citizens kept the pressure on. This strategy bore some fruit when Governor Cone called out the National Guard to avert the mob murder of Robert Hinds of Apalachicola.

In spite of this pressure, however, Florida governors never altered their fundamental series of reactions to lynchings. The national revulsion over the gruesome vigilante murders of Claude Neal and Joseph Shoemaker should have been enough to make Florida governors more aggressive in dealing with the lynching problem. Yet these incidents, in certain respects, had only marginal impact. During the second half of the thirties Florida governors were more willing to call out the National Guard to prevent lynchings; they also communicated more carefully with local officials when dangerous situations arose. Still, their basic response pattern of denunciation, a call for investigation, and then a decision to let the matter die locally never changed. No governor ever asked local authorities to reopen a closed lynching case or even to widen the scope of an ongoing inquiry. Apparently, none considered the idea of setting up a special commission to look into the lynching problem and offer legislative recommendations to stop this abuse; moreover, they all opposed federal antilynching legislation.

Florida governors allowed local officials to behave inappropriately in one lynch affair after another. In many cases, in fact, law enforcement personnel were almost certainly guilty of complicity. In almost every case, furthermore, police officers and deputies were careless with their black prisoners. A number of vigilante acts could have been prevented if officers had moved their charges to safer jails in other counties and other towns, or if they had been more circumspect about how and when they transferred their prisoners from one jail to another, or if they had provided them with more armed protection. Policemen and deputies were not eager to risk their safety by warding off lynchers. Many hapless officers simply had their black prisoners taken from them by small bands of well-armed vigilantes. Without exception, law officers were unable to identify any lynchers who had accosted them and kidnapped their charges.

Mobs often intimidated local law enforcement. On more than one occasion, vigilantes were allowed to search through jail facilities for their would-be victims. Indeed, in one particular case, a mob even went to the home of a county sheriff, woke him up in the middle of the night, and demanded to know the whereabouts of a certain black prisoner. Finally, it was not uncommon for motorized vigilantes to follow in hot pursuit behind a sheriff and his captive from one Florida jail to another. In several instances, however, law officers (in an effort to protect local reputations) held firm against would-be lynchers. For example, in the Claude Neal case, the Jackson County sheriff turned away an angry and threatening throng who came to his home; and in the same case, the sheriff of Washington County held off a hostile mob all night that was threatening to storm his jail and take Neal's two aunts out and lynch them.

Such opposition from local officials discouraged large, mass lynchings in Florida during the decade of the thirties. In fact, most extralegal executions at the time were carried out by private mobs (relatively small groups of five to twenty persons) that were closed, secretive, and fell into what one investigator called the "Bourbon" classification as "relatively exclusive and well-regulated" for the purpose of punishing a specific person for a specific crime "to assure white supremacy and maintain accepted mores."[4] And indeed, nearly all of the state's lynch victims were simply kidnapped from law officers and then shot to death by a small band of abductors in vigilante-style executions. These incidents took the form not of frenzied murders by uncontrolled rabble but of deliberate and carefully planned extensions of the administration of justice. Furthermore, Florida lynchers in the 1930s were most likely to kill their victims in out-of-the-way places without much ritual or ceremony. Moreover, it is difficult to determine in every instance how much community support there was for extralegal violence. Although newspaper editors (at least of larger urban dailies), as well as most state and local officials, consistently denounced lynchings, a closer look might reveal a good deal of support for extralegal executions by those who considered themselves ordinary, law-abiding citizens. For example, in the 1934 Claude Neal case, widespread public support by local Jackson County whites was obvious and well documented; in the 1937 Tallahassee double lynching, the written threat left by vigilantes clearly reaffirmed the traditional communal values of white supremacy and black subordination.

White public opinion in most Florida lynch communities in the thirties would have undoubtedly approved of vigilante actions, regardless of the specifics of each extralegal incident, as ultimately necessary to protect southern white womanhood. Allegations of rape, however, were not the cause of most lynchings in Florida. Only three of the thirteen black victims—Claude Neal, Otis Price, and Robert Johnson—were accused of raping white women. Two other blacks, Buckie Young and Reuben Stacey, were accused of nonsexual assaults on white women; Henry Woods, Richard Ponder, and Ernest Hawkins allegedly assaulted white police officers; and J. C. Evans was accused of a sexual crime against a white male child. Two brothers, Charlie and Richard Smoak, supposedly attacked a white coworker. And finally, Lee Snell accidentally killed a white child with his cab. All these alleged deeds were viewed as acts of black insolence and insubordination and in this manner, a threat to whites.

Florida mobs acquired their victims in a variety of ways. According to the data in table 6.4, seven victims were kidnapped from jail, one was kidnapped from his employer (with the latter's foreknowledge and cooperation), and one was murdered by the arresting posse. In several lynchings and one attempted lynching, there was a manhunt for the suspect; this usually consisted of motorized vigilantes riding around the back roads of northwest Florida in search of their prey. The lyncher's assumption was that blacks accused of lynchable offenses must be hunted down and killed like animals. In such cases, self-appointed manhunters, not law officers, dominated the search; consequently, they felt the fate of the captive was theirs to decide. In a distinctly carnival atmosphere, then, unrestrained lynchers freely indulged their desire to parade around the city and county carrying rifles, pistols, and ropes. For a brief period of time, no matter how low the lynchers' social standing, they were protectors of white womanhood and upholders of white supremacy.

In rural Florida lynchings, manhunts and kidnappings certainly offered a degree of "excitement" to otherwise culturally deprived southerners. The noted social critic H. L. Mencken said as much when he argued that the gala events surrounding lynchings were pathological substitutes for more normal community activities. The diversionary nature of some lynchings in Florida in the thirties is hinted at by the occurrence of so many of them during slack periods of farm work. Indeed, no verified rural extralegal killing occurred during April or May, the busy time on the farm; all took place during the summer (Smoak, Woods, Price) and the fall (Neal, Young, Evans), months when the crops had been laid by and picked.[5]

TABLE 6.4
*Florida Lynchings, 1930–40, by Victim, Alleged Crime,
Acquisition of Victims, and Manner of Killings*

Victim	Alleged Crime	Acquisition of Victim	Manner of Killing
Hodaz	Attempted murder	Kidnapped from police escort	Shot and hanged
Smoaks	Assault on white man	Kidnapped from employer	Shot to death
Woods	Car theft and murder of white police chief	Captured by posse	Shot and burned at the stake
Johnson	Sexual assault on white woman	Kidnapped from police escort	Shot to death
Neal	Rape and murder of white woman	Kidnapped from jail	Tortured, mutilated, and hung after death
Stacey	Assault on white woman	Kidnapped from police escort	Shot and hanged
Shoemaker	No crime	Kidnapped from jail	Flogged to death
Young	Assault on white woman	Kidnapped from police escort	Shot to death
Ponder & Hawkins	Assault on white police officer	Kidnapped from jail	Shot to death
Evans	Sexual assault on white boy	Kidnapped from police escort	Shot to death
Price	Sexual assault on white woman	Kidnapped from jail	Shot to death
Brown	Murder	Kidnapped from jail	Shot to death
Snell	Accidental manslaughter	Kidnapped from police escort	Shot to death

Source: Data compiled from Ames, *Changing Character of Lynching,* 36.

Still another significant factor in manhunts and kidnappings was the automobile. The auto played a key role in every Florida lynching of the decade, rural and urban and alike. Motorized mobs had replaced old-fashioned vigilantes who searched on foot through the woods and lowlands with dogs for their black quarry. Furthermore, they chased after their victims, who were often in the care of fleeing law officers, in every part of the state. The obvious capabilities of the automobile expanded the influence and scope of mob activity as lynchers found they could overcome police vehicles in high-speed chases to obtain their prey and could drive to other cities, counties, and even states (Neal) to kidnap victims. It also accelerated the pace of lynchings, as mobs overcame policemen on the open roads and highways and made quick getaways after they kidnapped and executed their victims—which discouraged, to some extent, old-fashioned ceremonial lynchings.[6]

The method of accomplishing mob murders in Florida at this time varied with the lynchers. The victim might be killed by beating, hanging, shooting, or some combination of these three methods. The deliberate, prolonged torture and mutilation that were part of any kind of ritual or ceremony were rare. Indeed, of the decade's fifteen lynch victims, only two —Claude Neal and Joseph Shoemaker—were tortured at length before death. The remaining thirteen were just taken off to a remote location and shot to death; two of these were hanged, however, and one was burned at the stake in addition to being shot. Anger at the victim sometimes caused the vigilantes to fire shots into the body, and death was almost always quick. Finally, one victim, John Hodaz, was apparently hung and shot simultaneously. And in several extralegal affairs, lynchers retained mementos of a lynching in the form of souvenirs, sometimes from the victim's body, as in the Neal case, where digits were taken from the corpse.

These dynamics of the group behavior of Florida lynch mobs may also reflect the status of race relations in various areas of the state.[7] Race relations were not uniform throughout Florida during the 1930s, as African Americans living in the largely rural northern area apparently experienced more racial hostility and white violence than did their counterparts farther south. In fact, nine of the thirteen lynch sites of the decade were located in north Florida, and all but two of the decade's black lynch victims were executed there as well. Thus, the record clearly indicates that most of the thirties' lynch killings did indeed occur in the northern part of the state, representing the continuation of the long-standing geographic and historic trend that ran from the 1880s through the 1920s. This geographic pattern may well be explained by the fact that north Florida was a former Old South region that even in the 1930s was living uneasily with the legacy of racial slavery and still embraced the values associated with white supremacy. In light of this situation, then, the caste theory of lynching (that extralegal violence was used to maintain white racial hegemony and black subordination) best helps to explain the motivation of southern white lynchers in northern Florida, even as extralegal violence became a fading tradition. And by way of contrast, that all of south Florida's lynchings were urban incidents, and that two of the four victims there were white, suggests that the theory of urban vigilantism (the use of fatal, illegal violence primarily to protect community standards and the political and social status quo) might be most applicable in explaining these affairs.

There is one theory, however, that aids in explaining all Florida lynchings, urban and rural, in northern and southern regions. The ethic of honor in Florida during the 1930s ultimately determined which crimes were lynchable offenses and which were not, so that in the final analysis, the state's southern code of honor lay behind every act of extralegal violence in the decade. Florida's white men were indeed quite concerned, no matter their class standing or regional location, with their honor as a function of their public reputations. As one historian stated the case, "Honor demands that a person always see himself through the eyes of others because personal worth was determined not by self-appraisal but by the worth others conferred."[8] Thus, protecting their honor, white Floridians struck back at those offending it. According to this code, they would not hesitate if physical violence was a necessary last resort to address wounded honor; if they hesitated they risked tarnishing their individual and collective reputations. Hence, honor-bound Floridians felt obliged to do away with suspects who provoked them, whether he was a white dynamiter in Plant City, a rebellious black youth in Calhoun County, or a determined political radical in Tampa.

Many factors contributed to the decline of lynch law after 1930 in Florida, and foremost among them was undoubtedly the antilynching actions of blacks themselves. In every lynching city and county of the state in the thirties, new interracial adjustments followed every act of extralegal violence against African Americans. In some cases, thoroughly alarmed blacks became exceedingly circumspect in their dealings with whites and went to great lengths to give the appearance of subservience and deference after mob murders. They relied on this time-tested technique of manipulation, acting out the role of being genial and ingratiating to whites in order to protect themselves and their families.[9] By way of contrast, urban blacks throughout the state defiantly struck a militant pose. Unafraid to vehemently protest lynchings and openly demand the arrest, conviction, and punishment of perpetrators, NAACP branches in such places as St. Petersburg, Pensacola, Miami, Jacksonville, Tampa, and Key West often joined the national office in antilynching outcries. Furthermore, black ministerial alliances in Tampa and Jacksonville regularly denounced extralegal violence to local authorities as well as to the governor's office. Additionally, well-known, eminent black Floridians such as Mary McCleod Bethune, educator and New Deal official, and J. R. E. Lee, president of the Florida Agricultural and Mechanical College for blacks, sometimes added their voices to the state's black urban antilynching chorus. Also, lynching during the thirties might have encouraged some blacks to leave the state and relocate in northern cities. That large numbers of blacks left the state during Florida's lynch era cannot be disputed; nevertheless, racial tension and extralegal violence was only one motivating factor because many migrated to the larger industrial cities outside the South to seek employment opportunities or to look for comparative freedom from discrimination and Jim Crow. The ultimate effect of black migration on white planters and employers who were fearful of losing cheap, reliable labor may have inhibited the impulse to lynch and kill African Americans.[10]

Understandably, the national black press aggressively attacked lynching abuses through the thirties. In several northern cities it kept the black community informed about Florida lynchings after 1933 by carrying details of these incidents in front-page pieces in papers such as the *Chicago Defender, Baltimore Afro-American, Norfolk Journal and Guide, Pittsburgh Courier, Atlanta Daily World*, and the *New York Age*. Black editors, moreover, penned scorching editorials protesting Florida's white vigilante murders of black citizens. Acting in accordance with the best traditions of black journalism set by Ida B. Wells-Barnett, they hoped that by monitoring lynchings in Florida and the South, they might stir northern blacks and liberal whites to pressure their congressmen and senators to support federal antilynching legislation.

While blacks were either protesting, fleeing, or withdrawing, the general public in Florida was becoming increasingly sensitive to the lynching problem, which helped to suppress its practice. This growing responsiveness was reflected in the state's press. During the early 1930s, Florida editors devoted very little space to this topic; editorial pages contained little about the first three extralegal murders of the decade, which occurred in Plant City, Calhoun County, and Hamilton County. During the second half of the decade, however, almost every lynching was given abundant space on the editorial pages of most of the state's larger newspapers. Adverse national press coverage of Florida lynchings, particularly the Neal and Shoemaker horrors, played a crucial role in sensitizing state editors and the public to this problem. Editors were embarrassed by the state's extralegal murders and distressed by damage to the state's good name and reputation in the North. Finally, many also feared that if they did not discourage lynching, Congress might pass a federal antilynching law.

These journalists were not the only white groups to work toward the goal of suppressing extralegal violence. In Florida, the ASWPL effectively opposed lynch law by developing a good working relationship with the state's governors. The Florida Council of the association and its allied organizations were active in the 1930s and by middecade boasted a membership of 753 women and 61 men throughout 47 counties and in over 100 cities and towns. Its executive committee worked out of Jacksonville, although strong chapters also existed in Tallahassee, Orlando, and Mineola. Jane Cornell, a committed activist, headed up the Florida branch, and her efforts were nicely complemented by various religious groups, including the Florida Convention of the Women's Missionary Council (Disciples of Christ), the Florida Conference of the Women's Missionary Council (Methodist Episcopal Church), and the Florida Baptist Convention (Southern Baptist Convention). By far the most aggressive of these groups, the Women's Missionary Council of the Methodist Episcopal Church, was led by Mrs. O. O. McCullom of Jacksonville. As the state's superintendent of social relations for the Methodist women's groups and as the chairwoman of her church's interracial committee, she was Cornell's most active ally.[11]

Economic changes of the period, like the actions of white organizations such as the ASWPL, helped to suppress Florida's mob spirit in the 1930s. New Deal agricultural programs profoundly influenced rural areas of the state through their subsidy and crop-reduction initiatives, which significantly sped up the modernization of southern agriculture. These changes predictably altered race relations in rural Florida, as the number of tenants and sharecroppers decreased and the army of wage laborers increased. Yet white planters, the traditional holders of power, easily managed to continue their dominance, albeit in ways that required less violent coercion. The courts and law officers increasingly replaced mobs as an instrumentality to discipline the labor force. Further, the passing of the long-standing plantation system in the Old South region of north Florida brought about a sharp decline of population in rural areas and the subsequent lessening of racial tensions and incidents of extralegal violence.[12]

A constant theme in Florida lynchings of the 1930s was the racial tension exacerbated by the economic urgency of the Great Depression.[13] No one understood this better than Walter White[14] of the NAACP and the activists of the ILD.[15] The Depression years witnessed an increase in southern lynch activities to which White and the ILD responded by strong protests and the fight for a federal antilynching law. For much of the decade White and the association competed with the leftist ILD, which had gained the upper hand early on by winning control of the legal defense of the nine Scottsboro defendants. Many blacks at this time did indeed take an interest in the radical alternative to the moderate NAACP, and this tended to pull White and the association to the left throughout the period.[16] This development manifested itself in Florida by way of the ILD's active role in the events surrounding Sunshine State extralegal executions in the late thirties. In these years Floridians and Americans generally became more aware of the issue of minority rights and civil liberties, owing to the publicity surrounding the actions of the racist fascists in Europe. The Florida ILD, based in Jacksonville and led by the able Margaret Bailey, took advantage of this growing awareness in their effort to fight lynch law. It championed traditional American democratic virtues, especially the rule of law and equal treatment for all under the law. The memberships of the ILD and the U.S. Communist Party in this southern state were small in number but maintained a high profile. The ILD kept up a steady correspondence with local, state, and federal officials in response to every lynching, and was usually given abundant newspaper coverage.[17] Margaret Bailey's close association with Vito Marcantonio, New York's radical congressman, also proved to be an invaluable aid to ILD effectiveness in Florida.[18]

The highly visible agitation of the ILD brought substantial pressure to bear on officials at all levels of government. In fact, ILD legal maneuvering in the Snell affair in Daytona Beach provoked public discussion in the press about the possibility that the Justice Department might involve itself in this case and claim jurisdiction in order to prevent a whitewash in a local trial before an all-white jury. ILD attorneys, with Congressman Marcantonio's assistance at the national level, actually brought the jurisdictional question before a federal judge, who finally ruled that Florida courts should handle the matter.[19] Nonetheless, just putting the issue before a federal judge and having that fact widely publicized in state newspapers had an important, if immeasurable, effect on those who might wish to lynch blacks. The federal government was slowly moving toward stronger measures that would suppress the lynch-law spirit in the South, and by 1939 the Department of Justice, acting through the FBI, began "informal investigations" into the lynchings of blacks.[20]

Without doubt, the antilynching activities of the ILD, NAACP, ASWPL, and the black and white press helped to bring an end to Florida extralegal violence. Another factor was the new forces in the national community that appeared with such strength in these years and tended to deprive lynchers of their sovereign gratifications. Modern technology in the form of news services and travel facilities for reporters removed the last protective cloak for those bent upon anonymous extralegal action through lynching. The media had the resources both to force their way into local areas and expose criminals. Thus it became obvious that persons and communities in which lynchings occurred would have to stand trial before public opinion for their misdeeds. Whereas an absence of effective opposition within the local community had once encouraged lynching, the new national community created by the news media could inhibit the practice. Newspaper coverage and editorial denunciation of Florida lynchings of the 1930s (and by the 1940s) grew steadily on an annual basis, and in the case of Claude Neal and Joseph Shoemaker may well have been the most complete for any lynchings in American history.[21]

There can be no doubt that lynchings, once exposed, became a source of embarrassment to leading citizens in all Florida lynching communities and, indeed, throughout the entire state. Fear of outside pressure probably also prompted many other persons in Florida who still secretly believed in old-time lynchings to comply outwardly with national norms. This may well explain, for instance, the antilynching actions of such a man as Governor Cone throughout the years of his administration. An editorial writer for the *Richmond Times-Dispatch*, who endorsed a federal antilynching bill in 1937, perceived the issue clearly when he declared the newspaper's support for legislation "to put a stop to the seemingly endless series of murders which have disgraced the South and America before the world."[22]

Another reason for the decline of lynchings in Florida and the South during the thirties and forties was the growing sensitivity to the moral evil of the practice. In this connection the NAACP, ASWPL, and ILD again had an important if incalculable effect. All of Florida's lynchings examined in this study served as catalysts for their cause. By November 1937, one perceptive southerner, Virginius Dabney, noted the upsurge of editorial condemnation of lynching and support for federal antilynching legislation in fifteen southern newspapers, including the prestigious *Birmingham Age-Herald*, *Louisville Courier Journal*, and *Richmond Times-Dispatch*. Writing in the *Nation* in 1937 Dabney ascribed major importance to the Neal episode in bringing about a change in attitudes among southerners. He wrote as follows some two years after Neal's death: "An incident which must have had enormous influence in swinging many citizens of Dixie over to the view that the time has come to stop playing around the fringes of the lynching problem was the sickening killing of Claude Neal."[23]

The "Neal affair," Dabney declared, was disillusioning for intelligent southerners because it provided "convincing evidence to unbiased minds that some southern states were wholly unwilling to proceed against lynchers."

Dabney believed that a sufficient number of southerners were also "disgusted over the situation, primarily due to the Neal lynching" and the "blow-torch barbarity at Duck Hill, Mississippi," that they had become convinced the answer was a federal law. He also noted that the South's best organized foe of lynching, the Commission on Interracial Cooperation, endorsed a federal bill for the first time, according to the findings of a Gallup poll in that year.[24] All the Florida lynchings that followed the Neal execution only served to reinforce this new way of thinking in the South.

Along with perceptible changes in public opinion in the South, the weight of that opinion could be more effectively exercised even in the increasingly remote areas of the South with the emergence of efficient highway patrol cars in several southern states.[25] This technical innovation was of significant value in deterring ceremonial lynching affairs. Jessie Daniel Ames credited the organization of efficient state patrolmen using radio communications in six southern states in 1938 as influencing both the reduction in numbers of lynchings and the decrease in the numbers of attempted lynchings.[26]

Still another major retaliatory force against mob violence toward blacks was the increasing determination of the federal government to abolish the practice of lynching. Although no lynching law passed during the New Deal, the general support of President and Mrs. Roosevelt on the issue, the appearance of two antilynching bills on the floor of both the House and Senate (1935, 1937)[27] and the capable leadership of the proponents of these bills, especially New York's senator Robert Wagner, had the effect of intimidating to some degree those who would lynch blacks. Walter White made repeated reference to the diminution of lynchings when passage of an antilynching bill was being considered by the Congress.[28] FDR's directive to the Justice Department in the early 1940s to investigate all deaths of blacks where there was a suspicion of lynching undoubtedly served the same effect.[29]

Lynching in Florida during the 1930s was a vicious practice in which a group of individuals took the law into their own hands. Southern lynchers in this state executed their victims in summary fashion and justified their actions as an effort to seek retribution for some wrongdoing. Although three whites were lynched during the period under study, lynch law in Florida was primarily a means to intimidate, degrade, and control black caste members in this southern state. This violent crime, as a brutal instrument of social control, revealed the contempt of white Floridians for black people as well as their disrespect for duly constituted legal procedures. Florida vigilantes and mobs exercised a ruthless sovereignty of sorts over all blacks in their state. Every time a band of lynchers vented their fury against one or more helpless black victims, white supremacy in the Sunshine State was blatantly displayed before a national audience. Indeed, lynching proved a ready instrument for enforcing white supremacy in Florida.

Lastly, the examination of extralegal violence in Florida during the thirties suggests new things about the nature of lynching as well as the reasons for its decline. For instance, the significant number of urban lynchings at this time contradicts the old assertion, made by scholars from Cash to McGovern, that after 1914 lynchings were always rural, small-town events in the South. Quite the contrary, modernization was clearly a contributing cause of mob violence in the Sunshine State. Further, because so many more blacks than whites were lynched in Florida cities and counties it appears that race was undoubtedly more important than class as the root cause of this form of violence. As expected, the evidence confirms the widely accepted claim that most lynchings were sparked not by rape but more often by some other violation of the strict sanctions of the southern racial caste system. Moreover, analysis confirms McGovern's assertion that the grisly Neal lynching played a key role in the disappearance of old-fashioned ceremonial lynchings. By the 1930s, lynchers in Florida regularly organized themselves into small, well-managed bands that, with few exceptions, carried out their horrible work quickly, decisively, and with as little fanfare as possible. They were also aided by the automobile, which fit well with the preferred means of acquiring victims (kidnapping) and the preferred means of execution (shooting, hanging, beating, or some combination of these three methods), and allowed quick getaways. Lastly, the black freedom struggle engaged the antilynching cause in the thirties as it pushed the nation along toward the goal of racial justice for all of its citizens.

EPILOGUE

From Lynching to Assassination

OF all southern states, Florida had the highest incidence of lynch law during the 1930s. Nonetheless, its leaders consistently objected to federal measures proposed by civil rights advocates that aimed to curtail this social problem. Florida's governors and U.S. senators—Doyle Carlton, David Sholtz, Fred Cone, Charles Andrews, and Claude Pepper—would not support a federal antilynching bill. Among this group of Floridians, the most eminent man, Claude Pepper, was quite effective in his opposition to the antilynching cause. And indeed, he figured prominently in concerted southern efforts to kill and bury antilynching legislation that came before Congress in 1937 and 1938.

In fact, Florida's lynching problem emerged as an important part of the congressional debate over the antilynching issue in 1938. Like many other southerners, the Florida senator displayed a defensive attitude about this gruesome custom. On 24 January, speaking on the floor of the Senate, he attacked the section of the bill providing legal sanctions against southern policemen negligent in their duties in lynching crimes. Pepper then brought up the Robert Hinds case, praising Governor Cone's act of calling out the National Guard in order to prevent an extralegal affair. He spoke boldly: "I know of my personal knowledge . . . that same governor [Cone] within the last four months [actually it was seven months] had called out the state militia to defend Negroes . . . against the hazards of lynching." He concluded: "I know from personal conversations with the governor . . . that there is not any governor in the whole country more determined to prevent lynchings in his state than he is."[1]

Pepper's invocation of the Hinds case rankled Senate supporters of the antilynching bill. Indeed, a few days after the Florida senator's speech, one of his colleagues called up another name notable from the annals of Florida lynch law: Claude Neal. Matthew Neely of West Virginia spoke in some detail about the grisly Neal killing, quoting at length from the Kester Report about this lynch sufferer's horrible ordeal at the hands of sadistic

149

tormentors. He read into the *Congressional Record* vivid, disturbing descriptions about how Neal was castrated and forced to consume his own genitals. Immediately after these emotional remarks, Neely pleaded with the Senate to vote for cloture to stop the southern filibuster. This plea, however, fell on deaf ears; unmoved southerners doggedly pressed on with their obstructionism.[2]

If Pepper felt any satisfaction in blocking passage of a federal antilynching bill, he could not have been pleased that white Floridians lynched three blacks in the first five years of the 1940s. The first of these victims, A. C. Williams, a man in his early twenties, was executed in Gadsden County on 14 May 1941. Furthermore, this affair was unique in Florida's lynch law history because Gadsden County lynchers kidnapped and assaulted this black man on two separate occasions in May 1941 before they actually succeeded in taking his life. In fact, acting without mercy on the second attempt, they stopped the ambulance transporting the injured Williams to a Tallahassee hospital, dragged him off a stretcher, and shot him to death.[3]

This malicious aspect of the Florida lynching was not the only factor that state and national condemnation focused on. That the Gadsden County execution occurred against the background of the Second World War, a war against racist fascism, was uppermost in the mind of thoughtful onlookers. The *New York Times*, for instance, stated that "nothing that can happen in this country is better grist for the Nazi propaganda mill than a lynching."[4] The NAACP and ASWPL also vehemently protested this crime as an international embarrassment to the United States.[5]

The wartime mood of the nation led to strong reactions against this lynching. A number of outraged clergymen and Florida citizens called on the state's new chief executive, Governor Spessard Holland, to deal forcefully with local officials who had failed to prevent this killing.[6] Moreover, the Associated Press dispatched a special correspondent to cover this southern lynching. The new governor readily showed determination to combat lynching by ordering state attorney Orion Parker and Gadsden County sheriff W. Luten to make thorough inquiries into this extralegal murder and report back to him. Further, he publicly expressed dismay over how local authorities could have offered lynchers a second opportunity.[7]

As the state attorney and sheriff worked on their reports, one Florida editorial after another denounced this slaying. Many resembled the piece featured in the *St. Petersburg Times* titled: "Once Again, Lynch Law." It read: "Lynch law has reared its ugly head once more in Florida, and as a result of this latest mob violence, a new stigma is attached to the state's reputation." The concluding remarks undoubtedly reflected the sentiments of many concerned Floridians: "We are not proud of Florida's record in recent years.

In fact, the state's history in respect to lynching has been about the blackest in the South."[8]

Condemnations from the black press dealt with the international implications of this tragedy. The *Baltimore Afro-American*, which dispatched a special correspondent to Quincy in Gadsden County, claimed that the lynching was "a story of bestiality and stupidity that rivals the crimes of Hitler."[9] An editorial in the *Pittsburgh Courier*, titled "Warlike Florida," followed up on this theme: "That Florida is very war-like was demonstrated . . . by the lynching on May 14 of a wounded and helpless colored man, A. C. Williams, who was snatched from an ambulance by a mob of white men." It added that "J. Edgar Hoover's FBI cannot cross state lines to grab and jail the war-like Floridians who hauled A. C. Williams out of an ambulance and murdered him, but it can hound aliens, snoop into citizen's private affairs and help break up labor unions in the name of patriotism."[10]

Even the press in Gadsden County wrote about the lynching in the context of Hitler and nazism, but with a different twist, reflected in the title "Hitler and Backers of Antilynching Bill in Congress Get a Break in Quincy." It stated: "A bunch of Nazi-minded citizens went berserk over the weekend, and succeeded in smearing the city across the pages of the newspapers of the nation as a lawless community." It added that "the Hitler-controlled press of Germany likes nothing better than this to deride America, and undoubtedly will take advantage of this opportunity given by these Fifth Columnists to attack the U.S. with venomous words." It also stated, "More important, the advocates of the long-pending antilynching bill in Congress, which would deny every community, North and South, its basic rights, will leap upon this Quincy scandal to support their case."[11]

The paper was keenly sensitive about damage to the county's reputation. Indeed, its editor expressed outrage when Westbrook Pegler, the Pulitzer prize-winning journalist, blasted Gadsden County and Florida in his nationally syndicated column. Pegler denounced Quincy and called northwest Florida a "social and intellectual slum which, according to the hearsay historians of Florida, was populated by low whites who fled from other southern states, notably Georgia and Alabama, to escape service in the Civil War." The editor of the *Times* said of this columnist, "His vigorous style of writing has led him into frequent controversies, but it is doubtful if he ever has aroused resentment among persons more familiar with the subject involved than in the present case."[12]

Not all northern journalists, however, were as belligerent as Pegler. For example, *New York Post* correspondent C. C. Nicolet wrote a balanced, well-informed exposé on Quincy. "Most people, when they think of Florida, think of beaches and palms. It [Gadsden County] is too far north for good ones." He observed that "it has instead towering live-oak trees, hung with Spanish moss, and century-old houses, including one or two of the finest examples of colonial architecture extant, and roses and wisteria and magnolias, and a general atmosphere of traditional gentility." He added that "the first free school in Florida was established there, and three of four major churches of the community are more than 100 years old." In answer to Pegler's false claim that Quincy was populated by those who wished to avoid participation in the Civil War, Nicolet declared that "before the courthouse stands a monument to the Confederate dead, and the cemeteries of the county are turned into masses of flowers on Confederate memorial day." He also refuted Pegler's charge of social backwardness. "Drop into one of the drugstores around the courthouse square which are conversation centers. . . . If the radio isn't bringing a European news broadcast, a man will probably start out by exchanging views on world developments from the morning newspapers. . . . Any of several may chime in with a quote from a *New York Times* editorial . . . and another will offer something from *Fortune.* Perhaps the talk will turn to college days, in which case the subject will probably be Emory at Atlanta, where three generations of one family have been among the local alumni." Nicolet concluded: "If it is a younger group, the University of Florida may be the subject. Quincy is definitely Old South, but it is not by any means backward South."[13] Local county leaders carefully read these pleasing remarks, as well as Pegler's predictable counterattacks.

After several weeks of such journalistic exchanges, furor subsided. The governor decided against formally disciplining the Gadsden County sheriff, who had been careless, if not negligent, with young Williams. In spite of the enlightened attitude of county spokesmen, such as the *Times* editor, no one was ever arrested or indicted for this lynching crime.

In all the articles and editorials written about the Williams affair, little was said about the underlying cause of the murder. Even if Quincy and Gadsden County were not backward or isolated areas, they were regions where whites maintained their superior social position over blacks through the threat of violence and intimidation. And if enlightened, articulate white opinion weighed against the lynching, there were apparently many other whites who approved of this extralegal execution. In all probability, they also approved of the message that the execution sent to the county's blacks: stay within prescribed social boundaries and, above all, do not commit the legal offense of which Williams was accused, robbery of the home of a white family. He paid the ultimate price for this alleged transgression, and many local whites certainly felt the accused black received just what he deserved.[14]

The Williams slaying was the first of three lynchings in Florida during the 1940s. The second such incident occurred in Jackson County in 1943; on 15 June four masked men took Cellos Harrison from the county jail and beat him to death. He had allegedly murdered a white man in 1940, and had avoided punishment for over three years through legal maneuvers.[15]

In the wake of this racial slaying, city officials took immediate steps to prevent demonstrations and disorder. They may have remembered the racial disturbances in Marianna that had followed the Claude Neal lynching nine years earlier; or the city fathers may have been sensitized to the possibility of trouble because of the wartime race riots occurring at this time all over the country. The sale of beer in Marianna during the day and night following the lynching was prohibited, and all city police were placed on patrol while Jackson County deputies were put on alert status. As events proved, authorities reported no disturbances of any kind.[16]

The county grand jury speedily convened to investigate the lynching. Grand jury testimony was substantially the same as that given at a coroner's inquest and resulted in the verdict that Harrison had come to his death at the hands of parties unknown.[17] The matter-of-course finding did not go unnoticed.

Outside observers expressed disgust over the predictable judicial outcome. When the Florida NAACP bitterly protested the lynching to the governor's office, Holland directed the state highway patrol to probe into the crime.[18] Their inquiry, however, uncovered no new evidence about the tragic affair. In the meantime, Florida editors indulged in unrestrained condemnation of the Harrison execution. According to a *St. Petersburg Times* editorial, "Democracy Has a Holiday," the "men guilty of this crime are no better than the enemies we are fighting [Germany and Japan], and the only way Florida can clear itself in this disgraceful matter is to bring to court and try for murder the persons responsible."[19] In a piece called "Murder of a Murderer," the *Tampa Tribune* cynically remarked that "It is customary for the press to urge in these cases that the authorities exert every effort to catch and prosecute the perpetrators—but that's wasted ink and paper, because it's never done."[20] Finally, the *Miami Herald* declared that "the [Harrison] killing is a disgrace to Florida," and added that "such acts place the South under the accusing finger of the rest of the nation."[21]

The outraged black press placed the Jackson County lynching in a national perspective. The *Chicago Defender,* the *Pittsburgh Courier,* and the *Baltimore Afro-American* cited this incident as just one of many instances of wartime interracial violence plaguing the country.[22] Within two weeks of the Harrison lynching, serious race riots broke out in Detroit and Beaumont (Texas) in which a score of blacks were killed and many more injured; four black soldiers were shot in Riverside, California, in a white restaurant; white

Mississippi highway patrolmen wounded three black soldiers and clubbed another; and at Ft. Benning, Georgia, a black staff sergeant was badly beaten by white police.[23]

The sharp differences between the lynching of Cellos Harrison in 1943 and Claude Neal in 1934 illustrate how changing conditions may have lessened the brutality of extralegal executions in one southern county. Unlike Neal, Harrison was not tortured, mutilated, or strung up by a white mob. He was quickly murdered without fanfare. Moreover, Harrison also had the opportunity to exercise his legal rights in the courts in a way not afforded to Neal. After the 1943 lynching, no racial violence broke out in Marianna the way it had in 1934 after the Neal killing. Finally, the Florida Highway Patrol was only in its infancy in the midthirties. In spite of all this, however, the striking similarity between the two affairs was that a group of whites took the law into their own hands and lynched a black man.

The third and final lynching of the forties in Florida occurred about two years after the Jackson County slaying. This time the black victim, Jesse James Payne, was kidnapped from jail and shot to death. Accused of sexually assaulting a five-year-old white girl in Greenville, Madison County, he was arrested on 4 July 1945, after a two-day search by numerous groups. Vigilant highway patrolmen kept angry crowds away from the wounded Payne—he had been shot by the same posse that tracked him down—as they moved him on to the state's maximum security prison, in Raiford, for safekeeping. He was kept in the state prison for several months until officials felt it was safe to return him to Madison County for trial.[24]

On 9 October 1945, authorities quietly returned the black suspect to the local county jail. At his arraignment hearing on the following day, he pled not guilty to the charge of rape. At this point Sheriff Lonnie Davis committed a serious error in judgment by placing his highly vulnerable prisoner in an unguarded jail. This proved to be an open invitation to lynch-minded citizens, who, on 10 October, kidnapped Payne from the county jail and riddled his body with bullets. Before the sheriff, who lived next door to the jail, discovered his prisoner was missing, a passing motorist came across the victim's body and reported it to authorities.

Needless to say, this lynching put Sheriff Davis in an embarrassing position. "All I know is that he was taken out of jail sometime before dark and daylight and was found dead seven miles south of here on the highway." Thrown on the defensive, he bluntly stated, "I never have any guard at the jail." Attempting to defend his actions, the sheriff admitted, "Things look bad on my part but I didn't have anything to do with it." Additional statements by Davis raised concerns about his men's role in this incident. He forthrightly proclaimed there were no indications that the jail doors had been forced, and added that he "really believed the keys were used." He declared that he had no idea how the keys could have fallen into the hands of lynchers, because only he and his deputies had jail keys.

Once again a new Florida governor, Millard Caldwell, found himself confronted with the unpleasant aftermath of an extralegal slaying. The governor's special investigator went right to work on this matter only to discover that state attorney A. K. Black had not been informed of the lynching until twelve hours after the body was found. The two government officials, nonetheless, promptly initiated a belated investigation into this affair. It went nowhere. "The sheriff told me the other prisoners who were in the jail claimed they were all asleep and did not hear anything during the night," said Black, who could find no witnesses willing to cooperate with him. Not surprisingly, neither the state attorney nor the governor's investigator uncovered sufficient evidence to identify and indict the lynchers.[25]

This predictable outcome disconcerted several observers who were already dismayed over the sheriff's incompetence in the matter. The searing editorial carried by the *St. Petersburg Times* merits quoting at length:

> Despite all this [the protection afforded the prisoner by the highway patrol and at Raiford] the sheriff of the county . . . brought this prisoner back and put him in an unguarded cell. This raises or should raise the question in the governor's mind of the fitness of the sheriff. Either he didn't care for the safety of the prisoner who shouldn't be left in an unguarded jail right after he was brought back from Raiford where he had been kept for the express purpose of preventing a mob from getting him.
>
> The sheriff's excuse that he never had a guard at the jail at night is pretty lame. The fact that other prisoners in the jail heard no noise indicates that the mobsters got in without any great commotion. Of course, no one has any idea who committed the murder.
>
> The sheriff of each county is sworn to up hold the Constitution and keep law and order. This sheriff obviously failed the job.

This editorial also compared the Payne lynching to the planned trial of war criminals. In an exposé called "Fair Trial for Nazis, Japs, but Lynch Law in Florida," the editor observed that "because Americans believe in law and order, we are setting up elaborate and democratic courts in Japan and Germany to give the accused war criminals a fair trial and to punish them for their guilt." Then he pointed out that "it would have been much easier for the military to line up the suspects and shoot them without trial, but, because we stand for law and order and due process of law so that no innocent man will suffer, we are going to give every man his day in court." He concluded: "This same desire for fair play, however, does not always burn so brightly in Florida. The lynching at Madison . . . is an example of how to flout the very ideals for which our army has been fighting."[26]

An editorial in the *Miami Herald* attempted to use the lynching to educate its reading public about the evils of "racial bigotry." It stated that "the lynching of a Negro this week at Madison, Florida, and the decision of the Daughters of the American Revolution to continue the ban against Negro artists in their Constitution Hall in Washington, emphasize anew that racial bigotry seethes tragically in this country." It went on to say, "Governor Caldwell owes it to this nation, to this state, to the honor of the white people of Florida to bring the lynchers to justice." It concluded, "Let's educate young America to Americanism, and there won't be Constitution Halls and lynchings."[27]

National pressure was brought to bear on Governor Caldwell. His office received telegrams from two New York City organizations—the Citizen's Non-Partisan Committee and the National Federation for Constitutional Liberties—that demanded the suspension of Sheriff Davis. The governor also learned at this time that a representative of the Justice Department might be sent to Florida to determine if Payne's "civil liberties" had been infringed upon. In addition, Congressman Vito Marcantonio of the American Labor Party wired a protest to the governor's office in his capacity as president of the ILD. He also offered a five hundred-dollar reward for information leading to the conviction of the lynchers.[28]

Black papers throughout the country expressed outrage over the Payne lynching. The *Atlanta Daily World* reported the astonishing statement made by the Madison County sheriff: "If I had wanted to kill the Negro, I could have shot him in jail. I wouldn't have to engineer a deal like this."[29] In an editorial sarcastically titled "That Innocent Florida Sheriff," the *Pittsburgh Courier* admonished blacks, "Let us get to work again to get such a law [antilynching bill] passed as soon as possible, so that there will be no more such disgraceful occurrences in Florida or anywhere else under the stars and stripes."[30]

These national protests led to an unprecedented development in Florida's lynching history. Governor Caldwell rejected the jury's findings that unknown lynchers had murdered Payne, and on 23 October he ordered Judge Rowe to impanel a new grand jury to reinvestigate this matter. This second investigative effort brought to light startling new information: the sheriff's brother had been on the first grand jury that had exonerated Davis; even more surprising, the sheriff was the uncle of the little girl involved in this affair. These dramatic revelations moved Florida attorney general Tom Watson to comment at a special press conference, "It is my opinion that there is sufficient evidence in the facts uncovered by the investigation so far to justify a conclusion that the sheriff did not exercise that degree of protection and care that he should have in seeing that the Negro was protected from what happened to him."[31]

The second grand jury completed its probe into the affair on 31 October. Like the first, it absolved the sheriff of responsibility for the lynching of Payne, finding no negligence on his part. It also reported no new evidence about who lynched the black victim. Perhaps speaking for the state, the *St. Petersburg Times* expressed a profound sense of disappointment that many must have felt at the time, stating that Madison County officials "have let us all down."[32]

Governor Caldwell studied the grand jury findings for about one week before he responded. He then blasted the Madison County sheriff: "I have examined the reports covering the Jesse James Payne death, and have concluded that the disgraceful occurrence resulted from the stupid inefficiency of the sheriff and not from his abetting or participation." Barely restraining his anger, he pointed out, "A crime of this nature is not essentially local in character. Its significance transcends the borders of both the county and state and draws unfavorable attention to Florida. . . . Florida and Madison County have suffered a loss of standing in the country as a result of this affair. There was no excuse for it." He then revealed, with a sense of frustration over his predicament, his decision regarding the sheriff: "Although Sheriff Davis has in this case proven his unfitness for office, he was, nevertheless, the choice of the people of Madison County. Stupidity and ineptitude are not sufficient grounds for the removal of an elected official by the governor." Finally, Caldwell issued a warning: "I want now . . . to serve notice upon the officials of Florida that in the future, particularly in cases of this kind [potential lynching situations], I expect the highest degree of care to be exercised."[33]

National sensitivity about lynching abuses in 1945 was such that Governor Caldwell's handling of the Payne incident displeased many observers. This displeasure, however, turned into outrage when Florida's chief executive made some controversial, ill-timed public remarks about the case. On the defensive, he maintained that technically the Payne slaying was not a lynching because there was no evidence to indicate that more than one individual (there had to be two or more to qualify as an a "lynching") illegally executed the victim. No witness, he claimed, ever saw a mob, or even a small group, take the black man from a completely unguarded jail. Furthermore, he highlighted the potential tragedy of bringing the child victim into court to testify about the alleged rape.[34]

National journalists immediately responded to these pronouncements. In January 1946, *Time* magazine ran a short story titled "Two Governors," which attacked the Florida leader. It told how Governor R. Gregg of North Carolina had commuted a death sentence to life imprisonment for a fourteen-year-old black who had robbed and raped a white woman. By way of contrast, the national magazine reported that in response to the Payne killing, Governor Caldwell failed to consider the crime a lynching, and "he condoned the shooting [of Payne] by saying that it saved a lot of trouble."[35] And in February 1946 *Colliers* carried a similar piece. It declared that "Governor Millard Caldwell of Florida said he didn't consider this [the Payne execution] a lynching. He went on to opine that the mob had saved the courts, etc., considerable trouble."[36]

Governor Caldwell and other prominent Floridians angrily lashed out at *Time* and *Colliers*, objecting to what they considered "unfair" treatment. *Time* editors promptly reconsidered their appraisal of the Florida governor and printed a retraction. They readily admitted to being "less than fair" to the governor, and "by way of apology, hereby set the record straight." They stated: "Governor Caldwell did not consider the killing of Jesse James Payne a lynching, because there was no evidence that Payne had been abducted and shot by a mob. Presumably the crime was committed by one man, as yet unidentified." Finally, the editors concluded that the governor "did not say the shooting saved a lot of trouble. He did observe that the ordeal-by-open-court for victims of rape was a problem 'society has not found a solution to.'"[37]

The editors of *Colliers*, on the other hand, refused to print any kind of retraction. In response, a determined Caldwell, bolstered by the *Time* retreat, filed a libel suit against the magazine, asking for $500,000 in damages. The governor claimed that the editorial in question falsely pictured him as condoning lynching, and he called "entirely false" the statement attributed to him that the mob "had saved the courts, etc., considerable trouble." According to all reliable sources, his exact words were as follows: "The ordeal of bringing a young and innocent victim of rape into open court and subjecting her to detailed cross-examination could easily be as great an injury as the original crime. This fact probably accounts for a number of killings [like the Payne slaying] which might otherwise be avoided."[38]

The libel trial understandably attracted a good deal of attention in Florida and throughout the nation. Representatives of *Colliers* insisted in their testimony that there was no "ill will" behind the editorial criticizing Caldwell, and they held fast to the position that what the editorial said was fair commentary, drawn by inference, from the governor's statements. This claim, however, failed to convince the jury, which awarded Caldwell $237,000 in damages in 1947. Nonetheless, before he could collect this sum, the U.S. Circuit Court of Appeals reversed the decision and thereby denied Caldwell his legal victory.[39]

In the years after the Payne lynching, black leaders in Florida struggled toward the goal of equality and attacked the caste system. They found that white southerners in their state overlooked the racial implications of World War II (a war against fascists and racists) and the cold war (with America as global champions of freedom and fair play for all people), clinging tenaciously to the traditional values, associated with white supremacy. They also found that the white South still regularly resorted to literacy tests, poll taxes, discrimination, exclusion, and even violence to maintain the Jim Crow racial order. In response to this oppressive situation, the courageous and committed state NAACP leader Harry T. Moore stepped forward and acted. He organized the Florida Progressive Voters League in a concerted effort to register black voters throughout the state; indeed, the total number of blacks on the state's books jumped from 49,000 in 1947 to over 116,000 in 1950. Furthermore, the determined Moore went to court, seeking to equalize the salaries of white and black teachers in Florida. In 1949 he turned his attention to a disturbing racial crisis that unfolded in Lake County.[40]

The Groveland affair, which has been called the Sunshine State's "little Scottsboro," was "an episode that put Florida racial justice on trial before the nation and the world." On 16 July 1949, four black men were alleged to have raped a seventeen-year-old white woman named Norma Padgett near the community of Groveland in Lake County. Three of the black suspects— Walter Irvin, Sammy Shepherd, and Charles Greenlee—were quickly arrested, but the fourth, Ernest Thomas, evaded capture for more than a week and then was shot and killed by Lake County sheriff Willis McCall and his posse. Further, the sheriff prevented a large lynch mob, estimated to number over five hundred angry white men, from taking his prisoners from jail and executing them. He could not, however, stop them from terrorizing the local black community in Groveland by burning and shooting into some of their homes. This outbreak of white racial violence prompted Governor Fuller Warren to send in the National Guard to restore peace and order in this riot-torn town in central Florida. Lynch-minded whites, at this point, adopted the attitude of waiting in sullen silence to see if the courts would do the work of the mob.[41]

Almost immediately the national office of the NAACP involved itself in this matter by sending a young lawyer, Franklin Williams, to Florida to handle the defense of the three Groveland defendants. He promptly discovered that the case against his new clients was clearly weak; the sheriff had allowed (or ordered) his deputies to use torture to obtain a confession from two of the three men, and then he had publicly announced the confessions to a white press eager to spread the word. He also learned that the alleged victim, Norma Padgett, might not have been raped at all. More likely, her husband, from whom she was separated because of physical abuse, "had beaten her for refusing to grant him 'matrimonial rights' and subsequently he implored his wife to claim she had been raped by blacks or her family would take revenge upon him" (9).

The trial of the three Groveland defendants was a classic "legal lynching" in the tradition of Scottsboro and Robert Hinds from the 1930s. A hastily impaneled grand jury indicted the three defendants for rape, a capital crime; and local circuit court judge Truman G. Futch rushed the case to trial amidst a lynch-spirit atmosphere best illustrated by an *Orlando Sentinel* cartoon that showed electric chairs awaiting the guilty culprits. Judge Futch turned down motions for a change of venue and for more time for defense attorneys to prepare their case. In the sham trial that followed, the state failed to introduce any medical evidence that a rape had even occurred, and the confessions extracted by torture were not introduced, perhaps for fear of making public the conditions under which they were obtained. Despite the best of intentions, the defense was not adequate; it failed to challenge the damning testimony of Norma Padgett, nor did it introduce any medical testimony of its own. Predictably, the all-white, local jury took only one hour and a half to reach the verdict of guilty, with the recommendation of the death penalty for Irvin and Shepherd, and life imprisonment for the sixteen-year-old Greenlee (16–19).

In the aftermath of the trial and conviction there was a federal investigation of the torture of the three black defendants.[42] And although evidence was uncovered that indicated abuse by the Lake County sheriff, the U.S. district attorney Herbert Phillips of Tampa, refused to move forward with the findings, perhaps because of his sympathies for the lawmen. In any case, the *St. Petersburg Times*, a progressive paper, presented a series of pieces clearly showing that one defendant, Greenlee, had been miles away at the time of the alleged rape and could not have been a party to the crime. The St. Petersburg newspaper also raised other doubts about the guilty verdict, but these exposés had no influence on the deliberations of the Florida Supreme Court, which turned down all appeals for a new trial. When the case came before the U.S. Supreme Court, however, the guilty verdict was overturned, paving the way for a new trial. According to Justice Robert Jackson, the pretrial publicity was "one of the best examples of one of the worst menaces to American justice."[43]

Local authorities grumbled and denounced the Supreme Court ruling. Sheriff McCall, however, was prepared to do more than complain: in

November 1951, as he transported Irvin and Shepherd from state prison, he simply pulled off to the side of a deserted road, pulled the two men out of the car, and shot them. Shepherd died, but somehow Irvin survived the attempt on his life. In spite of several investigations of this incident, the sheriff held on to his job. In response to this shooting, the NAACP stepped up its efforts on behalf of Irvin and the still-incarcerated Greenlee and assigned new lawyers to the case, including Thurgood Marshall, future associate justice on the U.S. Supreme Court. The shooting temporarily became an international incident when Andrei Vishinsky, a high-ranking United Nations official from the Soviet Union, asserted that the United States "had a nerve talking about human rights and upbraiding other nations while Negroes were shot down by an officer of the law while in custody." In a *Crisis* article the NAACP added that "Samuel Shepherd is no better off for this American hypocrisy . . . nor are his fifteen million fellow Americans who happen not to be white" (20).

Just weeks after the Shepherd killing, state NAACP leader Harry T. Moore was felled by assassins. From the outset of the Groveland affair Moore had publicized its injustice, raised funds for the defendants, and called on Governor Fuller Warren to suspend Sheriff McCall. Retaliating against this activist and civil rights leader, assassins picked Christmas eve to dynamite his home; the explosion killed Moore immediately, and his severely injured wife died soon afterwards. The NAACP maintained that "his death fits into the pattern of terror which has centered around the town of Groveland . . . and advertises to the world that though we preach democracy abroad we cannot practice it at home." The dynamiters were never captured or punished. Shortly after Moore's assassination, Irvin was retried, found guilty, and sentenced to death. Although the U.S. Supreme Court did not hear the appeal this time, a racially moderate governor, LeRoy Collins, commuted the death sentence to life imprisonment. After the entire Groveland tragedy had slipped out of the public mind in Florida Greenlee was paroled in 1962 and moved to Tennessee, and Irvin was paroled in 1968 by Governor Claude Kirk and relocated to Miami. In 1973 Governor Reuben Askew suspended Sheriff McCall for kicking a black prisoner to death (23–24).

The meaning of Groveland is best stated by scholars who put the matter in its proper historical perspective: "The social changes and ideological battles surrounding World War II and the Cold War made little difference to the Lake County officials charged with trying the Groveland case. Attacks by black men upon white women, or even the suspicion of such assaults, could not be tolerated or second-guessed." They concluded that "To do so would pose a challenge to the traditional assumptions governing race relations in the postwar South, assumptions that remained little changed as Florida prosecuted the Groveland case" (26).

Few lynchings occurred in the South of the 1950s, and those which did, such as those of Emmett Till (1955) and Mack Charles Parker (1959), led to national outcries against the practice. But the killing of Sammy Shepherd and the assassination of Harry T. Moore in 1951 showed that mob spirit lived on in Florida through the forties into the fifties. As lynch law declined in the Sunshine State, the factor of race remained the most significant source of Florida vigilantism. The circumstances that contributed to this violence against blacks were unquestionably numerous. Practitioners of lynch law at one time or another may have suffered an excess of the frontier spirit, economic frustration, or fear of threats to the establishment order. They may have also been motivated in large part by a consciousness of their sense of honor and duty to punish any affront to family and community.[44] Yet none of these factors singly or even collectively can explain why blacks suffered disproportionately compared with whites. That the dissolution of the caste system in the South during the civil rights era prompted a temporary revival of lynching and antiblack violence,[45] strongly suggests that the classical theory of white social control—that blacks were lynched to maintain white supremacy and dominance—may, after all, best explain the phenomenon of southern lynchings

In recent decades Americans have come to understand the tradition of extralegal violence in an almost trivial way. Images in popular Hollywood productions in the fifties and sixties served basically to glorify lynchings as a justifiable practice of the Old West to bring order out of chaos, and more recently vigilantism in an urban setting has been glorified in movies devoured by millions of Americans anxious over the deeply troubling urban problems of race, poverty, and crime.[46] Few of these people understand that it was not until the 1960s that the federal government moved to abolish the southern racial caste system, grant African Americans their Fourteenth and Fifteenth Amendment rights, and protect them from extralegal violence. In the 1960s the civil rights movement confronted white racism on a massive scale and forced Congress to act.

As the twentieth century draws to a close, it stands as a barbaric period that witnessed terrible violence of all sorts. Admittedly, lynching in the state of Florida,[47] and even in the South[48] generally, seems less than impressive alongside other twentieth-century events such as the well-known genocide against Armenians, Jews, and Cambodians. Nonetheless, extralegal violence, in the words of one scholar, "epitomizes the hypocrisy of a nation that prided itself on respect for the natural rights of humanity."[49]

Notes

Introduction

1. Richard Hofstadter, "Reflections on Violence in the United States," in *American Violence: A Documentary History*, ed. Richard Hofstadter and Michael Wallace (New York, 1971), 5, 7.

2. Emma Lou Thornbrough, *T. Thomas Fortune: Militant Journalist* (Chicago, 1972), 14–17.

3. W.E.B. Du Bois, *Dusk of Dawn* (New York, 1968), 67.

4. W.E.B. Du Bois, *The Souls of Black Folk* (New York, 1903; reprint, New York, 1982), 141.

5. Robert A. Hill, ed., *The Marcus Garvey and Universal Negro Improvement Association Papers* (Berkeley, 1983), 2:438.

6. For a review of this ASWPL finding, see *Miami Daily News*, 2 April 1939.

7. The strong inclination of southerners in Florida to take the law into their own hands has been well established in Robert P. Ingalls, *Urban Vigilantes in the New South: Tampa, 1882–1936* (Knoxville, Tenn., 1988). For a broad discussion of the issues of southern violence, violation of honor, and vigilantism, see Bertram Wyatt-Brown, *Southern Honor: Ethics and Behavior in the Old South* (New York, 1983); Dickson D. Bruce, Jr., *Violence and Culture in the Antebellum South* (New York, 1979); and John Hope Franklin, *The Militant South, 1800–1861* (Cambridge, Mass., 1956).

8. Records of blacks lynched in Florida during the 1930s are in the files titled "Lynching by Counties," Negro Collection, Files of the Association of Southern Women for the Prevention of Lynching, Woodruff Library, Atlanta University Center, Atlanta, Ga. See also the Papers of the National Association for the Advancement of Colored People (NAACP) C-351, 352, 353, Manuscript Division, Library of Congress; and Jessie Daniel Ames, *The Changing Character of Lynching: Review of Lynching, 1931–1941* (Atlanta; reprint, New York, 1973), 36.

9. This definition was standardized in 1940, Lynching Records, Tuskegee Institute Archives, Tuskegee, Ala.

10. For scholarly accounts of the American criminal justice system's failure to deliver "equal treatment" under the law to blacks and its failure to prosecute lynchers, see Mary Frances Berry, *Black Resistance/White Law: A History of Constitutional Racism in America* (New York, 1971); and Richard Bardolph, ed., *The Civil Rights Record: Black Americans and the Law, 1849-1970* (New York, 1970), 168-189.

11. For useful treatments of lynching in American history, see Richard Maxwell Brown,

Strain of Violence: Historical Studies of American Violence and Vigilantism (New York, 1975), 214–18; Herbert Shapiro, *White Violence, Black Response: From Reconstruction to Montgomery* (Amherst, Mass., 1988); Alfred Percy, *Origins of Lynch Law, 1780* (Madison Heights, Va., 1959); and John Raymond Ross, "At the Bar of Judge Lynch: Lynching and Lynch Mobs in America" (Ph.D. diss., Texas Tech University, 1983), 55–57.

12. The classic histories of lynching are James Elbert Cutler, *Lynch-Law: An Investigation into the History of Lynching in the United States* (New York, 1905); Walter White, *Rope and Faggot: A Biography of Judge Lynch* (New York, 1929); and Frank Shay, *Judge Lynch: His First Hundred Years* (New York, 1938; reprint, Montclair, N.J., 1969). The classic studies of the antilynching movement are Jacquelyn Dowd Hall, *Revolt against Chivalry: Jessie Daniel Ames and the Women's Campaign against Lynching* (New York, 1979); and Robert L. Zangrando, *The NAACP Crusade against Lynching, 1909–1950* (Philadelphia, 1980).

13. Instances of lynch law in the Old South have been examined in Clement Eaton, "Mob Violence in the Old South," *Mississippi Valley Historical Review* 19 (December 1942): 361–89. See also U. B. Phillips, *American Negro Slavery* (New York, 1918), 460–63, 511; Winthrop Jordan, *White over Black: American Attitudes toward the Negro, 1550–1812* (Chapel Hill, N.C., 1968), 121, 473; John Blassingame, *The Slave Community: Plantation Life in the Antebellum South* (New York, 1979), 32–33, 155; and Eugene D. Genovese, *Roll, Jordan, Roll: The World the Slaves Made* (New York, 1976), 32–33.

14. By far the best historical treatment of lynching and vigilantism in an urban context, using a class-oriented perspective, is Ingalls, *Urban Vigilantes in the New South.* See also John V. Baiamonte, Jr., *Spirit of Vengeance: Nativism and Louisiana Justice, 1921–1924* (Baton Rouge, La., 1986).

15. This is clearly the perspective in C. Vann Woodward, *Origins of the New South, 1877–1913* (Baton Rouge, La., 1966), 351–52; and George Brown Tindall, *The Emergence of the New South, 1917–1945* (Baton Rouge, La.,1967), 170–75. See also Peter Daniel, *Standing at the Crossroads: Southern Life in the Twentieth Century* (New York, 1986), 28, 56–58, 142–43; Edward Ayers, *Vengeance and Justice: Crime and Punishment in the Nineteenth-Century American South* (New York, 1984), 238–39.

16. It was the *Chicago Tribune* that first began to keep lynching statistics as of 1882, and in the 1890s Alabama's Tuskegee Institute took up the task. Finally, the National Association for the Advancement of Colored People undertook a comprehensive accounting of this deadly practice that extended into the present century in its *Thirty Years of Lynching in the United States.* All published official statistics undercount lynchings insofar as many such incidents went unreported. For a list of all lynchings up to 1968, see *The Negro Almanac* (New York, 1971), 270. It should be noted that the Tuskegee Institute's statistics suggest that the NAACP records may have undercounted America's total lynching numbers by well over one thousand cases; see Daniel T. Williams, "The Lynching Records at the Tuskegee Institute," in *Eight Negro Bibliographies* (New York, 1970), pt. 5, 1–15.

17. NAACP, *Thirty Years of Lynching in the United States*, 41, 53–56.

18. Shay, *Judge Lynch*, 250; and Ames, *The Changing Character of Lynching*, 36.

19. For a brief analysis of these reasons for the decline of lynchings in the United States, see Mary Frances Berry and John Blassingame, *Long Memory: The Black Experience in America* (New York, 1982), 125.

20. As an instrument of enforcement, lynching was part of the general southern pattern of racial segregation. An excellent recent study of this phenomenon is Neil R. McMillen, *Dark Journey: Black Mississippians in the Age of Jim Crow* (Urbana, Ill., 1989).

21. W. Fitzhugh Brundage, *Lynching in the New South: Georgia and Virginia, 1880–1930* (Urbana and Chicago, 1993), 8.

22. James R. McGovern, *Anatomy of a Lynching: The Killing of Claude Neal* (Baton Rouge, La., 1982), 3, 15.

23. Terence Robert Finnegan, "At the Hands of Parties Unknown: Lynching in Mississippi and South Carolina, 1881–1940" (Ph.D. diss., University of Illinois, 1993), 329–31.

24. For a discussion of Cassity's thesis in *Chains of Fear* (Westport, Conn., 1984), see Dennis B. Downey and Raymond M. Hyser, *No Crooked Death: Coatesville, Pennsylvania, and the Lynching of Zachariah Walker* (Urbana and Chicago, 1991), 5–6.

25. Arthur F. Raper, *The Tragedy of Lynching* (Chapel Hill, N.C., 1933; reprint, New York, 1969); John Dollard, *Caste and Class in a Southern Town* (Garden City, N.Y., 1957); Oliver C. Cox, *Caste, Class, and Race* (Chicago, 1948); W. J. Cash, *The Mind of the South* (New York, 1941); Gunnar Myrdal, *An American Dilemma: The Negro Problem and Modern Democracy* (New York, 1944); and White, *Rope and Faggot.*

26. Allison Davis, Burleigh B. Gardner, and Mary Gardner, *Deep South: A Social Anthropological Study of Caste and Class* (Chicago, 1941); Cox, *Caste, Class, and Race;* Dollard, *Caste and Class;* and more recently Charles L. Flynn, *White Land, Black Labor: Caste and Class in Late-Nineteenth-Century Georgia* (Baton Rouge, La., 1983).

27. George M. Fredrickson, *The Black Image in the White Mind* (New York, 1971), 272.

28. Hubert Blalock, *Toward a Theory of Minority-Group Relations* (New York, 1967), 107–61; Allen D. Grimshaw, "Interpreting Collective Violence: An Argument for the Importance of Social Structure," in *Collective Violence,* ed. James F. Short, Jr., and Marvin E. Wolfgang (Chicago, 1972); James E. Inverarity, "Populism and Lynching in Louisiana, 1889–1896: A Test of Erikson's Theory of the Relationship between Boundary Crises and Repressive Justice," *American Sociological Review* 41 (April 1976): 262–80; John Shelton Reed, *The Enduring South: Subcultural Persistence in Mass Society* (Chapel Hill, N.C., 1974), 45; and H.C. Bearley, "The Pattern of Violence," in *Culture in the South,* ed. W. T. Couch (Chapel Hill, N.C., 1934), 678.

29. For an account of the ongoing debate over various lynching theories, see John Shelton Reed, "Percent Black and Lynching: A Test of Blalock's Theory," *Social Forces* 50 (March 1972): 356–67; Jay Corzine, James Creech, and Lin Corzine, "Black Concentration and Lynchings in the South: Testing Blalock's Power-Threat Hypothesis," *Social Forces* 61 (March 1983): 774–96; and more recently, Stewart Tolnay, E. M. Beck, and James L. Massey, "Black Lynchings: The Power-Threat Hypothesis Revisited," *Social Forces* 67 (March 1989): 605–23; John Shelton Reed, "Comment on Tolnay, Beck, and Massey," *Social Forces* 67 (March 1989): 624–25; James Creech, Jay Corzine, and Lin Huff-Corzine, "Theory Testing and Lynching: Another Look at the Power-Threat Hypothesis," *Social Forces* 67 (March 1989): 626–30; H. M. Blalock, Jr., "Percent Black and Lynching Revisited," *Social Forces* 67 (March 1989): 631–33; Stewart Tolnay, E. M. Beck, and James Massey, "The Power-Threat Hypothesis and Black Lynching: 'Whither' the Evidence," *Social Forces* 67 (March 1989): 634–39. See also Richard P. Bagozzi, "Populism and Lynching in Louisiana," *American Sociological Review* 42 (April 1977): 355–58; Ira M. Wasserman, "Southern Violence and the Political Process," *American Sociological Review* 42 (April 1977): 359–62; and Whitney Pope and Charles Ragin, "Mechanical Solidarity, Repressive Justice, and Lynchings in Louisiana," *American Sociological Review* 42 (April 1977): 363–68.

30. E. M. Beck and Stewart Tolnay, "The Killing Fields of the Deep South: The Market for Cotton and the Lynching of Blacks, 1882–1930," *American Sociological Review* 55 (August 1990): 526–39.

31. Finnegan, "At the Hands of Parties Unknown."

32. Neil Smelser, *Theory of Collective Behavior* (New York, 1962); Roger Brown, *Social Psychology* (New York, 1965); T. W. Adorno, et. al., *The Authoritarian Personality* (New York, 1950),

384–89. See also, Stewart E. Tolnay, E. M. Beck, James L. Massey, et al., "Black Lynching: An Article and Commentary," *Social Forces* 67 (March 1989): 605–40.

33.   For a provocative treatment of lynchings using psychoanalytical (perhaps even metaphysical) categories, see Joel Williamson, *The Crucible of Race: Black-White Relations in the American South since Emancipation* (New York, 1984), 183–89, 289–90, 318–19. See also Beth Day, *Sexual Life between Blacks and Whites: The Roots of Racism* (New York, 1972); Joel Kovel, *White Racism: A Psychohistory* (New York, 1970); Earl E. Thorpe, *The Old South: A Psychohistory* (Durham, N.C., 1973); Peter Loewenberg, "The Psychology of Racism," in *The Great Fear: Race in the Mind of America*, ed. Gary B. Nash and Richard Weiss (New York, 1970); and Jonathan M. Wiener, "The 'Black Beast Rapist': White Racial Attitudes in the Postwar South," *Reviews in American History* 13 (June 1985): 226. For a Frankfurt School perspective on most forms of violence, see Erich Fromm, *The Anatomy of Human Destructiveness* (New York, 1973).

34.   Laurens van der Post, *Jung and the Story of Our Time* (New York, 1975) and *The Dark Eye in Africa* (New York, 1955); Walter Odajnyk, *Jung and Politics: The Political and Social Ideas of C. G. Jung* (New York, 1976). Perhaps the sharpest attack on psychohistory comes from David E. Stannard, *Shrinking History: On Freud and the Failure of Psychohistory* (New York, 1980).

35.   The best appraisal of Hall's groundbreaking working in interpreting lynching can be found in W. Fitzhugh Brundage, "Mob Violence North and South, 1865–1940," *Georgia Historical Quarterly* 75 (Winter 1991): 750–51.

36.   Wyatt-Brown, *Southern Honor.*

37.   Williamson, *The Crucible of Race.*

38.   Ayers, *Vengeance and Justice.*

Chapter 1. Lynch Law, Florida Style

1.   Ingalls, *Urban Vigilantes in the New South*, 11.

2.   Larry E. Rivers, "A Troublesome Property: Master/Slave Relations in Florida, 1821–1860" (paper, Southern Historical Association, 1993).

3.   Jerrell H. Shofner, *Nor Is It Over Yet: Florida in the Era of Reconstruction, 1863-1877* (Gainesville, Fla., 1974); and Shofner, *Jackson County, Florida: A History* (Marianna, Fla., 1985).

4.   R. M. Brown, *Strain of Violence*, 100, 308.

5.   Edward C. Williamson, *Florida Politics in the Gilded Age, 1877-1893* (Gainesville, Fla., 1976), 133–43, 193.

6.   Joel Williamson, *The Crucible of Race*; Fredrickson, *The Black Image in the White Mind*; and especially Loewenberg, "The Psychology of Racism."

7.   Jeffrey S. Adler, "Black Violence in the New South: Patterns of Conflict in Late-Nineteenth-Century Tampa" (paper, Southern Historical Association, 1993); and NAACP, *Thirty Years of Lynching in the United States*, 53–54.

8.   NAACP, *Thirty Years of Lynching in the United States*, 53–54.

9.   Pauli Murray, *States' Laws on Race and Color* (Cincinnati, 1951), 77; C. Vann Woodward, *The Strange Career of Jim Crow* (New York, 1955), 67–68; NAACP, *Thirty Years of Lynching in the United States*, 55–56.

10.   Undoubtedly, one reason for the decline of lynching in the twenties was that Florida officials hoped to use the criminal justice system to punish blacks charged with a lynchable offense. For example, in 1917 Governor Sidney J. Catts paid a $150 reward to Sheriff W. E. Law of Hernando County for the capture of Dave Dunbar, a black man who had allegedly shot and killed Deputy Sheriff Wiggins of DeSoto County. Law to Catts, 2 March 1917;

Catts to Law, 6 March 1917, Sidney J. Catts records, office of the governor, correspondence of the governors, 1909–25, RG 101, series 603, box 5, file #6, Florida State Archives, Tallahassee, Fla.

11. For statistics on Florida lynchings in the 1920s, see ASWPL, "Are the Courts to Blame?" (n.p., February 1934).

12. *Tampa Tribune*, 25 April 1930; and *Tampa Times*, 25 April 1930.

13. *Tampa Tribune*, 25 April 1930; and *Tampa Times*, 25 April 1930.

14. *Tampa Tribune*, 28 April 1930.

15. Ibid.; *Tampa Times*, 28 April 1930.

16. *Tampa Tribune*, 28 April 1930; and *Tampa Times*, 28 April 1930.

17. *Tampa Times*, 25 April 1930.

18. Ibid.; *Tampa Tribune*, 25 April 1930.

19. *Tampa Tribune*, 27 April 1930; *Tampa Times*, 28 April 1930.

20. *Tampa Tribune*, 27 April 1930; *Tampa Times*, 28 April 1930.

21. *Tampa Tribune*, 27 and 28 April 1930. Investigators found only one clue that Hodaz may have been helped by an accomplice: they spotted an extra set of footprints in the garden around Willaford's house. *Tampa Times*, 28 April 1930.

22. *Tampa Tribune*, 28 April 1930.

23. One Tampa journalist, a child at the time of the Hodaz execution, recalls that the victim was lynched at a spot on the road between Thonotassassa and Zephyrhills (off of present-day Highway 301). He also reports that it took place somewhere in the vicinity of what is now Hillsborough State Park. For a generation, vivid memories of this affair were associated in the minds of Hillsborough County residents with the lynch tree widely known as the "Hodaz Oak." Author's interview with Leland Hawes, *Tampa Tribune* staff writer and editor, 11 March 1988. The Hodaz lynching was, in the words of one observer, "conducted with precision pointing almost to rehearsal." The same commentator noted that "there were no signs of hurried preparation" by the vigilantes in this carefully planned execution. *Tampa Tribune*, 29 April 1930. Since neither the governor nor the grand jury investigated this crime, the only detailed accounts of it were published by Tampa's two newspapers. *Tampa Times*, 28 April 1930.

24. *Tampa Times*, 28 April 1930.

25. *Tampa Tribune*, 29 April 1930.

26. U.S. Department of Commerce, *Fifteenth Census of the United States: 1930. Population* (Washington, D.C., 1932), 3:423.

27. Quintilla Geer Bruton and Diard E. Baily, Jr., *Plant City: Its Origins and History* (St. Petersburg, Fla., 1977), 71; Ernest L. Robinson, *History of Hillsborough County* (St. Augustine, Fla., 1928), 83–88.

28. As the central marketplace for eastern Hillsborough County, Plant City was strategically located at the hub of six rail lines. Further, this community claimed an accredited high school and four grammar schools with an enrollment of hundreds of students. It also boasted a thriving social and cultural life, including its own music and opera house. Bruton and Baily, *Plant City*, 71; Robinson, *Hillsborough County*, 54, 87. See also Charles S. Johnson, *Statistical Atlas of Southern Counties: Listing and Analysis of Southern Counties* (Chapel Hill, N.C., 1941), 77.

29. Brown, *Strain of Violence*, 144–79.

30. The distribution of the county's ethnic population in 1930 can be broken down in the following way: native whites, 70.1 percent; foreign-born whites, 10.9 percent; blacks, 18.9 percent. U.S. Department of Commerce, *Fifteenth Census: Population*, 3:413, 423.

31. The eastern European population in 1930 in Hillsborough County numbered as

follows: 91 Poles, 52 Czechs, 101 Austrians, and 268 Russians. Only a handful of the 1,347 Hungarians who lived in Florida at the time resided in this urban county. Ibid., 402, 425.

32. One recent study of Tampa's ethnic history examines ethnic and class divisions in urban Hillsborough County. The authors state that the "white power structure jealously guarded and retained control" of the community. Gary R. Mormino and George E. Pozzetta, *The Immigrant World of Ybor City: Italians and Their Latin Neighbor in Tampa, 1885–1985* (Urbana, Ill., 1987), 55–57.

33. Ibid.

34. Ingalls, *Urban Vigilantes in the New South*.

35. By 1930 Hillsborough County agriculture was clearly feeling the sting of the Great Depression. Hundreds of agricultural laborers were unemployed, and those still working often suffered wage cuts. Overall, the county's farmers in 1930 planted fewer crops of all kinds than in previous years. In addition, there was also a sharp decline in the number of acres of strawberries planted and quarts harvested. U.S. Department of Commerce, *Fifteenth Census of the United States: 1930 Agriculture*, vol. 2, pt. 2 (Washington, D.C., 1932), 238–50.

36. *Tampa Tribune*, 29 April 1930.

37. Ibid.

38. Of the ten lynchings that occurred in 1929, four took place in Florida, three in Texas, and one each in Kentucky, Tennessee, and Mississippi. Ibid.

39. Ibid.

40. Ibid.

41. *Orlando Sentinel*, 30 April 1930.

42. *Tampa Tribune*, 1 May 1930.

43. Ibid., 2 May 1930.

44. Ibid.

45. *St. Petersburg Times*, 29 April 1930.

46. *Miami Herald*, 29 April 1930.

47. *Tampa Tribune*, 7 and 8 May 1930.

48. Hodaz was the only white man lynched in 1930. Raper, *The Tragedy of Lynching*, 469–71.

49. Raymond Wolters, *Negroes and the Great Depression* (Westport, Conn., 1970), 116–17.

50. Ann Wells Ellis, "The Commission on Interracial Cooperation, 1919–1944: Its Activities and Results" (Ph.D. diss., Georgia State University, 1975), 59–105.

51. Raper, *The Tragedy of Lynching*, 14.

52. For an account of the origins, development, and impact of antilynching sentiment in the twentieth-century South, see Wilma Dykeman and James Stokely, *Seeds of Southern Change: The Life of William Alexander* (Chicago, 1962).

53. George F. Milton, "The Impeachment of Judge Lynch," *Virginia Quarterly Review* 8 (April 1932): 250–52; Howard Odum, "Lynching, Fears, and Folkways," *Nation*, 30 December 1931, 719–20; Alex Spence, "Lynching and the Nation," *Commonweal*, 13 April 1932, 658–59.

54. Ellis, "The Commission on Interracial Cooperation," 72–73.

55. Carlton's antilynching stance was not surprising in light of his educational background. He attended such prestigious northern schools as Columbia University and the University of Chicago. His opposition to the practice of lynching, however, was based primarily on his recognition of the damage it did to the state's reputation in the North, discouraging visitors with their tourist dollars from coming to Florida for vacations. A brief but enlightening portrait of this governor can be found in Charlton Tebeau, *A History of Florida* (Coral Gables, Fla., 1971), 395–99.

56. By way of contrast, Carlton's successor, Governor David Sholtz, took all of these listed steps in response to the 1934 lynching of Robert Johnson. Walter T. Howard, "'A Blot on Tampa's History': The 1934 Lynching of Robert Johnson," *Tampa Bay History* 6 (Fall 1984): 5–18.

57. George F. Milton to Governor Carlton, 18 October 1930, Carlton records 1928–32, lynching file, administrative correspondence, Florida State Archives, Tallahassee, Fla.

58. Carlton to Milton, 23 October 1930. Ibid.

59. Jessie Daniel Ames to Carlton, 3 November 1930, ASWPL Papers, special collections, Woodruff Library, Atlanta University Center, Atlanta, Georgia.

60. Carlton to Ames, 10 November 1930, ibid.

61. Rowland H. Rerick, *Memoirs of Florida* (Atlanta, Ga., 1902), 328.

62. W. T. Cash, *The Story of Florida*, 4 vols. (New York, 1938), 1:773.

63. U.S. Department of Commerce, *Fifteenth Census: Agriculture*, 2:667.

64. U.S. Department of Commerce, *Fifteenth Census: Population*, 3:411.

65. Jerrell H. Shofner, "Postscript to the Martin Talbert Case: Peonage as Usual in the Florida Turpentine Camps," *Florida Historical Quarterly* 60 (October 1986): 161–73.

66. For an account of this case, see Peter Daniel, *The Shadow of Slavery: Peonage in the South, 1901-1969* (Urbana, Ill., 1977), 8–10, 34.

67. Shofner, "Postscript to the Martin Talbert Case," 161–73.

68. "Report Concerning Lynching of Charlie and Richard Smoak in Calhoun County, Florida, August 28, 1931," from State Attorney John H. Carter to Governor Carlton, 5 March 1932, Carlton records, lynching file.

69. Carter to Carlton, 5 March 1932, Carlton records, lynching file.

70. *St. Petersburg Times*, 1 September 1931; *Tampa Tribune*, 30 August 1931; *Miami Herald*, 1 September 1931; *Tallahassee Democrat*, 30 August 1931.

71. *St. Petersburg Times*, 1 September 1931.

72. Alexander to Carlton, 30 August 1931; Carlton records, lynching file.

73. Dr. Brazell to Carlton, 3 September 1931, ibid.

74. K. I. Hamway to Carlton, 31 August 1931, ibid.

75. Smoak to Carlton, 26 October 1931, ibid.

76. Carlton to Carter, 30 October 1931, ibid.

77. Carter to Carlton, 5 November 1931, ibid.

78. Carlton to Smoak, 30 October 1931, ibid.

79. "Report Concerning Lynching of Charlie and Richard Smoak," 15–17, ibid.

80. Carter to Carlton, 5 March 1932, ibid.

81. Carlton to Carter, 14 March 1932, ibid.

82. Carter to Carlton, 28 May 1932, ibid.

83. Carlton to Carter, 31 May 1932, ibid.

84. Arnold Rose, *The Negro in America* (New York, 1964), 171–72.

85. Raper, *The Tragedy of Lynching*, 472.

86. U.S. Department of Commerce, *Fifteenth Census: Population*, 3:412.

87. U.S. Department of Commerce, *Fifteenth Census: Agriculture*, 2:668. See also, Rerick, *Memoirs of Florida*, 338; Cash, *The Story of Florida*, 770.

88. U.S. Department of Commerce, *Fifteenth Census: Population*, 3:412.

89. Florida State Planning Board, *Statistical Abstract of Florida Counties*, Hamilton County, (n.p., n.d.); Johnson, *Statistical Atlas of Southern Counties*, 79.

90. Will Alexander to Carlton, 13 August 1932, Carlton records, lynching file.

91. *Tampa Tribune*, 7 June 1932.

92. George M. Scoefield to Will Alexander, 27 June 1932.

93. Alexander to Carlton, 13 August 1931, ibid.
94. B. Joyce Ross, *J. E. Spingarn and the Rise of the NAACP, 1911-1939* (New York, 1972), 186–98.
95. Ibid.; Dan T. Carter, *Scottsboro: A Tragedy of the Modern South* (Baton Rouge, La., 1969), 56–63.
96. Zangrando, *The NAACP Crusade against Lynching*, 98–100.

Chapter 2. Protecting White Women

1. The year 1933 was the only lynch-free year in Florida during the thirties. In the rest of the South, however, twenty-four blacks and four whites were lynched. Raper, *The Tragedy of Lynching*, 369.
2. For a brief evaluation of this book, see Ellis, "The Commission on Interracial Cooperation," 79.
3. Chadbourn to Sholtz, 4 January 1934; Sholtz to Chadbourn, 16 January 1934, David Sholtz records, lynching file, administrative correspondence, Florida State Archives, Tallahassee, Fla.
4. Sholtz's statements were quoted in a telegram from Jessie Daniel Ames to Sholtz, 31 January 1934, ibid.
5. James H. Chadbourn, *Lynching and the Law* (Chapel Hill, N.C., 1933), 153–54.
6. *Tampa Tribune*, 31 January 1934. The explosive issue of sex between black men and white women in the South of the 1930s has been analyzed in many studies. Two of the best are Dollard, *Caste and Class*, and McGovern, *Anatomy of a Lynching*.
7. In 1935 Tampa policemen were indicted in the Joseph Shoemaker flogging case as actual participants in the lynching of this Tampa socialist. Robert P. Ingalls, "The Tampa Flogging Case: Urban Vigilantism," *Florida Historical Quarterly* 56 (July 1977): 13–27.
8. The account that follows was reported in the *Tampa Tribune*, 31 January 1934.
9. Sholtz to Farrior, 31 January 1934; Sholtz records, lynching file.
10. Sholtz to Spencer, 31 January 1934, ibid.
11. *Tampa Tribune*, 31 January 1934.
12. *Tampa Tribune*, 1 February 1934.
13. Ibid.
14. *Tallahassee Democrat*, 3 February 1934.
15. Merlin G. Cox, "David Sholtz: New Deal Governor of Florida," *Florida Historical Quarterly* 43 (October 1964): 149–51.
16. Mary McCleod Bethune to Sholtz, 31 January 1934, Sholtz records, lynching file.
17. Lee to Sholtz, 31 January 1934, ibid.
18. J. H. Adams to Sholtz, 7 February 1934, ibid.
19. Key West branch of the NAACP to Sholtz, 5 February 1934, ibid.
20. M. M. White to Sholtz, 2 February 1934, ibid.
21. Mrs. E. S. Garnett to Sholtz, 31 January 1934, ibid.
22. Martha Stallo to Sholtz, 31 January 1934, ibid.
23. Mrs. E. Elchleff to Sholtz, 6 February 1934, ibid.
24. *Tampa Tribune*, 1 February 1934.
25. Ibid.
26. U.S. Department of Commerce, *Fifteenth Census: Population*, 3:421.
27. The extent of segregated life in Tampa at this time was spelled out in detail in a

study commissioned by the Tampa Welfare League and the Tampa YMCA. It was compiled by representatives of the National Council of the YMCA and by the CIC. Raper, *A Study of Negro Life in Tampa* (Tampa, Fla., 1927), Florida Collection, University of South Florida Library, Tampa.

28. Ibid.

29. Ibid. Major black occupational groups were domestic service, personal service, laborers, operatives, and service workers. U.S. Department of Commerce, *Sixteenth Census of the United States, 1940, Population*, vol. 2, *Characteristics of the Population—Florida* (Washington, D.C., 1940), 157.

30. Raper, *Negro Life in Tampa*, 48–52.

31. According to Raper, it was the unions of skilled workers, such as carpenters, painters, and paperhangers, that discriminated most thoroughly against blacks. Ibid., 48–49.

32. Black neighborhoods included West Hyde Park, Scrub, Robles Pond, Central Avenue, Garrison, and College Hill. Ibid., 4–5, 7–17.

33. Although it did not deal with social segregation in any great detail, the Raper study made it clear that interracial contacts were "limited to those of a business nature," and that "orthodox Southern traditions as to race relations prevail in Tampa." Ibid., 1.

34. Florida State Planning Board, *Statistical Abstract of Florida Counties*, Hillsborough County (n.p., n.d).

35. Raper, *Negro Life in Tampa*, 50–51.

36. For an account of blacks on relief, see Emma O. Lundberg, *Social Welfare in Florida* (Tallahassee, Fla., 1934).

37. *Tampa Tribune*, 1 February 1934.

38. Tampa Urban League to Sholtz, 3 February 1934; Tampa branch of the NAACP to Sholtz, 1 February 1934, Sholtz records, lynching file.

39. William M. Davis to Sholtz, 3 February 1934, ibid.

40. *Chicago Defender*, 3 February 1934; *Baltimore Afro-American*, 3 February 1934; *Pittsburgh Courier*, 3 February 1934; and *Atlanta Daily World*, 31 January 1934.

41. *Pittsburgh Courier*, 17 February 1934.

42. *Crisis* 41 (February 1934): 7.

43. Ames to Sholtz, 31 January 1934; Sholtz to Ames, 1 February 1934. ASWPL papers.

44. Zangrando, *The NAACP Crusade against Lynching*.

45. White to Sholtz, 2 February 1934, Sholtz records, lynching file.

46. Zangrando, "The Efforts of the NAACP to Secure Passage of a Federal Antilynching Law, 1920–1940" (Ph.D. diss., University of Pennsylvania, 1963), 307–8.

47. White to Sholtz, 2 February 1934, Sholtz records, lynching file.

48. Sholtz to Walter White, 15 February 1934, ibid.

49. Howard, "'A Blot on Tampa's History,'" 15.

50. Sheriff Spencer to Sholtz, 31 January 1934, Sholtz records, lynching file.

51. Farrior to Sholtz, 15 March 1934, ibid.

52. White to William Rosenwald, 16 November 1934, NAACP papers, Manuscript Division, Library of Congress, C-78, 79.

53. Raper, *Tragedy of Lynching*, 483.

54. Although Jackson County was linked both by rail and by numerous roads with all parts of Florida and by roads with Georgia and Alabama, few of its residents owned cars or used trains. Few read national magazines. The local newspapers, the *Times-Courier* and the *Floridan*, were both weeklies and were both almost entirely concerned with Jackson County

news. Jackson County provided less than 0.3 percent of Florida's manufactured goods in 1933. Florida State Planning Board, *Statistical Abstract of Florida Counties*, Jackson County (n.p., n.d.), and U.S. Department of Commerce, *Fifteenth Census: Population*, 3:406.

55. Howard Odum, *Southern Regions of the United States* (New York, 1969), 276.

56. For nostalgic glimpses of the old days, see *Jackson County Floridan*, 26 June 1931. The dated but revealing study of this county is J. Randall Stanley, *History of Jackson County* (Marianna, Fla., 1950). But the recent definitive work is Jerrell H. Shofner's penetrating *Jackson County, Florida*. See also Shofner, *Nor Is It Over Yet: Florida in the Era of Reconstruction* (Gainesville, Fla., 1974).

57. U.S. Department of Commerce, *Fifteenth Census: Population*, 3:406, 418.

58. There are many indexes of poverty. Jackson County's ratio of inhabitants to cars was 14:1, and its car owners represented less than 0.1 percent of persons owning cars in the state of Florida in the 1930s. Florida State Planning Board, *Statistical Abstract of Florida Counties*, Jackson County. Only 0.2 per cent of the population paid income tax, ibid. Nearly one out of five children suffered from hookworm; see Johnson, *Statistical Atlas of Southern Counties*, 78.

59. McGovern, *Anatomy of a Lynching*, 30–31.

60. Chambliss to Sholtz, 31 October 1934, Sholtz records, lynching file. Sheriff Chambliss made a detailed report of the entire incident upon request of Governor Sholtz. George Cannidy, Lola's father, owned twenty acres, two mules, and one cow, according to tax lists, 1934, Jackson County Courthouse.

61. *Jackson County Floridan*, 26 October 1934.

62. Chambliss to Sholtz, 31 October 1934, Sholtz records, lynching file.

63. *Panama City Pilot*, 25 October 1934.

64. J. D. Smith to Sholtz, 2 November 1934, Sholtz records, lynching file.

65. *Pensacola Journal*, 26 October 1934.

66. Ibid.

67. Ibid. Interview of Hugh M. Caffey, solicitor of Escambia County, Alabama, with Sheriff G. S. Byrne (n.p., 1934), in papers of Governor B. M. Miller, Alabama State Archives, Montgomery. Caffey obtained interviews in response to a demand by Governor Miller for an investigation of Neal's capture in Brewton. Gandy's decision to relocate Neal in Brewton was a fateful step because Brewton was a small town with an inadequate jail. Neal probably would have been safe in Mobile, Alabama, or at the federal facility for detention at Fort Barrancas near Pensacola.

68. Chambliss to Sholtz, 31 October 1934, Sholtz records, lynching file.

69. *Brewton Standard*, 1 November 1934.

70. Interview of Hugh M. Caffey with jailer Jack Shanholter (n.p., 1934), Miller papers.

71. Interviews of Hugh M. Caffey with Sheriff G. S. Byrne and T. J. Criggers, operator of Gulf filling station in Brewton (n.p., 1934), ibid.

72. Interview of Hugh M. Caffey with Jack Shanholter (n.p., 1934), ibid.

73. *United States Statutes at Large* 47 (1933): stat. 326.

74. *Dothan* (Alabama) *Eagle*, 26 October 1934. On radio reports, see "The Lynching of Claude Neal," NAACP papers, C-352.

75. The lynchers also spread the word that the site for the lynching would be the Cannidy farm. *Pensacola Journal*, 27 October 1934. See also *Tallahassee Democrat*, 28 October 1934.

76. *Dothan Eagle*, 26 October 1934.

77. *Boston Herald*, 29 October 1934.

78. Telegrams from White to Sholtz, 26 October 1934; Alexander to Sholtz, 26 October 1934; Cornell to Sholtz, 26 October 1934, Sholtz records, lynching file.

79. J. P. Newell to Mrs. Walter S. Jones, 1 November 1934, Sholtz records, lynching file. See also *Montgomery Advertiser,* 27 October 1934.

80. *Tallahassee Democrat,* 1 November 1934.

81. *Montgomery Advertiser,* 27 October 1934. Nearly every person interviewed who knew members of the mob confirms that its leaders came from the "good citizens" of Jackson County. All sources must remain confidential. Howard Kester, who investigated the incident for the NAACP, reported, "I have it from the most authoritative sources that certain prominent businessmen and leaders from the best families were in the mob." Kester to Walter White, 8 November 1934, NAACP papers, C-352.

82. Erich Fromm observes that "the person who ha[s] complete control over another living being makes that being into a thing, his property, while he becomes the other being's god." He also notes that racial minorities, if powerless, offer this opportunity to majorities. See Fromm, *The Anatomy of Human Destructiveness,* 289–90.

83. Author's interview with confidential source.

84. Kester to Walter White, 7 November 1934, NAACP papers, C-352.

85. "The Lynching of Claude Neal," NAACP papers, C-352, 8.

86. Tindall, *The Emergence of the New South,* 551.

87. White to Sholtz, 22 November 1934, Sholtz records, lynching file.

88. "The Lynching of Claude Neal," NAACP papers, C-352, 5.

89. For a vivid and chilling account of mob activities at the Cannidy's, see McGovern, *Anatomy of a Lynching,* 81–83.

90. "The Lynching of Claude Neal," NAACP papers, C-352.

91. One man reportedly offered to divide a finger with a friend as a "special favor," while another had one finger preserved in alcohol. Three fingers from one hand and two from the other hand had been amputated from Neal's body, besides other mutilations. Ibid.

92. Chambliss to Sholtz, 31 October 1934, Sholtz records, lynching file.

93. Author's interview with Arthur Jensens, 21 July 1977.

94. Chambliss to Sholtz, 31 October 1934, Sholtz records, lynching file.

95. *Jackson County Floridan,* 2 November 1934.

96. More than twenty calls were made by concerned persons in Marianna to the governor's office between 1:30 P.M. and 4:00 P.M., 27 October 1934. "Marianna Mob," in Sholtz records, lynching file.

97. Ibid .

98. Author's interview with Filmore Sims, 27 September 1977.

99. Interview by James R. McGovern with a group of blacks who were victims in the riots, Marianna, 15 July 1977 (confidential sources).

100. Author's interview with Tommy Smith, 7 July 1977.

101. A prominent Marianna physician who was in constant contact with the governor's office reported to Sholtz that the situation was "worse than can be imagined" and that the mob was "threatening to burn out all Negro quarters tonight." Dr. N. A. Baltzell to Sholtz, 28 October 1934; and "Marianna Mob," Sholtz records, lynching file.

102. Quotes from "The Lynching of Claude Neal," NAACP papers, C-352, 48.

103. *Tallahassee Democrat,* 28 October 1934.

104. The editor of the *Montgomery Advertiser,* Tom Brown, Jr., went to Marianna during the period of the National Guard occupation. He reported to the Florida governor that the guard was well behaved at all times. Brown to Sholtz, 7 November 1934, Sholtz records, lynching file.

105. The council also passed City Ordinance 120A, which stated: "It shall be unlawful to make, develop, publish, sell, or exhibit within the City of Marianna any picture, photo-

graph, or likeness of any person who has met his death by lynching or mob violence." Such a crime was punishable by a fine of one hundred dollars or not more than sixty days in jail. Marianna, Florida, *Minutes of the City Council, 1934*, 395. See also *Jackson County Floridan*, 2 November 1934.

106. *Montgomery Advertiser*, 29 October 1934.

107. Ibid

108. "The Lynching of Claude Neal," NAACP papers, C-352, 7–8.

109. Sholtz asked for a complete investigation and report from Sheriff Chambliss and State Attorney John H. Carter. However, he accepted the sheriff's report with "you did all you possibly could" and accepted without protest a complete whitewashing of the Neal lynching from the Jackson County grand jury. See *Tallahassee Democrat*, 1 November 1934. See also Sholtz to Carter, 27 October 1934, Sholtz records, lynching file.

110. *Jackson County Floridan*, 18 November 1934.

111. Ibid

112. Burton managed to find a basis for community esteem in Marianna's riot when he inquired of Governor Sholtz, "In the final analysis, don't you really think that the city of Marianna is entitled to some credit for staging a 'bloodless riot'?" Burton to Sholtz, 30 October1934, Sholtz records, lynching file.

113. Chambliss added, "That mob crowd who tried to seize Bud Gammons [black riot victim] was led by a bunch of ———— rascals, and some of them were from Alabama." *Montgomery Advertiser*, 29 October 1934.

114. *Tallahassee Democrat*, 1 November 1934.

115. Ibid., 28 October 1934.

116. Public statements released by Sholtz's office, 27 October 1934, Sholtz records, lynching file.

117. Walter White to Sholtz, 30 October 1934, Sholtz records, lynching file. See also "The Lynching of Claude Neal," 3, which records headlines in fifteen major newspapers in different parts of the country. Telegrams from Writers' League against Lynching to Sholtz, 24 October 1934, ibid., describe radio broadcasts in New York preceding the lynching.

118. *New York Times*, 28 October 1934; *Chicago Defender*, 3 November 1934. See also Kenneth O'Reilly, "A New Deal for the FBI: The Roosevelt Administration, Crime Control, and National Security," *Journal of American History* 69 (December 1982): 638–58, for a discussion of the Justice Department's attitudes that led to its minimizing involvement in state matters of criminal justice whenever possible.

119. Walter White to Franklin D. Roosevelt, 20 November 1934; White to Cummings, 20 November 1934; Cummings to Roosevelt, 22 December 1934, Franklin D. Roosevelt papers, Franklin D. Roosevelt Library, Hyde Park, N.Y. See also *Crisis*, December 1934, 386; and Mary Frances Berry, *Black Resistance/White Law: A History of Constitutional Racism in America* (New York, 1971).

120. *Crisis*, December 1934, 386.

121. Ibid. Telegram from Copeland to Roosevelt, 2 November 1934, Franklin D. Roosevelt papers.

122. White to Mrs. L. Posner, 14 December 1934; and White to Roy Wilkins, 14 December1934, NAACP papers, C-78, 79.

123. Edward M. Wayland, ed., *The Papers of Howard Kester* (14 reels), documents all these activities of Kester's, Southern Historical Collection, University of North Carolina at Chapel Hill.

124. McGovern, *Anatomy of a Lynching*, 130–32.

125. *New York Times,* 28 October 1934, 2.

126. Walter White to Boake Carter, 27 October 1934, NAACP papers, C-352.

127. James R. McGovern and Walter T. Howard, "Private Justice and National Concern: The Lynching of Claude Neal," *Historian* 43 (August 1981): 554.

128. White to Eleanor Roosevelt, 8 November 1934, Eleanor Roosevelt papers, ser. 100, 1352, Franklin D. Roosevelt Library, Hyde Park, N.Y.

129. Eleanor Roosevelt to White, 20 November 1934, ibid.

130. Ibid.

131. Zangrando, "The Efforts of the NAACP," 326–29.

132. McGovern, *Anatomy of a Lynching,* 128–29. See also Walter White, *A Man Called White: The Autobiography of Walter White,* 167–70.

133. *Punishment for the Crime of Lynching: Hearing before a Subcommittee on the Judiciary,* United States Senate, 74th Cong., 1st sess., 14 Feb. 1935, vol. 5, 141–46.

134. White to Eleanor Roosevelt, 10 April 1935, NAACP papers, C-352.

135. For an excellent treatment entitled "Art Commentary on Lynching," see McGovern, *Anatomy of a Lynching,* 131–35.

136. Allan Freelon to White, 2 February 1935, NAACP papers, C-206.

137. McGovern, *Anatomy of a Lynching,* 131–35.

Chapter 3. Florida Vigilantism at Mid-decade

1. Cornell to Sholtz, 25 March 1935, Sholtz records, lynching file.

2. Sholtz to Levy County sheriff, 22 March 1935, ibid.

3. Sholtz to Collins, 22 March 1935, ibid.

4 Cornell to Sholtz, 10 April 1935; Sholtz to Cornell, 12 April 1935, ibid.

5. Ames to Sholtz, 1 May 1935. The governor replied: "Your suggestion will receive every consideration." Sholtz to Ames, 3 May 1935, ASWPL papers.

6. *Ft. Lauderdale Daily News,* 20 July 1935.

7. Broward County Grand Jury Report, 22–23, Sholtz records, lynching file. A copy of the grand jury report was forwarded to Governor Sholtz at his request.

8. Ibid.; *Ft. Lauderdale Daily News,* 20 July 1935.

9. *Miami Herald,* 20 July 1935. Hill testified for less than five minutes before the grand jury. She identified Stacey as the attacker and briefly described how he had assaulted her. Grand Jury Report, 1–3, Sholtz records, lynching file.

10. *Ft. Lauderdale Daily News,* 20 July 1935.

11. Philip J. Weidling and August Burghard, *Checkered Sunshine: The Story of Ft. Lauderdale, 1793–1955* (Gainesville, Fla., 1966), 182–94.

12. U.S. Department of Commerce, *Fifteenth Census: Population,* 3:791; Florida State Planning Board, *Statistical Abstract of Florida Counties,* Broward County (n.p., n.d).

13. The racial caste system in Ft. Lauderdale was typical of the segregation found in other southern cities. Wali Kharif, "The Refinement of Racial Segregation in Florida after the Civil War" (Ph.D. diss., Florida State University, 1966), 93.

14. *Ft. Lauderdale Daily News,* 20 July 1935. Grand Jury Report, 4, 26, 36–37, Sholtz records, lynching file.

15. Grand Jury Report, 5–6, ibid.

16. Ibid., 8; *Ft. Lauderdale Daily News,* 20 July 1935.

17. Grand Jury Report, 14, Sholtz records, lynching file.

18. *Ft. Lauderdale Daily News,* 20 July 1935.
19. Ibid.
20. Cornell to Sholtz, 19 July 1935, Sholtz records, lynching file.
21. Newell to Cornell, 20 July 1935, ibid.
22. McCullom to Sholtz, 20 July 1935, ibid.
23. Newell to . McCullom, 21 July 1935, ibid.
24. Newell to Clark, 20 July 1935; and Newell to Maire, 20 July 1935, ibid.
25. Maire to Newell, 20 July 1935. Sheriff Clark also wired the governor's office on 20 July saying he would cooperate fully in the investigation of this lynching. Clark to Newell, 20 July 1935, ibid.
26. Grand Jury Report, 13-14, Sholtz records, lynching file.
27. Maire to Sholtz, 26 July 1935, Sholtz records, lynching file.
28. *Ft. Lauderdale Daily News,* 20 July 1935.
29. *Tampa Tribune,* 21 July 1935.
30. *Tallahassee Democrat,* 21 July 1935.
31. *Atlanta Daily World,* 20 July 1935.
32. *Pittsburgh Courier,* 20 July 1935.
33. *New York Age,* 27 July 1935.
34. Shay, *Judge Lynch,* 291.
35. Ingalls, "The Tampa Flogging Case," 20.
36. For a detailed account of the backgrounds of the principals in this case, see Ingalls, *Urban Vigilantes,* 179–81.
37. Ingalls, "The Tampa Flogging Case," 21.
38. Ibid. See also Ingalls, *Urban Vigilantes,* 181–82.
39. Ingalls, "The Tampa Flogging Case," 13; Shay, *Judge Lynch,* 291.
40. Quoted in Ingalls, "The Tampa Flogging Case"; see also Ingalls, *Urban Vigilantes,* 183.
41. Quoted in Ingalls, "The Tampa Flogging Case," 14.
42. The files of Florida governors in the midthirties are overflowing with correspondence of protest and concern over the Shoemaker case.
43. The present members of Metcalf's church still remember him as something of a "moral hero," and in 1986 they celebrated his civic leadership in a special program. Author's interview with Rob Ralph (church historian), 12 January 1986. The historic papers of the First Congregational Church (now called First United Church of Christ) are in Special Collections, University of South Florida Library, Tampa, Florida. See also *Tampa Tribune,* 11 January 1986.
44. Author's interview with Dr. Adliel Moncrief, 11 January 1986.
45. Quoted in Robert P. Ingalls, "Lynching and Establishment Violence in Tampa, 1858–1935," *Journal of Southern History* 53 (November 1987): 638.
46. Ingalls, "The Tampa Flogging Case," 18–19.
47. Ingalls, "Lynching and Establishment Violence," 639.
48. Ingalls, "The Tampa Flogging Case," 22.
49. Author's interview with John Metcalf (Walter Metcalf's son), 12 January 1986.
50. Ingalls, "The Tampa Flogging Case," 24.
51. Defense attorneys won a change of venue by arguing that the publicity surrounding the case would make it difficult to get a fair trial in Tampa. Ibid., 25.
52. For an excellent, detailed account of the trial, see Ingalls, *Urban Vigilantes,* 189–99.
53. Quoted in Ingalls, "The Tampa Flogging Case," 26.

54. *New York Times,* 22 October 1937.

55. Farrior to Cone, 11 January 1938, Cone records, 1936–40, lynching file, administrative correspondence, ser. 371, box 40, Florida State Archives, Tallahassee, Fla.

56. Dewell to Cone, 18 January 1938, ibid.

57. Ingalls, "The Tampa Flogging Case," 27.

58. Jack E. Davis, "'Whitewash' in Florida: The Lynching of Jesse James Payne and Its Aftermath," *Florida Historical Quarterly* 68 (January 1990): 279–80; and Jack E. Davis, "Shades of Justice: The Lynching of Jesse James Payne and its Aftermath" (Master's thesis, University of South Florida, 1988).

59. U.S. Department of Commerce, *Sixteenth Census: Population,* 2:442; and Florida State Planning Board, *Statistical Abstract of Florida Counties* (n.p., n.d.).

60. *Atlanta Daily World,* 15 September 1936.

61. *St. Petersburg Times,* 11 September 1936; and *Tampa Tribune,* 11 September 1936.

62. *Atlanta Daily World,* 15 September 1936; and *Madison-Enterprise Recorder,* 18 September 1936.

63. Shapiro, *White Violence,* 282–84.

Chapter 4. Mob Spirit in the Panhandle

1. For a brief account of this governor's character and administration, see James W. Dunn, "The New Deal and Florida Politics" (Ph.D. diss., Florida State University, 1971), 260–70. There is a very thin biographical file on Governor Cone in the Florida State Archives, and no collection of personal papers. An interview with his widow, Mildred Holmes, revealed many interesting personal stories but little about substantive issues. Author's interview with Mildred Holmes, July 1978. See also Jerrell H. Shofner, "The White Springs Post Office Caper," *Florida Historical Quarterly* 56 (January 1978): 339–47.

2. Cone's antilynching stance did not prevent him from committing gaffes that clearly sanctioned a vigilante ethic. *New York Times,* 23 October 1937; *Daily Worker,* 23 October 1937; *New York Post,* 23 October 1937; *St. Petersburg Times,* 25 October 1937; and *Chicago Defender,* 30 October 1937. For an excellent account of how the ASWPL interacted with southern governors, see Hall, *Revolt against Chivalry.*

3. Floridians lynched five blacks and one white during Cone's years in office, 1936–40. A brief description of these extralegal murders can be seen in Ames, *The Changing Character of Lynching,* 56–58.

4. *Tallahassee Democrat,* 17 May 1937.

5. *Panama City News-Herald,* 18 May 1937.

6. Hall, *Revolt against Chivalry,* 228–29, 324.

7. Telegrams from Mrs. O. O. McCullom to Cone, 19 May 1937; E. L. Vordermark to Cone, 19 May 1937; Jacksonville Ministerial Alliance to Cone, 20 May 1937; Cone to McCullom, May 21, 1937; Cone to Vordermark, 21 May 1937; Cone to Jacksonville Ministerial Alliance, 21 May 1937, Cone records, lynching file.

8. Cone to Robbins, 20 May 1937, Cone records, lynching file.

9. *Tallahassee Democrat,* 10 June 1937.

10. For summaries of this county's history, see Tebeau, *A History of Florida,* 145, 211; Rerick, *Memoirs of Florida,* 2:336–37; Dovell, *Florida: Historic, Dramatic, Contemporary,* 2:623–24.

11. Department of Commerce, *Fifteenth Census: Agricultural,* 2:442, 667. An interesting, if

unflattering, description of Apalachicola can be found in Omar Bradley, *A Soldier's Story* (New York, 1951). 26. Florida State Planning Board, *Statistical Abstract of Florida Counties, Franklin County* (n.p., n.d.). For an account of economic distress and relief efforts in this county, see Lundberg, *Social Welfare in Florida*, 45.

12. U.S. Department of Commerce, *Fifteenth Census: Population*, 3:498.

13. Kharif, "The Refinement of Racial Segregation in Florida after the Civil War," 93.

14. *Tallahassee Democrat*, 10 June 1937.

15. *Jacksonville* (Florida) *Times-Union*, 11 June 1937.

16. U.S. Department of Commerce, *Fifteenth Census: Population*, 3:421; Florida State Planning Board, *Statistical Abstract of Florida Counties*, Leon County (n.p., n.d.); Johnson, *Statistical Atlas of Southern Counties*, Leon County; Lundberg, *Social Welfare in Florida*, 49.

17. U.S. Department of Commerce, *Fifteenth Census: Population*, 3:413; Polk's *Tallahassee City Directory* (Jacksonville, Fla., 1936).

18. *Tallahassee Democrat*, 31 June 1937.

19. Ibid., 2 July 1937.

20. Johnson to Escambia County Sheriff's Office, 30 June 1937, case no. 620, *State of Florida v. Robert Hinds*, Circuit Court Records, microfilm no. 562–712, Leon County Courthouse, Tallahassee, Fla.

21. *Tallahassee Democrat*, 6 July 1937.

22. This aspect of southern jurisprudence is discussed by Carter, *Scottsboro*, 115; and much earlier by Ames, *The Changing Character of Lynching*; see also Myrdal, *An American Dilemma*, 179–80. and Raper, *The Tragedy of Lynching*, 46.

23. *Tallahassee Democrat*, 6 July 1937.

24. An editorial in the *Pensacola Journal* on 8 July 1937 expressed this very viewpoint.

25. *Tallahassee Democrat*, 6 July 1937. The *Democrat* carried detailed accounts of the day's testimony; the narrative that follows is taken from that account.

26. Ibid., 7 July 1937

27. Details of the history of Florida's electric chair can be found in Gene Miller, *Invitation to a Lynching* (New York, 1975), 13–16.

28. *Tallahassee Democrat*, 23 July 1937.

29. Hall, *Revolt against Chivalry*, 324; Zangrando, *The NAACP Crusade against Lynching*, 139–65.

30. Carter, *Scottsboro*, 11–50.

31. Ibid.

32. For a discussion of how Leibowitz handled the Scottsboro trials, see ibid., 192–242, 281–302, 340, 342, 369–76.

33. Myrdal, *An American Dilemma*, 179–80.

34. Howard, "In the Shadow of Scottsboro: The 1937 Robert Hinds Case," *Gulf Coast Historical Review* 4 (Fall 1988): 76.

35. Ames, *The Changing Character of Lynching*, 36–37; Shay, *Judge Lynch*, 250; *Tallahassee Democrat*, 24 July 1937.

36. Kelly was immediately hospitalized and reported in fair condition later that morning. *Tallahassee Democrat*, 20 July 1937. Little is known about the two youths. Residents remember that they were two Tallahassee-born teenagers from the Smokey Hollow area and that they were younger than eighteen years of age, perhaps as young as fourteen. Ponder and Hawkins are remembered as "mischievous" youths, but not as criminals, and there is no record of their involvement with the law prior to the alleged burglary. Author's interview with two Tallahassee blacks (who wish to remain anonymous) who recall the incident, 9 and 15 May 1988.

37. State attorney Orion C. Parker compiled a detailed report of the entire incident upon the request of Governor Cone. Parker to Cone, 4 August 1937, Cone records, lynching file.

38. In 1927 the Florida legislature enacted a law that authorized the city of Tallahassee to confine its prisoners in the Leon County jail. Under this arrangement city police were given a key that permitted officers to enter the jail during all hours of the night. Officials believed that under these circumstances a night guard at the county facility was unnecessary. *Tallahassee Democrat,* 21 July 1937.

39. According to Fairbanks, two of them were dressed in "overcoats," the other two in "raincoats." All wore masks made of "bags" in which eyeholes had been cut. Ibid., 20 July 1937.

40. Parker to Cone, 4 August 1937, Cone records, lynching file.

41. The details of the affair were described in two special reports to Governor Cone. Parker and Sheriff Stoutamire prepared lengthy formal accounts of this extralegal execution. *Tallahassee Democrat,* 20 July 1937.

42. *Newsweek,* 31 July 1937.

43. Stoutamire to Cone, 4 August 1937, Cone records, lynching file; *Tallahassee Democrat,* 20 July 1937. Later that morning, after the coroner's inquest, sheriff's deputies buried the bodies in Tallahassee's black cemetery.

44. The sheriff was reported in the local press as declaring that neither he nor his men were guilty of any carelessness. *Tallahassee Democrat,* 20 July 1937.

45. Ibid., 22 July 1937.

46. Johnson to Cone, 24 July 1937, Cone records, lynching file.

47. Wesson also stated that "this city is cooperating with the sheriff in an endeavor to ascertain the identity of the guilty parties." Wesson to Cone, 26 July 1937, ibid.

48. Offering Cone "friendly" counsel, Johnson stated, "I earnestly ask that you refrain from entering an order of suspension against Sheriff Stoutamire until you get the evidence that would sustain such a suspension. I ask this for three reasons: 1. If such a suspension was without competent evidence it would mean his re-election at the next general election, 1938. 2. It would mean that the state of Florida would have to pay his entire compensation during the period of suspension. 3. It would be a calamity to disrupt the sheriff's force at this time." Johnson to Cone, 25 July 1937, ibid.

49. *Tallahassee Democrat,* 25 July 1937.

50. Stoutamire to Wesson, 24 July 1937, Cone records, lynching file.

51. *Tallahassee Democrat,* 25 July 1937.

52. Stoutamire to Cone, 4 August 1937, Cone records, lynching file.

53. The state attorney never requested any indictments. *Tallahassee Democrat,* 22 July 1937.

54. Ibid., July 20, 1937.

55. Tallahassee "lies 170 miles from Jacksonville, 200 from Pensacola, 240 from Tampa, 245 from Orlando, 460 from Miami, and 606 from Key West. It lies only 20 miles from the Georgia line." Hampton Dunn, *Yesterday's Tallahassee* (Miami, Fla., 1974), 27–28.

56. For a brief discussion of how deeply rooted Old South traditions influenced the residents of Tallahassee during the 1930s, see Tom Wagy, *Governor LeRoy Collins: Spokesman of the New South* (University, Ala., 1985), 4–6, 11–12, 18–19. For a history of Tallahassee as an Old South community, see Bertram Groene's *Antebellum Tallahassee* (Tallahassee, Fla., 1971).

57. U.S. Department of Commerce, *Fifteenth Census: Population,* 3:416.

58. The racial segregation in Tallahassee on the eve of this lynching was typical of the segregation that existed in Florida in the early decades of the twentieth century. Racial

segregation and Jim Crow during the thirties are well documented in Polk's *Tallahassee City Directory*. Black labor was crucial to Tallahassee's economy. Black women held most of the domestic service jobs in the city, and black workers outnumbered whites almost ten to one in the general urban labor category. Florida State Planning Board, *Statistical Abstract of Florida Counties*, Leon County (n.p., n.d.).

59.   Terry E. Lewis, "Frenchtown: A Geographical Survey of an All-Negro Business District in Tallahassee, Florida" (Master's thesis, Florida State University, 1966), 8.

60.   All words in the sign were spelled correctly except where *negros* appeared, and in several words the letter *s* was turned backward. *Tallahassee Democrat,* 20 July 1937.

61.   Judge Johnson wrote Cone saying, "Governor, these negroes were not charged with what is termed a lynching crime. After I heard that the two negroes had been arrested, and that they had confessed, it never crossed my mind that there would be any attempt to take them out and lynch them. I dare say that you would not have thought so." Johnson to Cone, 24 July 1937, Cone records, lynching file.

62.   Most of the correspondence to Cone was like the letter from the Reverend LeRoy Cooley, Penny Farms, Florida, which called "for the suspension of the officers involved." Another from Mrs. John Drake of Philadelphia, Pennsylvania, informed the governor that if action was not taken against the lynchers, she and her family would spend their winter vacation somewhere other than Florida. One man from New York City predicted that Cone would "go down in history as our greatest governor" if he could obtain convictions in this case. For other correspondence to Cone, see the telegrams from the Chicago and Northern District Association of Colored Women, 25 July 1937; letter from Mrs. O. O. McCullom, n.d.; and telegram from Hayden Crosby, 21 July 1937, ibid.

63.   Albert Kissling to Cone, 23 July 1937, ibid.

64.   *St. Petersburg Times,* 21 July 1937.

65.   *Tampa Tribune,* 22 July 1937.

66.   *Miami Herald,* 22 July 1937.

67.   *Miami Daily Times,* 21 July 1937.

68.   *Tallahassee Democrat,* 21 July 1937.

69.   *New York Times,* 21 July 1937; *Washington Post,* 23 July 1937; *Chicago Tribune,* 21 July 1937; *Atlanta Constitution,* 21 July 1937; *St. Louis Post-Dispatch,* 23 July 1937; *Boston Herald,* 23 July 1937.

70.   *St. Louis Post-Dispatch,* 23 July 1937.

71.   Cone was informed of this broadcast in a telegram. J. H. Ingram to Cone, 23 July 1937, Cone records, lynching file.

72.   Telegram from Wilkins to Cone, 28 July 1937, NAACP papers, C-342.

73.   *Chicago Defender,* 24 July 1937; *Baltimore Afro-American,* 24 July 1937; *Atlanta Daily World,* 24 July 1937 *Norfolk Journal and Guide,* 31 July 1937.

74.   The *Norfolk Journal and Guide* also ran an editorial contrasting Cone's failings in this case to the success of the governor of Tennessee, who took decisive steps to prevent a lynching at about this time in his state, 11 September 1937.

75.   *Crisis,* January 1938, 13.

76.   Cornell to Cone, 28 July 1937, Cone records, lynching file.

77.   New York Congressman Joseph Gavigan's proposed bill (H.R. 1507), supported by the NAACP, would have invoked action by the U.S. District Court thirty days after a lynching, if state and local officials had failed to respond. Local officers found guilty of conspiring or cooperating with the lynchers could be imprisoned from five to twenty-five years. The House passed the bill in April 1937. The Senate bill, Wagner-Van Nuys, carried the same penalties as the House proposal. Zangrando, *The NAACP Crusade against Lynching,* 141–43.

78. *New York Times*, 21 July 1937; *Washington Post*, 21 July 1937; *Atlanta Constitution*, 21 July 1937.

79. Zangrando, *The NAACP Crusade against Lynching*, 145.

80. Ibid., 139–45, 154–58.

81. For an account of Roosevelt's attempt to distance himself from the bills, see McGovern and Howard, "The Lynching of Claude Neal," 554–55.

82. McGovern, *Anatomy of a Lynching*, 115–24; see also James T. Patterson, *Congressional Conservatism and the New Deal: The Growth of the Conservative Coalition in Congress, 1933–1939* (Lexington, Ky., 1967), 156–57; and Nancy J. Weiss, *The National Urban League, 1910–1940* (New York, 1974), 265–66.

83. *Congressional Record*, 75th Cong., 1st sess., 12 August 1937, 8756. This was also the last piece of civil rights legislation that Claude Pepper opposed, although he continued to support the concept of white supremacy. James. C. Clark, "The 1944 Florida Democratic Senate Primary," *Florida Historical Quarterly* 66 (April 1988): 365.

84. *Congressional Record*, 75th Cong., 2d sess., 18 November 1937, vol. 82, pt. 1, and 22 November 22, 1937, 208.

85. Ibid., 75th Cong., 3d sess., 24 January 1937, vol. 81, pt. 1, 974.

86. Zangrando, *The NAACP Crusade against Lynching*, 152–53.

87. Shay, *Judge Lynch*. This was the eighth and final lynching of 1937.

88. *Pensacola Journal*, 5 October 1937.

89. *Milton Gazette*, 7 October 1937.

90. While the county was serviced by a railroad and a few good roads, few persons owned cars or used trains. In 1930, only about 2 in 100 Santa Rosa County residents subscribed to national magazines, and by 1940 only 12.4 percent of the rural population had electric lights and only 506 individuals had radios in their homes. U.S. Department of Commerce, *Fifteenth Census: Population*, 3:415, 433; and Florida State Planning Board, *Statistical Abstract of Florida Counties*, Santa Rosa County (n.p., n.d.).

91. Only 0.2 percent of the population paid income tax and there was a high illiteracy rate among whites as well as blacks. Santa Rosa County's ratio of inhabitants to cars was 15:1. Its car owners represented less than 0.4 percent of persons owning cars in the state of Florida. Johnson, *Statistical Atlas of Southern Counties*, Santa Rosa County.

92. U.S. Department of Commerce, *Fifteenth Census: Population*, 3:433.

93. Shofner, "Custom, Law, and History: The Enduring Influence of Florida's 'Black Codes'," *Florida Historical Quarterly* 55 (January 1977): 277–98; Cash clearly ties this frontier ethic to lynchings in the rural South. Cash, *Mind of the South*, 32–34, 49–52, 115–23.

94. *Pensacola Journal*, 5 October 1937. There are no detailed reports of this lynching in the files of Governor Cone.

95. *Tallahassee Democrat*, 4 October 1937.

96. *Pensacola Journal*, 5 October 1937.

97. *Tallahassee Democrat*, 4 October 1937. Details of this execution were also carried nationally in the *New York Times*, 5 October 1937, and the *Washington Post*, 5 October 1937.

98. *Pensacola Journal*, 5 October 1937.

99. *Tallahassee Democrat*, 5 October 1937.

100. *Pensacola Journal*, 5 October 1937.

101. *Tallahassee Democrat*, 4 October 1937.

102. *Miami Herald*, 5 October 1937.

103. *St. Petersburg Times*, 6 October 1937.

104. Wilkins to Cone, 5 October 1937, NAACP papers, C-342.

105. Telegram from White to Cone, 8 October 1937, ibid.

106. *Miami Herald,* 6 October 1937.

107. *Miami Daily News,* 5 October 1937.

108. Jane Cornell to Cone, 6 October1937, Cone records, lynching file.

109. Mrs. O. O. McCullom to Cone, n.d. [1937], Cone records, lynching file.

110. Cone to White, 11 October 1937; Cone to Jane Cornell, 11 October 1937, Cone records, lynching file.

111. *Norfolk Journal and Guide,* 9 October 1937.

112. *Baltimore Afro-American,* 16 October 1937.

113. *Christian Century* 55 (12 January, 1938): 35.

Chapter 5. Kidnapped from the Police

1. *Tallahassee Democrat,* 6 February 1937; *Panama City News-Herald,* 6 February 1937. Cone's remarks came only three days after Wes Johnson, a black Alabama youth, became the nation's first lynching victim of 1937.

2. *Ocala Banner,* 11 February 1937. See also unidentified and undated news clippings in the biographical file of Governor Cone, Florida State Archives, Tallahassee, Florida.

3. Author's interview with Carl Gray (Bay County's representative in the state legislature during the 1930s), 6 June 1976.

4. In one instance, the six-foot Cone actually shoved another official into a chair during a cabinet meeting. *Panama City News-Herald,* 9 February 1937.

5. *New York Times,* 22 October 1937.

6. The ACLU was referring to an incident where the Ku Klux Klan, in full attire, officiated at the funeral of one of their members in St. Petersburg. Soon afterward, the Klan raided a Miami nightspot, where they smashed furniture and stole $360. This later crime was also described by David Chalmers, *Hooded Americanism: The First Century of the Ku Klux Klan, 1865–1965* (Garden City, N.Y., 1955), 311.

7. *Daily Worker,* 23 October 1937.

8. Ralph Harden to Cone, 7 December 1937, Cone records, lynching file.

9. *New York Times,* 24 October 1937.

10. *New York Post,* 23 October 1937.

11. *St. Petersburg Times,* 25 October 1937.

12. White also observed that the governor's words "demonstrate conclusively that if lynching is to be checked we must have a federal antilynching law." *Norfolk Journal and Guide,* 30 October 1937.

13. *Chicago Defender,* 30 October 1937; *Baltimore Afro-American,* 30 October 1937; *Norfolk Journal and Guide,* 30 October 1937.

14. Department of State, Bureau of Laws, *Acts, Resolutions and Memorials of the Legislature,* 1937, 715.

15. ACLU to Cone, 10 May 1937; League of American Writers to Cone, 3 May 1937; John Wesley to Cone, 4 May 1937, Cone records, lynching file.

16. Howard, "Beaches and Hanging Trees: Lynch Law in Florida, 1930–1940," *Carver* 10 (Spring 1992): 7–20.

17. Bailey to Cone, 24 September1938, Cone records, lynching file.

18. Roger Baldwin to Cone, 26 September 1938, American Civil Liberties Union papers, Firestone Library, Princeton University, Princeton, N.J.

19. Walter White to Cone, 26 September 1938; Modern American Youth Club (Jacksonville) to Cone, 26 September 1938, Cone records, lynching file.

20. Branch Cone sent this letter to Margaret Bailey, Roger Baldwin, Walter White, and the Modern American Youth Club, 29 September 1938, ibid.

21. Branch Cone to Wilson, 29 September 1938, ibid.

22. Wilson to Cone, 6 October 1938, ibid.

23. Ibid.

24. *Daily Worker*, 19 September 1938.

25. *Chicago Defender*, 24 September 1938; *Norfolk Journal and Guide*, 24 September 1938.

26. *Crisis*, 1938, 302.

27. *Baltimore Afro-American*, 24 September 1938.

28. *St. Petersburg Times*, 28 September 1938, *Tampa Tribune*, 28 September 1938; *Jacksonville Times-Union*, 28 September 1938; *Tallahassee Democrat*, 28 September 1938.

29. *St. Petersburg Times*, 28 September 1938.

30. *Tallahassee Democrat*, 6 October 1938.

31. *Tampa Tribune*, 28 September 1938.

32. Unsigned letter to Cone, 17 October 1938, Cone records, lynching file.

33. U.S. Department of Commerce, *Sixteenth Census*, 2:229.

34. Florida State Planning Board, *Statistical Abstract of Florida Counties*, Taylor County (n.p., n.d.).

35. This lynching reflects the insight found in the assertion of Herbert Shapiro that "violence against black labor was the heart of the racial caste system." See Shapiro, *White Violence*, 253.

36. Margaret Bailey to Branch Cone, 10 October 1938; Reverend Myles D. Blanchard to Governor Cone, 7 October1938; International Workers' Order Local no. 142 to Governor Cone, 12 October 1938, Cone records, lynching file.

37. *Panama City News-Herald*, 17, 18, and 19 January 1939.

38. U.S. Department of Commerce, *Sixteenth Census*, 2:231.

39. W. T. Cash, *The Story of Florida*, 2:765–66; author's interview with Tommy Smith, 6 June 1977.

40. *Panama City News-Herald*, 22 January 1939.

41. Ibid., 30 March 1939; 1 April 1939.

42. Ibid., 2 April 1939.

43. Ibid.

44. *Tallahassee Democrat*, 2 April 1939.

45. *Panama City News-Herald*, 18 April 1939.

46. Ibid., 3 April 1939.

47. *Miami Herald*, 2 April 1939.

48. *St. Petersburg Times*, 4 April 1939.

49. *Miami Daily News*, 2 April 1939.

50. *Tampa Tribune*, 2 April 1939.

51. *New York Times*, 2 April 1939; *St. Louis Post-Dispatch*, 2 April 1939; *Washington Post*, 2 April 1939; *Richmond Times-Dispatch*, 2 April 1939.

52. *Chicago Defender*, 8 April 1939; *Baltimore Afro-American*, 8 April 1939; *Norfolk Journal and Guide*, 8 April 1939; *Pittsburgh Courier*, 8 April 1939; *Atlanta Daily World*, 8 April 1939.

53. *Chicago Defender*, 8 April 1939.

54. *Norfolk Journal and Guide*, 8 April 1939.

55. Hovers to Cone, 2 April 1939, Cone records, lynching file. Hovers replaced Cornell in 1938 when the latter resigned over Ames's steadfast opposition to a federal antilynching bill.

56. *Tallahassee Democrat*, 2 April 1939.

57. *Crisis*, May 1939, 149.

58. *Daytona Beach Evening News*, 30 April 1939.

59. Ibid., 1 May 1939. The account that follows is from this news article.

60. Ibid., 3 May 1939.

61. U.S. Department of Commerce, *Sixteenth Census*, 2:232; Florida State Planning Board, *Statistical Abstract of Florida Counties*, Volusia County (n.p., n.d.).

62. On southern white violence toward economically self-sufficient blacks, see Donald L. Grant, *The Anti-Lynching Movement, 1883-1932* (San Francisco, 1975).

63. *Daytona Beach Evening News*, 30 April 1939.

64. Southern Workers' Defense League to Governor Cone, 29 April 1939, Cone records, lynching file.

65. *Daytona Beach Evening News*, 1 May 1939.

66. Ibid .

67. Ibid., 5 May 1939.

68. Ibid., 7 May 1939.

69. Ibid.

70. Ibid., 2 May 1939.

71. Ibid., 17 May 1939.

72. Ibid., 21 May 1939.

73. Ibid., 26 May 26 1939

74. Ibid .

75. Ibid., 28 May 1939. The account of the trial that follows is taken from this news report.

76. *Miami Daily News*, 29 May 1939. See also *Tampa Tribune*, 29 May 1939; *St. Petersburg Times*, 30 May 1939; and *Miami Herald*, 29 May 1939.

77. *Chicago Defender*, 3 June 1939.

78. *Norfolk Journal and Guide*, 3 June 1939.

Chapter 6. Trends and Patterns of a Fading Tradition

1. These "typical" lynching counties have been described in the Southern Commission on the Study of Lynching, *Lynchings and What They Mean: General Findings of the Southern Commission on the Study of Lynching* (Atlanta, Ga., 1931), 31–32. One classical analysis of the American South asserted that "after 1914 lynchings in all southern towns of more than 10,000 people, regardless of their location by states, became so rare as practically to be nonexistent." Cash, *The Mind of the South*, 307. Historians have embraced this inaccurate description even into the 1980s; see McGovern, *Anatomy of a Lynching*, 2.

2. U.S. Department of Commerce, *Fifteenth Census: Population*, 395. For a brief account of rapid urbanization in the 1920s, see Tebeau, *A History of Florida*, 377–92; and Stanton T. Dietrich, "The Urbanization of Florida's Population: An Historical Perspective of County Growth, 1830–1970" (Gainesville, Fla., 1978), 17–18.

3. Brundage, *Lynching in the New South*, 86.

4. Hadley Cantril, *The Psychology of Social Movements* (New York, 1941), 94.

5. H. L. Mencken, *Prejudices: Second Series* (New York, 1920), 151; Ames, *The Changing Character of Lynching*, 42–43.

6. For another account of the decline of ceremonial lynchings, see McGovern, *Anatomy of a Lynching*, 140–48.

7. The case for variable race relations in the modern South has been made by Howard Rabinowitz, *Race Relations in the Urban South, 1865–1890* (New York, 1978).

8. Quoted in Brundage, *Lynching in the New South*, 50.

9. These patterns of behavior have been explored in detail by Cox, *Caste, Class, and Race*, 550–51.

10. Booker T. Washington once commented that "for every lynching that takes place . . . a score of colored people leave . . . for the city," quoted in Floretti Henri, *Black Migration: Movement North, 1900–1920* (New York, 1976), 57; Shofner, "Florida and the Black Migration," *Florida Historical Quarterly* 57 (January 1979): 267. Several authorities conclude that persecution, and its ultimate expression in lynching, was not nearly such an important motivation for migration as the hope of economic betterment. Emmet J. Scott, *Negro Migration during the War* (New York, 1920), 22; Gilbert Osofsky, *Harlem: The Making of a Ghetto, Negro New York, 1890–1930* (New York, 1966), 22.

11. ASWPL, "Southern Women Look at Lynching," 34, Sholtz records, lynching file. Correspondence from McCollum's organization and other Florida antilynching groups is scattered through the lynching files of Governors David Sholtz and Fred Cone.

12. Peter Daniel, *Breaking the Land: The Transformation of Cotton, Tobacco, and Rice Cultures* (Urbana, Ill., 1985), chap. 11; Jack Temple Kirby, *Rural Worlds Lost: The American South, 1920–1960* (Baton Rouge, La., 1987), chap. 2; Theodore Saloutous, *The American Farmer and the New Deal* (Ames, Iowa, 1982); and Gavin Wright, *Old South, New South: Revolutions in the Southern Economy since the Civil War* (New York, 1986), 236.

13. Some analysts believe that lynchings are closely related to the struggle between blacks and whites in the lower-class job market. White, *Rope and Faggot*, 28; Ames, *The Changing Character of Lynching*, 15–16; and Wolters, *Negroes and the Great Depression*, 116–17.

14. White, *A Man Called White*.

15. For an account of ILD activities in the South during the 1930s, see, Carter, *Scottsboro*, 149–53. The ILD chronicled its own history in the organization's organ, the *Legal Defender*, June 1935. See also Charles W. Martin, "The International Labor Defense and Black America," *Labor History* 26 (Spring 1985): 165–94.

16. An excellent analysis of this competition can be found in Shapiro, *White Violence, Black Response*, 273–74.

17. The Florida ILD's activities were well covered in the official organ of the national ILD in New York City; see *Equal Justice* (formerly *Legal Defender*), October 1938, March 1939, and June 1939. For recent accounts of U.S. Communist Party activity in the South of the thirties, see Robin D. G. Kelley, *Hammer and Hoe: Alabama Communists during the Great Depression* (Chapel Hill, N.C.. 1992), and Fraser M. Ottanelli, *The Communist Party of the United States from the Depression to World War II* (New Brunswick, N.J., 1991), 39–43.

18. The ILD in Florida paid a high price for their notoriety. In the aftermath of the Otis Price lynching case, local vigilantes fell on ILD offices in Jacksonville, smashing their furnishings. Undaunted, Margaret Bailey and her staff promptly moved into new offices in a big downtown office building, and proudly displayed their name on the door and on the building directory billboard. *Equal Justice*, May 1939; and for Marcantonio's role in racial problems of the South, see Gerald Meyer, *Vito Marcantonio: Radical Politician, 1902–1954* (New York, 1991).

19. Southern Workers Defense League to Governor Cone, 29 April 1939, Cone records, lynching file.

20. FBI director J. Edgar Hoover vehemently opposed passage of any kind of antilynching bill. Furthermore, in the 1950s he attempted to prove to the Eisenhower administration no

such federal law was needed because "the number of lynchings had dropped from twenty to less than three per year since the FBI had begun informal investigations in 1939." Taylor Branch, *Parting the Waters: America in the King Years, 1954–1963* (New York, 1988), 182.

21. The NAACP files contain many more newspaper clippings and headlines about the Neal lynching than about any other lynching of a black. Most major newspapers reported the event and many, including the *New York Times* (28 October 1934), devoted front-page coverage. Editorials appeared in the *Baltimore Evening Sun, Birmingham News, Boston Herald, Chattanooga News, Cleveland Plain Dealer, Macon Telegraph, Montgomery Advertiser, Richmond Times-Dispatch, Washington Post,* and *New Republic.* NAACP papers, C-352. The lynching files of Florida governors in the 1930s contain more correspondence and newspapers clippings about the Shoemaker and Neal slayings than about any other lynchings.

22. *Richmond Times Dispatch,* 2 February 1937.

23. Virginius Dabney, "Dixie Rejects Lynching," *Nation,* 27 November 1937, 581; *Congressional Record,* 74th Cong., 1st sess., 15 April 1937, vol. 81, pt. 4, 3523.

24. McGovern and Howard, "The Lynching of Claude Neal," 557.

25. Ames, *The Changing Character of Lynching,* 16.

26. McGovern and Howard, "The Lynching of Claude Neal," 558.

27. Jesse W. Reader, "Federal Efforts to Control Lynchings" (Master's thesis, Cornell University, 1952), 90–98.

28. See Walter White's remark in *Punishment for the Crime of Lynching,* U.S. Senate, 35–39, and Walter White to President Roosevelt, 17 June 1938, Franklin D. Roosevelt Library, presidential personal file 1336, Hyde Park, N.Y.

29. Robert K. Carr, *Federal Regulations of Civil Rights: Quest for a Sword* (Ithaca, N.Y., 1947), 164.

Epilogue: From Lynching to Assassination

1. *Congressional Record,* 75th Cong., 3d sess., 24 January 1938, vol. 83, pt. 1, 974.

2. The liberal press criticized Pepper for these and other remarks he made in opposition to the antilynching bill. The *Christian Century* lamented that "Senator Pepper also invoked the spirit of 'liberalism' against the measure. He contended that a federal antilynching bill was out of harmony with the New Deal and it runs counter to 'progressive democracy'." Taylor Merrill, "Lynching and the Antilynching Bill," *Christian Century,* 23 February 1938, 238. See also *Congressional Record,* 75th Cong., 3d sess., 24 January 1938, 974.

3. Ames, *The Changing Character of Lynching,* 37; *St. Petersburg Times,* 14 May 1941; *Tampa Tribune,* 14 May 1941.

4. *St. Petersburg Times,* 14 May 1941.

5. Walter White to Governor Holland, 20 May 1941; Jessie Daniel Ames to Governor Holland, 29 May 1941, Governor Spessard Holland records, 1941–45, administrative correspondence, lynching file, ser. 406, box 71, Florida State Archives, Tallahassee, Fla.

6. *Gadsden County Times,* 22 May 1941; *Tallahassee Democrat,* 22 May 1941; *Baltimore Afro-American,* 24 May 1941.

7. Gadsden County Times, 22 May 1941.

8. The *St. Petersburg Times* also referred to the Gadsden County affair as a "two-day lynching," 14 May 1941. The *Tampa Tribune,* 14 May 1941, called it a "double-barreled lynching."

9. *Baltimore Afro-American,* 24 May 1941.

10. *Pittsburgh Courier*, 24 May 1941.
11. *Gadsden County Times*, 15 May 1941.
12. Ibid.
13. *New York Post*, 29 May 1941.
14. *Jackson County Floridan*, 4 June 1943.
15. Ibid.
16. Ibid.
17. Ibid., 24 June 1943.
18. Harry T. Moore to Governor Holland, 12 July 1943, Holland records, lynching file.
19. *St. Petersburg Times*, 17 June 1943.
20. *Tampa Tribune*, 18 June 1943.
21. *Miami Herald*, 18 June 1943.
22. *Chicago Defender*, 19 June 1943; *Pittsburgh Courier*, 19 June 1943; and *Baltimore Afro-American*, 19 June 1943.
23. *Chicago Defender*, 19 June 1943.
24. *St. Petersburg Times*, 12 October 1945. The account that follows is from this newspaper report.
25. Ibid., 13 October 1945.
26. Ibid.
27. *Miami Herald*, 13 October 1945.
28. *St. Petersburg Times*, 18 October 1945.
29. *Atlanta Daily World*, 13 October 1945.
30. *Pittsburgh Courier*, 20 October 1945.
31. *St. Petersburg Times*, 24 October 1945.
32. Ibid., 2 November 1945.
33. Ibid.
34. Ibid.
35. *Time*, 7 January 1946, 16.
36. *Colliers*, 23 February 1946, 16.
37. *Time*, 4 February 1946, 4.
38. *St. Petersburg Times*, 30 June 1949.
39. Davis, "'Whitewash' in Florida," 277–98.
40. Steven F. Lawson, David R. Colburn, and Darryl Paulson, "Groveland: Florida's Little Scottsboro," *Florida Historical Quarterly* 65 (July 1986): 1–2; and Steven F. Lawson, *Black Ballots: Voting Rights in the South, 1944–1969* (New York, 1976).
41. Lawson, Colburn, and Paulson, "Groveland," 1–2.
42. For a treatment of limited federal involvement in racial conflicts of the South of the 1940s, see Dominic J. Capeci, "The Lynching of Cleo Wright: Federal Protection of Constitutional Rights during World War II," *Journal of American History* 72 (March 1986): 859–87.
43. Lawson, Colburn, and Paulson, "Groveland," 16.
44. McGovern, *Anatomy of a Lynching*, chap. 1.
45. For accounts of lynchlike murders of civil rights workers in the 1950s and 1960s, see David J. Garrow, *Bearing the Cross: Martin Luther King, Jr., and the Southern Christian Leadership Conference* (New York, 1986).
46. Brundage, *Lynching in the New South*, 259.
47. The subject of Florida lynchings and vigilantism directed against blacks, whites, and ethnics has attracted much scholarly attention. See McGovern, *Anatomy of a Lynching*; Ingalls, *Urban Vigilantes in the New South*; Ingalls, "Lynching and Establishment Violence in

Tampa"; Ingalls, "The Tampa Flogging Case"; Ingalls, "General Joseph B. Wall and Lynch Law in Tampa," *Florida Historical Quarterly* 63 (July 1984); 51–70; Jerrell H. Shofner, "Murders at 'Kiss-Me-Quick': The Underside of International Affairs," *Florida Historical Quarterly* 62 (January 1984): 332–38; Jerrell H. Shofner, "Judge Herbert Rider and the Lynching at LaBelle," *Florida Historical Quarterly* 59 (January 1981): 292–306; and McGovern and Howard, "The Lynching of Claude Neal."

48.   The New South has always been a violent place, and the rich literature reflects this reality: Sheldon Hackney, "Southern Violence," *American Historical Review* 74 (February 1969): 906–25; George C. Rable, *But There Was No Peace: The Role of Violence in the Politics of Reconstruction* (Athens, Ga., 1984); Albert C. Smith, "'Southern Violence' Reconsidered: Arson as Protest in Black Belt Georgia, 1865–1910," *Journal of Southern History* 51 (November 1985): 527–64; William F. Holmes, "Whitecapping: Agrarian Violence in Mississippi, 1902–1906," *Journal of Southern History* 35 (May 1968), 165–85; Holmes, "Moonshining and Collective Violence: Georgia, 1889–1895," *Journal of American History* 67 (December 1980): 589–611; William L. Montel, *Killings: Folk Justice in the Upper South* (Lexington, Ky., 1986); Altina L. Waller, *Feud: Hatfields, McCoys, and Social Change in Appalachia, 1860–1900* (Chapel Hill, N.C., 1988); Allen W. Trelease, *White Terror: The Ku Klux Klan Conspiracy and Southern Reconstruction* (New York, 1971); Howard Smead, *Blood Justice: The Lynching of Mack Charles Parker* (New York, 1986); Stephen J. Whitfield, *A Death in the Delta: The Story of Emmett Till* (New York, 1988); and George C. Wright, *Racial Violence in Kentucky, 1865–1940: Lynchings, Mob Rule, and "Legal Lynchings"* (Baton Rouge, La., 1990).

49.   Brundage, *Lynching in the New South*, 259.

Bibliography

Manuscript Collections

American Civil Liberties Union. Papers. Firestone Library, Princeton University, Princeton, N.J.

ASWPL (Association of Southern Women for the Prevention of Lynching) Papers. Special collections. Woodruff Library, Atlanta University Center, Atlanta, Ga.

Carlton, Doyle. Records, 1928–32. Administrative correspondence. Florida State Archives, Tallahassee, Fla.

Catts, Sidney J. Records, 1909–25. Correspondence of the governors. Florida State Archives, Tallahassee, Fla.

Cone, Fred. Records, 1936–40. Administrative correspondence. Florida State Archives, Tallahassee, Fla.

Holland, Spessard. Records, 1940–44. Administrative correspondence. Florida State Archives, Tallahassee, Fla.

Kester, Howard A. Papers. Southern Historical Collection. University of North Carolina, Chapel Hill, N.C.

Lynching records. Tuskegee Institute Archives, Tuskegee, Ala.

Miller, Governor B. M. Papers. Alabama State Archives, Montgomery, Ala.

NAACP (National Association for the Advancement of Colored People) Papers. Manuscript Division, Library of Congress.

Roosevelt, Eleanor. Papers. Franklin D. Roosevelt Library, Hyde Park, N.Y.

Roosevelt, Franklin D. Papers. Franklin D. Roosevelt Library, Hyde Park, N.Y.

Sholtz, David. Records, 1932–36. Administrative correspondence. Florida State Archives, Tallahassee, Fla.

Government Documents

Circuit Court Records. Leon County Courthouse, Tallahassee, Fla.

Department of State, Bureau of Laws. *Acts, Resolutions and Memorials of the Legislature.* 1937. Florida State Archives, Tallahassee, Fla.

Florida State Planning Board. *Statistical Abstract of Florida Counties*. Tallahassee, Fla., n.d.

Jackson County Records. Jackson County Courthouse, Marianna, Fla.

Punishment for the Crime of Lynching: Hearing Before a Subcommittee of the Committee on the Judiciary, United States Senate. 74th Cong., 1st sess., on S. 24, 14 February 1935.

U.S. Department of Commerce. *Fourteenth Census of the United States, 1920: Population*. Vol. 3. Washington, D.C., 1922.

———. *Fifteenth Census of the United States, 1930: Agriculture*. Vol. 3. Washington, D.C., 1932.

———. *Fifteenth Census of the United States, 1930: Population*. Vol. 3. Washington, D.C., 1932.

———. *Sixteenth Census of the United States, 1940: Population*. Vol. 2. Washington, D.C., 1940.

Books and Reports

Adorno, T. W., et. al. *The Authoritarian Personality*. New York, 1950.

Ames, Jessie Daniel. *The Changing Character of Lynching*. Atlanta, 1942; reprint, New York, 1973.

ASWPL (Association of Southern Women for the Prevention of Lynching). "Are the Courts to Blame?" ASWPL papers, special collections, Woodruff Library, Atlanta University Center. Atlanta, Ga., 1939.

———. *Southern Women Look at Lynching*. Atlanta, Ga., 1937.

Ayers, Edward. *Vengeance and Justice: Crime and Punishment in the Nineteenth-Century American South*. New York, 1984.

Baiamonte, John V., Jr. *Spirit of Vengeance: Nativism and Louisiana Justice, 1921–1924*. Baton Rouge, La., 1986.

Bardolph, Richard, ed. *The Civil Rights Record: Black Americans and the Law*. New York, 1971.

Berry, Mary Frances. *Black Resistance/White Law: A History of Constitutional Racism in America*. New York, 1971.

Berry, Mary Frances, and John Blassingame. *Long Memory: The Black Experience in America*. New York, 1982.

Blalock, Hubert. *Toward a Theory of Minority-Group Relations*. New York, 1967.

Blassingame, John. *The Slave Community: Plantation Life in the Antebellum South*. New York, 1979.

Bradley, Omar. *A Soldier's Story*. New York, 1951.

Branch, Taylor. *Parting the Waters: America in the King Years, 1954–1963*. New York, 1988.

Brown, Richard Maxwell. *Strain of Violence: Historical Studies of American Violence and Vigilantism*. New York, 1975.

Brown, Roger. *Social Psychology*. New York, 1955.

Bruce, Dickson D., Jr. *Violence and Culture in the Antebellum South*. Austin, Tex., 1979.

Brundage, W. Fitzhugh. *Lynching in the New South: Georgia and Virginia, 1880–1930*. Urbana and Chicago, 1993.

Bruton, Quintilla Geer, and Diard E. Baily, Jr. *Plant City: Its Origins and History*. St. Petersburg, Fla., 1977.

Cantril, Hadley. *The Psychology of Social Movements*. New York, 1941.

Carr, Robert K. *Federal Protection for Civil Rights: Quest for a Sword*. Ithaca, N.Y., 1947.

Carter, Dan T. *Scottsboro: A Tragedy of the Modern South.* Baton Rouge, La., 1969.

Cash, W. J. *The Mind of the South.* New York, 1941.

Cash, W. T. *The Story of Florida.* 4 vols. New York, 1938.

Cassity, Michael. *Chains of Fear.* Westport, Conn., 1984.

Chadbourn, James H. *Lynching and the Law.* Chapel Hill, N.C., 1933.

Chalmers, David. *Hooded Americanism: The First Century of the Ku Klux Klan, 1865–1965.* Garden City, N.Y., 1955.

Cox, Oliver C. *Caste, Class, and Race.* New York, 1948.

Cutler, James Elbert. *Lynch-Law: An Investigation into the History of Lynchings in the United States.* New York, 1905.

Daniel, Peter. *Breaking the Land: The Transformation of Cotton, Tobacco, and Rice Cultures.* Urbana, Ill., 1985.

———. *The Shadow of Slavery: Peonage in the South, 1901–1969.* Urbana, Ill., 1977.

———. *Standing at the Crossroads: Southern Life in the Twentieth Century.* New York, 1986.

Davis, Allison, Burleigh B. Gardner, and Mary R. Gardner. *Deep South: A Social Anthropological Study of Caste and Class.* Chicago, 1941.

Day, Beth. *Sexual Life between Blacks and Whites: The Roots of Racism.* New York, 1972.

Dietrich, Stanton T. "The Urbanization of Florida's Population: An Historical Perspective of County Growth, 1830–1970." Gainesville, Fla., 1978.

Dollard, John. *Caste and Class in a Southern Town.* Garden City, N.Y. 1957.

Dovel, J. E. *Florida: Historic, Dramatic, Contemporary.* 2 vols. New York, 1982.

Downey, Dennis B., and Raymond M. Hyser. *No Crooked Death: Coatesville, Pennsylvania, and the Lynching of Zachariah Walker.* Urbana and Chicago, 1991.

Du Bois, W. E. B. *Dusk of Dawn.* New York, 1968.

———. *The Souls of Black Folk.* New York, 1903; reprint, New York 1982.

Dunn, Hampton. *Yesterday's Tallahassee.* Miami, Fla., 1974.

Dykeman, Wilma, and James Stokely. *Seeds of Southern Change: The Life of William Alexander.* Chicago, 1962.

Flynn, Charles L. *White Land, Black Labor: Caste and Class in Late-Nineteenth-Century Georgia.* Baton Rouge, La., 1983.

Franklin, John Hope. *The Militant South, 1800–1860.* Cambridge, Mass., 1956.

Frederickson, George M. *The Black Image in the White Mind: The Debate on Afro-American Character and Destiny, 1871–1914.* New York, 1971.

Fromm, Erich. *The Anatomy of Human Destructiveness.* New York, 1973.

Garrow, David J. *Bearing the Cross: Martin Luther King, Jr., and the Southern Christian Leadership Conference.* New York, 1986.

Genovese, Eugene D. *Roll, Jordan, Roll: The World the Slaves Made.* New York, 1976.

Grant, Donald L. *The Antilynching Movement, 1883–1932.* San Francisco, 1975.

Grimshaw, Allen D., ed. *Racial Violence in the United States.* Chicago, 1969.

Groene, Bertram. *Antebellum Tallahassee.* Tallahassee, Fla., 1971.

Hall, Jacquelyn Dowd. *Revolt against Chivalry: Jessie Daniel Ames and the Women's Campaign against Lynching.* New York, 1979.

Henri, Florette. *Black Migration: Movement North, 1900-1920*. New York, 1976.

Hill, Robert A., ed. *The Marcus Garvey and Universal Negro Improvement Association Papers*. Berkeley, Calif., 1983.

Ingalls, Robert P. *Urban Vigilantes in the New South: Tampa, 1882-1936*. Knoxville, Tenn., 1988.

Johnson, Charles S. *Statistical Atlas of Southern Counties: Listing and Analysis of Southern Counties*. Chapel Hill, N.C., 1941.

Jordan, Winthrop. *White over Black: American Attitudes toward the Negro, 1550-1812*. Chapel Hill, N.C., 1968.

Kelley, Robin D. G. *Hammer and Hoe: Alabama Communists during the Great Depression*. Chapel Hill, N.C., 1992.

Kirby, Jack Temple. *Rural Worlds Lost: The American South, 1920-1960*. Baton Rouge, La., 1987.

Kovel, Joel. *White Racism: A Psychohistory*. New York, 1970.

Lawson, Steven F. *Black Ballots: Voting Rights in the South, 1944-1969*. New York, 1976.

Lundberg, Emma O. *Social Welfare in Florida*. Tallahassee, Fla., 1934.

McGovern, James R. *Anatomy of a Lynching: The Killing of Claude Neal*. Baton Rouge, La., 1982.

McMillen, Neil R. *Dark Journey: Black Mississippians in the Age of Jim Crow*. Urbana, Ill., 1989.

Mencken, H. L. *Prejudices: Second Series*. New York, 1920.

Meyer, Gerald. *Vito Marcantonio: Radical Politician, 1902-1954*. New York, 1991.

Miller, Gene. *Invitation to a Lynching*. New York, 1975.

Montell, William L. *Killings: Folk Justice in the Upper South*. Lexington, Ky., 1986.

Mormino, Gary R., and George E. Possetta. *The Immigrant World of Ybor City: Italians and their Latin Neighbors in Tampa*, 1885-1985. Urbana, Ill., 1987.

Murray, Pauli. *States' Laws on Race and Color*. Cincinnati, Ohio, 1951.

Myrdal, Gunnar. *An American Dilemma: The Negro Problem and Modern Democracy*. New York, 1944.

NAACP (National Association for the Advancement of Colored People). "The Lynching of Claude Neal." New York, 1934.

————. *Thirty Years of Lynching in the United States, 1889-1918*. New York, 1919.

The Negro Almanac. New York, 1971.

Odajnyk, Walter. *Jung and Politics: The Political and Social Ideas of C. G. Jung*. New York, 1976.

Odum, Howard. *Southern Regions of the United States*. New York, 1969.

Osofsky, Gilbert. *Harlem: The Making of a Ghetto. Negro New York, 1890-1930*. New York, 1966.

Ottanelli, Fraser M. *The Communist Party of the United States from the Depression to World War II*. New Brunswick, N.J., 1991.

Patterson, James T. *Congressional Conservatism and the New Deal: The Growth of the Conservative Coalition in Congress, 1933-1939*. Lexington, Ky., 1967.

Percy, Alfred. *Origins of Lynch Law, 1780*. Madison Heights, Va., 1959.

Phillips, U. B. *American Negro Slavery*. New York, 1918.

Rabinowitz, Howard. *The First New South, 1865-1920*. Arlington, Ill., 1992.

————. *Race Relations in the Urban South, 1865-1890*. New York, 1978.

Rable, George C. *But There Was No Peace: The Role of Violence in the Politics of Reconstruction.* Athens, Ga., 1934.

Raper, Arthur F. *A Study of Negro Life in Tampa.* Tampa, Fla. 1927.

———. *The Tragedy of Lynching.* Chapel Hill, N.C., 1933. Reprint, New York, 1969.

Reed, John Sheldon. *The Enduring South: Subcultural Persistence in Mass Society.* Chapel Hill, N.C., 1974.

Rerick, Rowland. *Memoirs of Florida.* 2 vols. Atlanta, Ga., 1902.

Robinson, Ernest L. *History of Hillsborough County.* St. Augustine, Fla., 1928.

Rose, Arnold. *The Negro in America.* New York, 1964.

Rosenbaum, H. Jon, and Peter C. Sederberg, eds. *Vigilante Politics.* Philadelphia, 1976.

Ross, B. Joyce. *J. E. Spingarn and the Rise of the NAACP, 1911–1939.* New York, 1972.

Saloutous, Theodore. *The American Farmer and the New Deal.* Ames, Iowa, 1982.

Scott, Emmet J. *Negro Migration during the War.* New York, 1920.

Shapiro, Herbert. *White Violence, Black Response: From Reconstruction to Montgomery.* Amherst, Mass., 1988.

Shay, Frank. *Judge Lynch: His First Hundred Years.* New York, 1938. Reprint, Montclair, N.J., 1969.

Shofner, Jerrell H. *Jackson County, Florida: A History.* Marianna, Fla., 1985.

———. *Nor Is It Over Yet: Florida in the Era of Reconstruction, 1863–1877.* Gainesville, Fla., 1974.

Short, James F., and Mavin E. Wolfgang, eds. *Collective Violence.* Chicago, 1972.

Smead, Howard. *Blood Justice: The Lynching of Mack Charles Parker.* New York, 1986.

Smelser, Neil. *Theory of Collective Behavior.* New York, 1962.

Southern Commission on the Study of Lynching. *Lynchings and What They Mean: General Findings of the Southern Commission on the Study of Lynchings.* Atlanta, Ga., 1931.

Stanley, J. Randall. *History of Jackson County.* Marianna, Fla., 1950.

Stannard, David E. *Shrinking History: On Freud and the Failure of Psychohistory.* New York, 1980.

Tebeau, Charles W. *A History of Florida.* Coral Gables, Fla., 1971.

Thornbrough, Emma Lou. *T. Thomas Fortune: Militant Journalist.* Chicago, 1972.

Thorpe, Earl E. *The Old South: A Psychohistory.* Durham, N.C., 1973.

Tindall, George Brown. *The Emergence of the New South, 1917–1945.* Baton Rouge, La., 1967.

Trelease, Allen W. *White Terror: The Ku Klux Klan Conspiracy and the Southern Reconstruction.* New York, 1971.

van der Post, Laurens. *The Dark Eye of Africa.* New York, 1955.

———. *Jung and the Story of Our Time.* New York, 1975.

Wagy, Tom. *Governor LeRoy Collins: Spokesman for the New South.* Montgomery, Ala., 1985.

Waller, Altina L. *Feud: Hatfields, McCoys, and Social Change in Appalachia, 1860–1900.* Chapel Hill, N.C., 1988.

Weidling, Philip J., and August Burghard. *Checkered Sunshine: The Story of Ft. Lauderdale, 1793–1955.* Gainesville, Fla., 1966.

Weiss, Nancy J. *The National Urban League, 1910–1940.* New York, 1974.

White, Walter. *A Man Called White: The Autobiography of Walter White.* New York, 1948.

―――. *Rope and Faggot: A Biography of Judge Lynch.* New York, 1929.

Whitfield, Stephen J. *A Death in the Delta: The Story of Emmett Till.* New York, 1988.

Williams, Daniel T. *Eight Negro Bibliographies.* New York, 1970.

Williamson, Edward C. *Florida Politics in the Gilded Age, 1877–1893.* Gainesville, Fla., 1976.

Williamson, Joel. *The Crucible of Race: Black-White Relations in the American South Since Emancipation.* New York, 1984.

Wolters, Raymond. *Negroes and the Great Depression.* Westport, Conn., 1970.

Woodward, C. Vann. *Origins of the New South, 1877-1913.* Baton Rouge, La., 1966.

―――. *The Strange Career of Jim Crow.* New York, 1955.

Wright, Gavin. *Old South, New South: Revolutions in the Southern Economy since the Civil War.* New York, 1986.

Wright, George C. *Racial Violence in Kentucky, 1865–1940: Lynchings, Mob Rule, and "Legal Lynching."* Baton Rouge, La., 1990.

Wyatt-Brown, Bertram. *Southern Honor: Ethics and Behavior in the Old South.* New York, 1982.

Zangrando, Robert. *The NAACP Crusade against Lynching, 1909–1950.* Philadelphia, 1980.

Articles

Adler, Jeffrey S. "Black Violence in the New South: Patterns of Conflict in Late-Nineteenth-Century Tampa." Paper, Southern Historical Association, 1993.

Bagozzi, Richard P. "Populism and Lynching in Louisiana." *American Sociological Review* 42 (April 1977): 355–58.

Beck, E. M., and Steward Tolnay. "The Killing Fields of the Deep South: The Market for Cotton and the Lynchings of Blacks." *American Sociological Review* 55 (August 1990): 526–39.

Blalock, H. M., Jr. "Percent Black and Lynching Revisited." *Social Forces* 67 (March 1989): 631–33.

Bearley, H.C. "The Pattern of Violence." In *Culture of the South,* edited by W. T. Couch. Chapel Hill, N.C., 1934.

Brundage, W. Fitzhugh. "Mob Violence North and South, 1865–1940." *Georgia Historical Quarterly* 75 (Winter 1991): 748–70.

Capeci, Dominic J. "The Lynching of Cleo Wright: Federal Protection of Constitutional Rights during World War II." *Journal of American History* 72 (March 1986): 859–87.

Clark, James C. "The 1944 Florida Democratic Senate Primary." *Florida Historical Quarterly* 66 (April 1988): 365–84.

Corzine, Jay, James Creech, and Lin Corzine. "Black Concentration and Lynchings in the South: Testing Blalock's Power-Threat Hypothesis." *Social Forces* 61 (March 1983): 744–96.

Cox, Merlin G. "David Sholtz: New Deal Governor of Florida." *Florida Historical Quarterly* 43 (October 1964): 142–52.

Creech, James, Jay Corzine, and Lin Huff-Corzine. "Theory Testing and Lynching: Another Look at the Power-Threat Hypothesis." *Social Forces* 67 (March 1989): 626–30.

Dabney, Virginius. "Dixie Rejects Lynching." *Nation,* 27 November 1937, 579–81.

Davis, Jack E. "'Whitewash' in Florida: The Lynching of Jesse James Payne and its Aftermath." *Florida Historical Quarterly* 68 (January 1990): 277–98.

Eaton, Clement. "Mob Violence in the Old South." *Mississippi Valley Historical Review* 19 (December 1942): 361–89.

Grimshaw, Allen D. "Interpreting Collective Violence: An Argument for the Importance of Social Structure." In *Collective Violence*, edited by James F. Short, Jr., and Marvin E. Wolfgang. Chicago, 1972.

Hackney, Sheldon. "Southern Violence." *American Historical Review* 74 (February 1969): 906–25.

Hofstadter, Richard. "Reflections on Violence in the United States." In *American Violence: A Documentary History*, edited by Richard Hofstadter and Michael Wallace. New York, 1971.

Holmes, William F. "Moonshining and Collective Violence: Georgia, 1889–1895." *Journal of American History* 67 (December 1980): 589–611.

———. "Whitecapping: Agrarian Violence in Mississippi, 1902–1906." *Journal of Southern History* 35 (May 1968): 165–85.

Howard, Walter T. "Beaches and Hanging Trees: Lynch Law in Florida, 1930–1940." *Carver* 10 (Spring 1992): 7–20.

———. "'A Blot on Tampa's History': The 1934 Lynching of Robert Johnson." *Tampa Bay History* 6 (Fall 1984): 5–18.

———. "A Hillsborough County Tragedy: The 1930 Lynching of John Hodaz." *Tampa Bay History* 11 (Fall 1989): 34–51.

———. "In the Shadow of Scottsboro: The 1937 Robert Hinds Case." *Gulf Coast Historical Review* 4 (Fall 1988): 65–81.

———. "Vigilante Justice and National Reaction: The 1937 Tallahassee Double Lynching." *Florida Historical Quarterly* 66 (July 1988): 41–69.

Ingalls, Robert P; "General Joseph B. Wall and Lynch Law in Tampa." *Florida Historical Quarterly* 63 (July 1984): 51–70.

———. "Lynching and Establishment Violence in Tampa, 1858–1935." *Journal of Southern History* 53 (November 1987): 613–44.

———. "The Tampa Flogging Case, Urban Vigilantism." *Florida Historical Quarterly* 56 (July 1977): 13–27.

Inverarity, James E. "Populism and Lynching in Louisiana, 1889–1896: A Test of Erikson's Theory of the Relationship between Boundary Crises and Repressive Justice." *American Sociological Review* 41 (April 1976): 262–80

Lawson, Steven F., David R. Colburn, and Darryl Paulson. "Groveland: Florida's Little Scottsboro." *Florida Historical Quarterly* 65 (July 1986): 1–26.

Loewenberg, Peter. "The Psychology of Racism." In *The Great Fear: Race in the Mind of America*, edited by Gary B. Nash and Richard Weiss. New York, 1970.

Martin, Charles H. "The International Labor Defense and Black America." *Labor History* 26 (Spring 1985): 165–94.

McGovern, James R., and Walter T. Howard. "Private Justice and National Concern: The Lynching of Claude Neal." *The Historian* 43 (August 1981): 546–59.

Merrill, Taylor. "Lynching and the Antilynching Bill." *Christian Century* 55 (23 February 1938): 238–39.

Milton, George F. "The Impeachment of Judge Lynch." *Virginia Quarterly Review* 8 (April 1932): 250–52.

Odum, Howard. "Lynching, Fears, and Folkways." *Nation*, 30 December 1931, 719–20.

O'Reilly, Kenneth. "A New Deal for the FBI: The Roosevelt Administration, Crime Control, and National Security." *Journal of American History* 69 (December 1982): 638–58.

Pope, Whitney, and Charles Ragin. "Mechanical Solidarity, Repressive Justice, and Lynchings in Louisiana." *American Sociological Review* 42 (April 1977): 363–68.

Reed, John Sheldon. "Comment on Tolnay, Beck, and Massey." *Social Forces* 67 (March 1989): 624–25.

———. "Percent Black and Lynching: A Test of Blalock's Theory." *Social Forces* 50 (March 1972): 356–67.

Rivers, Larry E. "A Troublesome Property: Master/Slave Relations in Florida, 1821–1860." Paper, Southern Historical Association, 1993.

Shofner, Jerrell H. "Custom, Law, and History: The Enduring Influence of Florida's 'Black Codes'." *Florida Historical Quarterly* 55 (January 1977): 277–98.

———. "Florida and the Black Migration." *Florida Historical Quarterly* 57 (January 1979): 89–104.

———. "Judge Herbert Rider and the Lynching at LaBelle." *Florida Historical Quarterly* 59 (January 1981): 292–306.

———. "Murders at 'Kiss-Me-Quick': The Underside of International Affairs." *Florida Historical Quarterly* 62 (January 1984): 332–38.

———. "Postscript on the Martin Talbert Case: Peonage as Usual in the Florida Turpentine Camps." *Florida Historical Quarterly* 60 (October 1986): 161–73.

———. "The White Springs Post Office Caper." *Florida Historical Quarterly* 56 (January 1978): 339–47.

Smith, Albert C. "'Southern Violence' Reconsidered: Arson as Protest in Black Belt Georgia, 1865–1910." *Journal of Southern History* 51 (November 1985): 527–64.

Spense Alex. "Lynching and the Nation." *Commonweal*, 13 April 1932, 658–59.

Tolnay, Stewart E., E. M. Beck, and James L. Massey, et al. "Black Lynching: An Article and Commentary." *Social Forces* 67 (March 1989): 605–640.

———. "Black Lynchings: The Power-Threat Hypothesis Revisited." *Social Forces* 67 (March 1989): 605–23.

———. "The Power-Threat Hypothesis and Black Lynching: 'Whither' the Evidence." *Social Forces* 67 (March 1989): 634–39.

Wasserman, Ira M. "Southern Violence and the Political Process." *American Sociological Review* 42 (April 1977): 359–62.

Wiener, Jonathan M. "The 'Black Beast Rapist': White Racial Attitudes in the Postwar South." *Review in American History* 13 (June 1985): 226.

Theses and Dissertations

Davis, Jack E. "Shades of Justice: The Lynching of Jesse James Payne and Its Aftermath." Master's thesis, University of South Florida, 1988.

Dunn, James William. "The New Deal and Florida Politics." Ph.D. diss., Florida State University, 1971.

Ellis, Ann Wells. "The Commission on Interracial Cooperation, 1919–1944: Its Activities and Results." Ph.D. diss., Georgia State University, 1975.

Finnegan, Terence Robert. "At the Hands of Parties Unknown: Lynching in Mississippi and South Carolina, 1881–1940." Ph.D. diss., University of Illinois, 1993.

Howard, Walter T. "Vigilante Justice: Extra-legal Executions in Florida, 1930–1940." Ph.D. diss., Florida State University, 1987.

Kharif, Wali. "The Refinement of Racial Segregation in Florida after the Civil War." Ph.D. diss., Florida State University, 1966.

Lewis, Terry E. "Frenchtown: A Geographical Survey of an All-Negro Business District in Tallahassee, Florida." Master's thesis, Florida State University, 1966.

Mullin, Jack S. "Lynching in South Carolina, 1900-1914." Master's thesis, University of South Carolina, 1961.

Reader, Jesse W. "Federal Efforts to Control Lynchings." Master's thesis, Cornell University, 1952.

Ross, John Raymond. "At the Bar of Judge Lynch: Lynching and Lynch Mobs in America." Ph.D. diss., Texas Tech University, 1983.

Zangrando, Robert L. "The Efforts of the National Association for the Advancement of Colored People to Secure Passage of a Federal Antilynching Law, 1920-1940." Ph.D. diss., University of Pennsylvania, 1963.

Newspapers and Periodicals

Atlanta Constitution. 1937.

Atlanta Daily World. 1934–45.

Baltimore Afro-American. 1934–43.

Boston Herald. 1934, 1937.

Brewton (Alabama) *Standard*. 1934.

Chicago Defender. 1934–43.

Chicago Tribune. 1937.

Christian Century. 1937–39.

Colliers. 1946.

The Crisis. 1934–39.

Daily Worker. 1937, 1938.

Daytona Beach (Florida) *Evening News*. 1939.

Dothan (Alabama) *Eagle*. 1934.

Equal Justice. 1938–39.

Ft. Lauderdale Daily News. 1935.

Gadsden County (Florida) *Times*. 1941.

Jackson County Floridan. 1934, 1943.

Jacksonville (Florida) *Times-Union*. 1937-1938.

Legal Defender. 1935, 1938.

Madison (Florida) *Enterprise-Recorder.* 1936.

Marianna (Florida) *Times-Courier.* 1934.

Miami Daily News (Times). 1937–39.

Miami Herald. 1930–45.

Milton (Florida) *Gazette.* 1937.

Montgomery (Alabama) *Advertiser.* 1934.

New York Age. 1935.

New York Post. 1937, 1941.

New York Times. 1934–39.

Newsweek. 1937.

Norfolk (Virginia) *Journal and Guide.* 1937–39.

Ocala (Florida) *Banner.* 1937.

Orlando Sentinel. 1930

Panama City (Florida) *News-Herald.* 1937, 1939.

Panama City (Florida) *Pilot.* 1934.

Pensacola Journal. 1934, l937.

Pittsburgh Courier. 1934–45.

Richmond (Virginia) *Times-Dispatch.* 1937, 1939.

St. Louis Post-Dispatch. 1937–39.

St. Petersburg Times. 1930–45, 1949.

Tallahassee Democrat. 1931–41.

Tampa Times. 1930.

Tampa Tribune. 1930–40.

Time. 1946.

Washington Post. 1937–41.

Interviews

Gray, Carl, 6 June 1976.

Hawes, Leland, 11 March 1988.

Holmes, Mildred, 7 July 1978.

Jensens, Arthur, 21 July 1977.

Metcalf, John, 12 January 1986.

Moncrief, Dr. Adliel, 11 January 1986.

Ralph, Rob, 12 January 1986.

Sims, Filmore, 27 September 1977.

Smith, Tommy, 7 July 1977.

Index

978-0-595-37650-6
0-595-37650-9

Printed in the United States
65366LVS00004B/151-246

9 780595 376506